EVERY DISH
DELIVERS

Sandra Lee

EVERY DISH DELIVERS

365 Days of Fast, Fresh, Affordable Meals

This book belongs to:

_____

SL BOOKS
sandralee.com

HYPERION
NEW YORK

Copyright © 2013 Sandra Lee Semi-Homemade®

Printed in the United States of America.
For information address Hyperion,
1500 Broadway, New York, New York, 10036.

Library of Congress Cataloging-in-Publication
Data has been applied for.

ISBN: 978-1-4013-1084-4

PHOTOGRAPHY: Ben Fink

PHOTO RETOUCHING: Waterbury Publications, Inc.—
Des Moines, IA

PROP STYLING: Sarah Smart

FOOD STYLING: Jamie Kimm

HAIR AND MAKEUP: Alx Galasinao

WARDROBE STYLING: Amit Gajwani and
Annie Semenczuk

WARDROBE DESIGNERS: Ted Baker London,
Isaac Mizrahi, Max Studio, Jussara Lee, Kiton,
Candella, Jay Godfrey, Tahari, Moritz Glik, Vibes,
Nava Zahavi, Sethi Couture, Stella Flame

FIRST EDITION

THIS LABEL APPLIES TO TEXT STOCK

10 9 8 7 6 5 4 3 2 1

We try to produce the most beautiful books
possible, and we are also extremely concerned
about the impact of our manufacturing process
on the forests of the world and the environment
as a whole. Accordingly, we've made sure that all
of the paper we use has been certified as coming
from forests that are managed, to ensure the
protection of the people and wildlife
dependent upon them.

Dedication

With great appreciation and admiration for the amazing production teams that make the television shows incredible, the *Sandra Lee* magazine amazing, and all my books most beautiful. Thank you for all your helpful input, ideas, and inspirations for creating useful tips and tricks and making life better for everyone.

Contents

A Letter from Sandra

If you ask anyone in my family they would tell you my favorite thing to do is EAT. Then they would tell you I am already planning my next meal before I've even finished the meal in front of me. It's all true. I love to eat, I love to cook, and I love to bake. Being a great gourmet is not a requirement to enjoy eating or cooking, and being a good cook—even a great cook—is easy with wonderful recipes that come together without hassle or stress, and that is exactly what you have here.

Food is one of the true pleasures of life, and captivating dishes will always be in favor—the trick is to make them fresh, fast and make them simple and sensational. I created this book so you could savor every minute of every day your own unique way.

Every dish delivers, and the meals you make from these pages will become the family favorites you'll crave. So enjoy every day and every sensational bite.

Cheers to a happy, healthy home.

Sandra

"There is no sincerer love
than the love of food."
—George Bernard Shaw

PIZZA PARTY

Baileys Martini: Mix 2 ounces Baileys Original Irish Cream liqueur, .25 ounces Baileys with a Hint of Coffee, and .25 ounces Smirnoff No. 21 vodka into a shaker with ice. Shake and strain into martini glass. Makes 1 cocktail.

Crown Royal Apple Cider: Combine 1.5 ounces Crown Royal Maple Finished whisky, ½ teaspoon honey, and 3 ounces hot apple cider. Pour into a heatproof mug and garnish with a cinnamon stick. Makes 1 cocktail.

HOLIDAY AND BIRTHDAY CAKE DECORATING TIPS

EVERY DISH
DELIVERS

JANUARY

COLORFUL RICE

MAKES: 4 servings   **COOK:** 30 minutes

2½   cups low-sodium chicken broth

1   (6-ounce) package wild rice

Olive oil cooking spray

1   teaspoon chopped garlic

½   cup yellow onion, diced

½   cup diced celery

½   (8-ounce) package sliced white mushrooms, chopped

½   cup dried cranberries

½   cup chopped pecans

1   (8-ounce) can sliced water chestnuts, drained

Zest of ½ orange

1. Bring the chicken broth to a boil over medium heat. Add rice, cover, and turn heat down to low. Cook for 20 minutes or until rice has absorbed all the moisture and is tender.

2. Heat a large skillet over medium heat. Spray with olive oil cooking spray. Sauté garlic, onions, celery, and mushrooms until tender, about 5 to 7 minutes.

3. Add rice, cranberries, pecans, water chestnuts, and orange zest. Mix to combine and cook until all ingredients are heated through.

HONEY GLAZED PROSCIUTTO AND GORGONZOLA FIGS

MAKES: 8 servings   **COOK:** 10 minutes

4   large whole figs, quartered

4   teaspoons Gorgonzola cheese

1   (3-ounce) package prosciutto

3   tablespoons honey

¼   teaspoon pumpkin pie spice

1. Preheat oven to 400°F. Line a baking sheet with parchment paper and set aside.

2. Cut a small hole in the center of the flesh of each piece of fig. Fill each hole with ¼ teaspoon of Gorgonzola cheese.

3. Tear a prosciutto slice in half. Wrap one half diagonally around the fig, starting from the top. Tuck underneath at the ends. Repeat until all figs are wrapped, securing with a toothpick if necessary.

4. Place wrapped figs on prepared baking sheet, evenly spaced. In a small bowl, combine honey and pumpkin pie spice. Drizzle honey evenly over each fig. Place in the oven on the top rack and roast for 8 to 10 minutes. Remove and serve immediately.

JALAPEÑO QUESO CON TEQUILA

MAKES: 16 servings **COOK:** 3 to 4 hours

- 2 (10-ounce) cans condensed Fiesta Nacho Cheese soup—Campbell's
- 1 pound pepper jack cheese, shredded
- 2 (8-ounce) packages cream cheese, cut into cubes
- ½ cup salsa
- ½ tomato, diced
- 2 jalapeños, diced
- ¼ cup gold tequila—Jose Cuervo
- ⅛ cup chopped fresh cilantro, for garnish
- 1 bag tortilla chips

1. In a 4-quart slow cooker, combine all ingredients except cilantro and chips and mix thoroughly.
2. Cover and cook on low setting for 3 to 4 hours, stirring occasionally.
3. Garnish with cilantro and serve hot with tortilla chips.

JAPANESE EGGPLANT WITH WASABI VINAIGRETTE

MAKES: 4 servings **COOK:** 25 minutes

- 4 Japanese eggplants
- ½ cup wasabi soy & ginger vinaigrette, divided use
- 1 tablespoon wasabi paste
- 1 tablespoon mayonnaise
- 1 scallion, finely chopped
- 1 tablespoon toasted sesame seeds, for garnish

1. Cut each eggplant into thin lengthwise slices, leaving slices attached on stem end. Fan out on a baking sheet and coat with ¼ cup vinaigrette, carefully coating all slices. Let sit for 30 minutes. Stir remaining ¼ cup vinaigrette together with wasabi paste, mayonnaise, and scallion. Set aside until ready to serve.
2. Preheat oven to 375°F.
3. Roast eggplant fans for 20 to 25 minutes. Serve with wasabi vinaigrette and garnish with sesame seeds.

RISOTTO CAKES

MAKES: 4 servings   **COOK:** 10 to 12 minutes

3   cups mushroom risotto, cooked according
    to package directions
2   large eggs
½   cup frozen corn, thawed
½   cup panko bread crumbs
¼   cup grated Parmesan cheese
2   tablespoons canola oil
    Salt and pepper, to taste

1. Mix together the cooked risotto, eggs, corn, panko bread crumbs, and Parmesan cheese. Season with salt and pepper. Form into 6 patties.
2. Heat the oil in a large nonstick skillet over medium-low heat. Sauté the patties until golden brown and cooked through, about 5 to 6 minutes per side.

ROASTED VEGETABLE PASTA SALAD

MAKES: 4 servings   **COOK:** 1 hour

FOR THE ROASTED ROOT VEGETABLES:
2   tablespoons canola oil
2   carrots, cut into 3-inch pieces
2   russet potatoes, cut into 1-inch cubes
½   pound turnips, cut into wedges
1   red onion, sliced
1   teaspoon fresh rosemary, chopped
1   teaspoon fresh thyme, chopped

FOR THE VINAIGRETTE:
1   tablespoon spicy mustard
1   tablespoon cider vinegar
2   tablespoons olive oil

8   ounces penne pasta, cooked and cooled
1   small red onion, sliced
1   tablespoon fresh parsley, chopped
    Salt and pepper, to taste

1. Preheat oven to 400°F.
2. For the roasted root vegetables, toss vegetables in a bowl with canola oil, rosemary, and thyme and season with salt and pepper. Lay them on a baking sheet and roast for 30 minutes, then toss and roast for another 30 minutes.
3. For the vinaigrette, whisk the mustard, vinegar, olive oil, salt, and pepper in a small bowl.
4. Combine pasta with roasted root vegetables and sliced red onion. Toss pasta and vegetables with vinaigrette and chopped fresh parsley and refrigerate 1 hour to let flavors develop.

STEAMED PORK BUNS WITH HOISIN DIP

MAKES: 4 servings   **COOK:** 10 minutes

FOR THE STEAMED PORK BUNS:

- 1   cup prepared pulled pork
- 1   teaspoon chopped ginger
- 2   scallions, finely chopped
- 2   (7.5-ounce) canisters refrigerated biscuit dough, 20 biscuits

FOR THE HOISIN DIP:

- ¼   cup hoisin sauce
- ¼   cup low-sodium soy sauce
- 1   tablespoon apple cider vinegar
- 2   tablespoons water

1. Bring 2 cups of water to a simmer in a pot that will fit a steamer basket or a bamboo steamer.

2. In a medium bowl, mix together the pork, ginger, and scallions. Set aside.

3. Working with one dough canister (10 biscuits) at a time, roll out the biscuits with a rolling pin until they are about 3 inches in diameter. Place 1 heaping tablespoon of the pork mixture in the center of 5 of the biscuits. Cover with the remaining rolled-out biscuits. Gently press together the biscuits all the way around the filling and to the edges. Place a (2½- to 2 ¾-inch) biscuit cutter on top so that it is centered on the bun, and press down on the cutter to form a clean, sealed edge. Remove excess dough from around the outside of the biscuit cutter. Place the sealed buns onto a baking sheet and cover with plastic wrap. Repeat with the remaining ingredients.

4. Place the buns into the steamer basket. Depending on the size of your steamer, you may have to cook the buns in batches of 5. Place the steamer basket over the pot of simmering water, cover—and steam about 10 minutes. The buns will be puffed and the tops will look somewhat dry and shiny. Let cool 1 to 2 minutes.

5. While the buns are steaming, make the hoisin dipping sauce. In a small bowl, stir together the hoisin sauce, soy sauce, vinegar, and water. Serve warm buns with dipping sauce.

TUSCAN SOUP WITH TORTELLINI

MAKES: 6 servings   **COOK:** 1 hour

1   (14-ounce) bag frozen Italian vegetable blend
1   (15-ounce) can cannellini beans, drained
1   (14.5-ounce) can diced tomatoes
4   (14.5-ounce) cans beef broth
1   cup water
½   cup tomato sauce
2   teaspoons chopped garlic
1   tablespoon Italian seasoning
1   (16-ounce) bag frozen meat or cheese tortellini
     Salt and pepper, to taste

1. Preheat oven to 375°F.
2. Add all ingredients except tortellini to a 4-quart slow cooker. Cover and cook on high setting for 1 hour. In the last 10 minutes of cooking, add tortellini. Season with salt and pepper to taste.

WONTON SOUP

MAKES: 2 servings   **COOK:** 10 minutes

1   cooked pork sparerib, meat removed and finely chopped
1   carrot, grated
1   scallion, thinly sliced
12   wonton wrappers
2   (14.5-ounce) cans chicken broth
1   cup broccoli florets

1. Combine sparerib meat, carrot, and scallions in a small bowl. Make wontons by placing a tablespoon of filling in the center of each wrapper. Dampen edges with water, fold in half point to point, and seal. Wrap outside corners around and seal together.
2. Heat chicken broth in a medium saucepan over medium heat. When the broth has come to a simmer, add wontons and broccoli. Cook for 3 minutes and serve hot.

APPLE CHEDDAR CHICKEN BREASTS WRAPPED WITH BACON

MAKES: 4 servings   **COOK:** 35 minutes

Nonstick cooking spray

4 whole boneless, skinless chicken breasts, butterflied

4 ounces cream cheese, room temperature

1½ cups shredded sharp cheddar cheese, divided use

3 ounces apple, thinly sliced (about 18 slices)

4 thinly sliced smoked bacon slices

Salt and pepper, to taste

1. Preheat oven to 350°F. Spray a 9 × 13-inch baking pan with cooking spray.

2. Rinse chicken under cold water and pat dry with paper towels. Lay the butterflied chicken breasts out flat and season top and bottom lightly with salt and pepper. Spread 1 ounce (2 tablespoons) of cream cheese evenly over each chicken breast, leaving a border of about 1 inch. Sprinkle each breast with ½ cup cheese and top with thin apple slices, overlapping slightly. Reserve some apple slices for topping.

3. Roll up each chicken breast lengthwise and secure with a couple of toothpicks (just enough to hold it together while you wrap it with bacon). Wrap one slice of bacon in a spiral around each chicken breast and secure with toothpicks again. Remove first set of toothpicks.

4. Place in a single layer in the baking pan at least 1 inch apart. Bake for 30 minutes, then top with remaining slices of apple and broil for 2 minutes, 4 inches from the heat source. When time is up, lightly sprinkle a tablespoon of cheese over each breast and broil for 1 to 3 minutes more, until the cheese is crispy and golden brown.

BLACK TEA CHICKEN WITH EGGPLANT

MAKES: 4 servings   **COOK:** 11 minutes

2   black tea bags

2   cups boiling water

1   pound boneless, skinless chicken breasts

3   tablespoons canola oil

1   tablespoon chopped garlic

1   tablespoon chopped ginger

2   Asian eggplants, about 1 pound, cut into
    ¼-inch slices

3   tablespoons low-sodium soy sauce

1   tablespoon hoisin sauce

1. Steep the tea bags in boiling water for 5 minutes. Remove the bags and allow the liquid to cool.

2. Rinse chicken under cold water and pat dry with paper towels. Cut the chicken into bite-size strips. Put the strips into a bowl and cover with cooled tea. Refrigerate for 2 hours. When you are ready to cook, drain the chicken and pat it dry.

3. In a large skillet or wok over medium-high heat, add 2 tablespoons canola oil, then the chicken, garlic, and ginger. Stir-fry until just cooked through, about 4 to 5 minutes. Remove to a plate and set aside. Add the remaining 1 tablespoon of oil to the pan, add the eggplant, and stir-fry until the eggplant begins to brown and soften, 3 to 4 minutes. Return the chicken to the pan, and add the soy and hoisin sauces. Stir-fry until the chicken is cooked through, 2 to 3 minutes.

CHICKEN WITH LEMON BROCCOLI AND CANNELLINI BEANS

MAKES: 4 servings   **COOK:** 17 minutes

- 4   boneless, skinless chicken breasts
- 2   teaspoons Italian seasoning
- 1   teaspoon garlic salt
- 1   (12-ounce) bag steam-in-bag broccoli florets
- 3   tablespoons olive oil, divided use
- 3   tablespoons lemon juice
- 1   teaspoon chopped garlic
- ¼   teaspoon red pepper flakes
- 1   (15-ounce) can cannellini beans, drained

Salt and pepper, to taste

1. Rinse chicken breasts with cold water and pat dry with paper towels. Season with Italian seasoning and garlic salt. Set aside. Heat steam-in-bag broccoli in microwave on 100 percent power for 3 to 4 minutes. Remove and let cool for 1 minute. Open bag carefully to allow steam to escape. Set aside.

2. Heat 2 tablespoons oil in a large skillet over medium-high heat. Add chicken and cook 3 to 4 minutes on each side or until chicken is cooked through. Remove from pan. Stir remaining 1 tablespoon oil, lemon juice, garlic, and red pepper flakes into pan. Cook for 1 minute, scraping up browned bits. Add beans and broccoli to pan and sauté, stirring gently, for 2 to 4 minutes or until heated through. Season to taste with salt and pepper. Serve chicken hot with a side of broccoli and beans.

CONCHIGLIE WITH SAUSAGE AND ARTICHOKES

MAKES: 4 servings   **COOK:** 30 minutes

1   (16-ounce) box shell pasta

1   pound ground Italian sausage

1   tablespoon garlic puree

1   cup less-sodium chicken broth

1   (1.2-ounce) packet Creamy Pesto Sauce Mix—
Knorr

2   (6.5-ounce) jars marinated artichoke hearts

½   pound cherry tomatoes, halved

1. Cook pasta in a large pot of boiling water according to package directions, and drain.
2. While pasta cooks, brown sausage in a large skillet, stirring frequently to break up large clumps. Stir together garlic, broth, and pesto mix; pour into skillet. Add artichoke hearts and tomatoes, and bring to a boil. Reduce heat and simmer for 3 minutes, stirring occasionally.
3. Divide pasta among pasta bowls. Spoon sauce over top and serve.

CRISPY ORANGE BEEF WITH BROCCOLI

MAKES: 4 servings   **COOK:** 15 minutes

3   cups white rice

1¼   pounds beef chuck steak

½   cup canola oil

¼   cup cornstarch

¾   cup orange marmalade

1   tablespoon chopped garlic

2   tablespoons white vinegar

1   tablespoon peeled and chopped ginger

2   tablespoons soy sauce

½   cup orange juice

¾   head broccoli, cut into florets, stems sliced into ¼-inch rounds

1. Cook white rice according to package directions.
2. Thinly slice the chuck steak across the grain about ¼-inch thick. Cut slices into 3-inch-long strips.
3. Heat oil in a wok or large skillet over high heat. Toss the beef in cornstarch and shake off excess. Fry the beef in 2 batches in hot oil, turning once, until crispy and golden, about 2 minutes per side. Remove from pan and set aside on a paper towel. Carefully drain the oil from the skillet.
4. In a medium bowl, whisk together the marmalade, garlic, vinegar, ginger, soy sauce, and orange juice until well combined. Add to the wok and cook for 2 minutes. Add broccoli and cook for 3 to 5 minutes, until broccoli is slightly tender and sauce is thick. Stir in beef and serve immediately with rice.

GLAZED PORK CHOPS WITH LEMON-CILANTRO RICE

MAKES: 4 servings **COOK:** 40 minutes

FOR THE GLAZE:

    Nonstick cooking spray

3 whole chipotle chilies in adobo sauce

1 tablespoon chopped garlic

3 tablespoons honey

1 tablespoon water

¼ teaspoon salt

FOR THE PORK CHOPS:

4 thick-cut pork chops, bone-in, about 1 inch thick

1 tablespoon canola oil

    Salt and pepper, to taste

FOR THE RICE:

2 (8.8-ounce) packages precooked long grain rice

1½ tablespoons lemon juice

½ teaspoon salt

¼ cup minced cilantro

4 cilantro sprigs, for garnish

1. Preheat oven to 350°F. Spray a foil-lined rimmed baking sheet with cooking spray.

2. For the glaze, rinse chipotle chilies under running water. Slit them open, remove seeds, and pat dry. Mince and put in a small bowl. Add the garlic, honey, water, and salt. Whisk thoroughly to combine, and set aside.

3. To make the pork chops, heat a large ovenproof skillet over medium-high heat. Season pork chops with salt and pepper on both sides, and set aside.

4. Add oil to pan. When hot, add pork chops 2 at a time and brown, 2 minutes per side. As you finish each batch, place on baking sheet and brush both sides with glaze. Bake for 25 to 30 minutes, depending on thickness of chops. Internal temperature should be 155°F. Watch closely, as the honey glaze may scorch.

5. To make the rice, heat according to package directions. Pour into serving dish and stir in lemon juice, salt, and cilantro. Serve chops over the rice, and drizzle with any leftover pan juices. Garnish with cilantro sprigs.

ROASTED PEPPER CHICKEN BREAST

MAKES: 4 servings   **COOK:** 1 hour

FOR THE CHICKEN:

- 4   boneless, skinless chicken breasts
- 3   cups chicken broth
- ½   zest and juice of 1 lemon
- ½   cup frozen chopped onions, thawed
- 1   (0.37-ounce) Recipe Inspirations Spanish Chicken Skillet seasoning packet— McCormick
- 1   (12-ounce) jar roasted red peppers
     Salt and pepper, to taste

FOR THE LEMONY RICE:

- 2   cups low-sodium chicken broth
- 2   tablespoons olive oil
     Zest from ½ lemon
     1 lemon, juiced
- 2   (3.8-ounce) boxes whole-grain chicken-and-herb flavored rice
- ½   cup white wine

1. Rinse chicken under cold water and pat dry with paper towels. In a high-sided skillet over medium-low heat, bring the broth to a simmer. Add the lemon zest and juice, onions, and seasoning packet, and stir to combine. Add the chicken to the skillet and cover. Simmer on low until chicken is cooked through, about 20 minutes. Remove chicken from skillet and slice into ½-inch-thick slices. Add the peppers with the juice from the jar to a blender along with ⅓ cup of poaching liquid. Puree until smooth. If it is too thick, slowly add additional poaching liquid until it reaches desired consistency. Season with salt and pepper to taste. Transfer to a small pot and bring to a simmer. Serve the chicken topped with the roasted pepper sauce and alongside the Lemony Rice.

2. In a large saucepan over low heat, combine the chicken broth and olive oil and bring to a simmer. Add the lemon zest, lemon juice, rice, one of the rice seasoning packets, and the wine. Cover and cook until the rice is tender and the liquid is absorbed, 25 to 30 minutes.

PORK MEDALLIONS WITH GLAZED BRUSSELS SPROUTS

MAKES: 4 servings   **COOK:** 25 minutes

1¼ pounds pork tenderloin

2 teaspoons garlic salt

1 tablespoon citrus herb seasoning

1 (16-ounce) bag Brussels sprouts

½ cup plus 2 tablespoons tangerine juice, divided use

2 tablespoons canola oil

¼ cup honey

2 teaspoons stone-ground mustard

1. Rinse tenderloin under cold water and pat dry with paper towels. Cut into eight 1-inch medallions, season with garlic salt and citrus herb seasoning, and set aside. Heat Brussels sprouts and ½ cup tangerine juice in a medium saucepan over high heat. Bring to a full boil, then reduce heat and cover. Simmer for 7 to 9 minutes. Remove sprouts and drain well.

2. Heat oil in a large skillet over medium heat. Sauté medallions for 3 to 4 minutes per side, or until golden brown. Remove medallions from pan and set aside. Heat the honey with the remaining 2 tablespoons tangerine juice and mustard in the skillet until it begins to bubble at the edges. Add Brussels sprouts and toss to coat. Return medallions to skillet along with any accumulated juices, turning to coat with glaze. Cook 1 to 2 minutes or until heated through. Serve hot.

PRIME RIB AU JUS

MAKES: 4 servings   **COOK:** 2 to 3 hours

1   (4- to 5-pound) beef rib roast
5   cloves garlic, slivered
2   tablespoons spicy brown mustard
¼   cup peppercorn and garlic marinade
½   cup red wine
1   cup beef broth

1. Preheat oven to 350°F.
2. Using a paring knife, make small slits into roast about 3 inches apart and press the garlic slivers into the slits. Using a pastry brush, coat the entire roast with mustard. Sprinkle marinade to completely cover the roast. Place on a rack in a roasting pan and cook at 350°F until a thermometer inserted into the center reads 130°F. Remove from oven, cover with foil, and allow to rest for 10 to 15 minutes.
3. To make au jus, place roasting pan over stovetop burners on medium-low. Whisk in wine and scrape off the little brown bits from the bottom of the roasting pan. Reduce slightly and add broth. Bring to a simmer and reduce slightly. Serve along with sliced prime rib.

ROASTED CHICKEN WITH WINTER SQUASH

MAKES: 4 servings   **COOK:** 1 hour

1   (1.25-ounce) packet Bag 'n Season Chicken mix—McCormick, divided use
1   (20-ounce) package cut butternut squash, cut into 1-inch cubes
2   teaspoons pumpkin pie spice
2   tablespoons packed brown sugar
2½   pounds chicken breasts, thighs, and drumsticks

1. Preheat oven to 350°F.
2. Add 1 tablespoon chicken seasoning and the squash to a large oven bag, hold closed, and shake to coat inside of bag. Place bag in a 9 × 13-inch baking pan and set aside.
3. Combine remaining chicken seasoning, pie spice, and brown sugar in a small bowl. Rinse chicken under cold water and pat dry with paper towels. Season chicken well and place in a single layer over squash. Sprinkle in any remaining seasoning mixture.
4. Close oven bag with an ovenproof tie and cut 4 small holes in the top of the bag. Bake in the lower half of the oven for 1 hour. Let rest 5 minutes before cutting open bag. Serve hot.

ROASTED GARLIC MUSHROOM RISOTTO

MAKES: 4 servings   **COOK:** 1 hour 40 minutes

  1 head garlic
2½ teaspoons extra-virgin olive oil, divided use
  2 (14.5-ounce) cans chicken broth
  3 (14.5-ounce) cans water
  1 medium onion, chopped
  1 (8-ounce) package sliced mushrooms
2½ cups long grain rice
  2 tablespoons butter
  ½ cup grated Parmesan cheese
     Salt and pepper, to taste

1. Preheat oven to 350°F.
2. Slice the top off the head of garlic. Place exposed cloves on a square of aluminum foil and drizzle with 1 teaspoon extra-virgin olive oil. Wrap the foil around the garlic and put it in the oven until garlic is soft, about 50 minutes to 1 hour. Remove from the oven and let cool.
3. Pour broth into a saucepan and add water. Bring to a simmer.
4. In a large heavy-bottomed skillet, heat remaining olive oil over medium-high heat. Add the onion and sauté for 3 minutes. Add the mushrooms, season with salt and pepper, and cook until the mushrooms release their juices, about 5 minutes. Add the rice and cook for 1 minute to toast.
5. Add 2 ladlefuls of hot broth to the pan and gently stir the rice. Cook until most of the liquid has been absorbed. Adjust the heat so that the liquid is just gently bubbling. Continue adding broth and stirring until all the broth is used and the rice is cooked through but not mushy, about 20 to 25 minutes.
6. Once the rice has absorbed all the liquid and is nice and creamy, stir in the butter and Parmesan cheese, and garlic pulp. Cover and let rest for 2 minutes. Transfer to a serving dish and serve hot.

ROASTED LAMB WITH RED WINE REDUCTION

MAKES: 8 servings   **COOK:** 2 hours 40 minutes

10 garlic cloves, peeled

1 tablespoon chopped fresh rosemary

1 tablespoon Dijon mustard

¼ cup extra-virgin olive oil

1 tablespoon steak seasoning

1 (3 ½- to 4-pound) boneless rolled leg of lamb

1 bottle Merlot wine

1 (0.87-ounce) packet brown gravy mix

2 tablespoons cold butter, cut into 4 pieces

1. Preheat oven to 350°F.

2. Combine garlic and rosemary in a food processor and pulse to finely chop. Scrape down sides of bowl and add mustard. With the motor running, slowly drizzle in oil. Stir in steak seasoning. Poke holes all over lamb with a sharp knife, and rub garlic-rosemary paste over it, pushing paste down into holes.

3. Place lamb in a flameproof roasting pan and roast in preheated oven for approximately 2 hours for medium rare (135°F) or 2½ hours for medium (150°F). Remove roast to a cutting board and tent with foil. Internal temperature will continue to rise 5 to 10 degrees.

4. Carefully drain fat from roasting pan and place pan on stovetop over a medium flame. Reserve ½ cup wine and deglaze the pan with the remaining wine, scraping up the browned bits. Bring to a boil and reduce by half. Strain reduction into a small saucepan. Dissolve gravy mix in the reserved red wine and whisk into the reduction. Bring to a boil and reduce heat to a simmer for 1 minute. While sauce simmers, whisk in butter, 1 piece at a time.

5. Remove strings from roast and slice. Serve hot with red wine reduction sauce.

SAGE-PESTO ROAST CHICKEN STUFFED WITH RICE

MAKES: 4 servings **COOK:** 1 hour

FOR THE RUB:

- 1 (1.5-ounce) package fresh sage leaves, 4 whole leaves reserved
- 2 (3.5-ounce) jars pesto sauce, divided use

FOR THE RICE:

- 1 cup instant rice
- ½ cup less-sodium chicken broth

FOR THE CHICKEN:

- 1 (3- to 4-pound) roasting chicken
  Nonstick cooking spray

1. Preheat oven to 400°F. Line a baking sheet with foil and spray with cooking oil spray.

2. In a bowl, stir the rice, broth, and 1 tablespoon of the pesto sauce together. Set aside.

3. To make the rub, pulse the sage leaves and pesto in the food processor until smooth. Transfer to a small bowl.

4. To make the chicken, remove giblets from the cavity, if there are any. Rinse the chicken inside and out in cool water and pat dry with paper towels. Gently run your finger between the breast and skin of the bird, taking care not to detach the center where the skin meets the meat. Insert sage leaves at an angle under the skin, manipulating so they lie flat, 2 leaves on each side.

5. Rub whole chicken with pesto mixture inside and out. Spoon rice mixture into the cavity.

6. Place chicken on baking sheet and put in oven. Turn heat down to 350°F, and roast for 45 minutes to 1 hour or until golden. A thermometer inserted into the thickest part of the thigh should read 170°F. If the rice hasn't absorbed all the cooking liquid, strain it and pour over the cooked bird.

SOUTHWEST BEEF AND BLACK BEAN CHILI

MAKES: 4 servings **COOK:** 35 minutes

1 tablespoon canola oil

1 medium yellow onion, diced

1 tablespoon chopped garlic

½ pound ground beef

1 (28-ounce) can crushed tomatoes

1 (15-ounce) can black beans, drained

1½ tablespoons chili powder

2 cups water

¼ cup shredded Monterey Jack cheese

Salt and pepper, to taste

1. Heat a large saucepan over medium heat and add oil, diced onion, and garlic. Sauté until onions are golden, about 5 minutes. Add the beef and cook, breaking it up with a spoon, until it is not pink, about 3 to 5 minutes. Add tomatoes, black beans, chili powder, and water. Turn heat down and simmer for 30 minutes. Season with salt and pepper to taste. Serve hot. Sprinkle 1 tablespoon of cheese over each bowl of chili.

SWEET AND STICKY SPARERIBS WITH FRIED NOODLES

MAKES: 4 servings   **COOK:** 1 hour 40 minutes

FOR THE MARINADE:

1	tablespoon canola oil
2	tablespoons barbeque sauce
2	tablespoons sweet chili sauce
3	tablespoons white vinegar
¼	cup soy sauce
2	teaspoons finely chopped ginger
1	tablespoon chopped garlic
1	cup pineapple juice
¼	cup brown sugar

2 ½ pounds pork spareribs

FOR THE FRIED NOODLES:

½	(12-ounce) package wonton wrappers
1	cup canola oil
	Salt and pepper

1. Whisk together all ingredients to make marinade. Slice spareribs and place in a large zip-top bag. Pour marinade over spareribs and toss to coat. Place the bag into a large bowl and let marinate in the refrigerator for 2 hours.

2. Preheat oven to 300°F.

3. Remove spareribs from marinade. Reserve marinade and place spareribs on a baking sheet. Cover with foil, and poke holes to vent. Bake for 1½ hours or until spareribs are tender.

4. In the meantime, bring remaining marinade to a boil in a saucepan, reduce to a simmer, and cook until thick, about 30 minutes.

5. Remove foil from spareribs and raise oven temperature to 400°F. Baste spareribs with reduced marinade and roast in oven for 5 minutes. Turn and baste with remaining sauce, and roast for an additional 5 minutes.

6. For the fried noodles, heat 1 cup canola oil in a medium saucepan. Cut wonton wrappers into ½-inch-wide strips. Fry in batches until golden brown and drain on a plate lined with a brown paper bag. Serve hot with the spareribs.

VEGETABLE LO MEIN

MAKES: 4 servings **COOK:** 7 minutes

1 (8-ounce) package lo mein noodles
2 tablespoons vegetable oil
2 teaspoons chopped garlic
1 teaspoon peeled and chopped ginger
1 (16-ounce) bag frozen stir-fry vegetables
¼ cup soy sauce
1 teaspoon sugar
¼ teaspoon salt
2 scallions, finely sliced
1 tablespoon sesame oil

1. Cook the noodles according to package directions. Drain, rinse with cold water, and drain again.
2. In a large skillet over medium-high heat, add the vegetable oil. When it is hot, add the garlic and ginger, and cook for 30 seconds. Add the vegetables and stir-fry until heated through, about 3 minutes. Add the noodles and mix well. Mix together the soy sauce, sugar, and salt, and stir into the noodles. Stir in the scallions and sesame oil and serve.

TUSCAN VEGGIE POT PIE

MAKES: 4 servings **BAKE:** 45 minutes

1 box pie crust mix (any brand that makes enough for two crusts)
3 cups Select Harvest Chicken Tuscany soup—Campbell's Select Harvest
1 tablespoon all-purpose flour
1 cup frozen pearl onions
½ cup frozen peas
1 egg

1. Preheat oven to 350°F.
2. Prepare pie crust according to package directions. Divide in half. Roll out one portion and put into bottom of a 9-inch pie plate or tin.
3. Stir together soup, flour, onions, and peas and pour into the prepared pie crust. Roll out the second portion of the dough and place on top of pie. Crimp edges to seal, and slash steam vents into the top. Beat egg and brush over top and edges of crust.
4. Place pie on a baking sheet and bake for 40 to 45 minutes or until crust is golden brown. Remove from oven and allow to cool slightly before serving warm.

ZESTY STRIP STEAKS AND ROASTED FINGERLING POTATOES

MAKES: 4 servings **COOK:** 20 minutes

4 (1-inch-thick) New York strip steaks

⅓ cup Italian salad dressing

⅓ cup steak sauce

⅓ cup barbeque sauce

1 tablespoon steak seasoning

1 tablespoon butter, melted

3 tablespoons extra-virgin olive oil, divided use

1½ pounds fingerling potatoes, washed and patted dry

1 tablespoon lemon zest

½ teaspoon onion salt

1 teaspoon garlic sea salt

½ teaspoon poultry seasoning

1. Rinse steaks with cold water and pat dry with paper towels. Place in a large zip-top bag and set aside. In a bowl, stir together salad dressing, steak sauce, and barbeque sauce. Pour into bag with steaks. Make sure steaks are coated, squeeze air from bag, and seal. Marinate in refrigerator for 1 hour.

2. Preheat oven to 425°F. Line a baking sheet with foil and set aside.

3. Remove steaks from marinade, scraping off excess, and let them come to room temperature for 30 minutes. Discard marinade. Pat steaks dry with paper towels and season with steak seasoning. Set aside.

4. Stir together melted butter and 1 tablespoon oil in a large microwave-safe bowl. Add potatoes and toss together. Cover and cook in microwave on 100 percent power for 8 minutes. Remove cover carefully, and cool for 5 minutes.

5. Combine zest, onion salt, garlic salt, and poultry seasoning in a small bowl. Sprinkle over potatoes and toss to coat thoroughly. Place potatoes on prepared baking sheet.

6. Heat a heavy ovenproof pan over medium-high heat for 5 minutes. When the pan is very hot, add remaining oil and sear the steaks for 4 to 5 minutes on one side. Turn the steaks and place the pan in the oven along with the potatoes. Cook for 7 minutes for medium rare and 9 minutes for medium. The potatoes will take 12 minutes or until a fork inserts easily into the center. Remove steaks from oven and let rest while potatoes finish cooking. Serve hot.

FORTUNE COOKIES

MAKES: 24 cookies   **BAKE:** 10 minutes

½   cup all-purpose flour

1   teaspoon cornstarch

½   cup sugar

2   large egg whites

1   teaspoon vanilla extract

2   tablespoons canola oil

1   tablespoon water

    Nonstick cooking spray

1. Write your fortunes on 24 pieces of paper that are about ½-inch wide and 2 ½-inches long.

2. Preheat oven to 300°F.

3. In a small bowl, sift together the flour, cornstarch, and sugar.

4. In a medium bowl, whisk together the egg whites, vanilla, oil, and water until smooth. Add the dry ingredients into the wet and mix until a smooth batter is formed.

5. Working in batches of 4, drop batter by tablespoonfuls onto a nonstick baking sheet lightly coated with cooking spray. Tilt the baking sheet in a circular motion to spread batter into 4-inch-diameter circles.

6. Bake for 10 minutes or until edges of cookies are golden brown. Remove from oven and, working quickly, use a spatula to remove the cookies from the baking sheet. Place the fortune into the center of a cookie, and fold the cookie in half. Bring the points together with open seams on the outside. Place into a muffin tin to help keep shape while cooling.

7. Repeat with remaining fortunes and cookies. Transfer to a serving bowl and serve.

MINI PARTY CAKES

MAKES: 12 mini cakes   **BAKE:** 25 minutes

1   (18.25-ounce) box cherry chip cake mix—
    Betty Crocker

3   eggs

⅓   cup vegetable oil

1¼ cups cran-cherry juice

3   tablespoons butter

1½ (7-ounce) jars marshmallow cream

1   teaspoon cherry extract

FOR THE VOLCANO:

12 waffle or sugar ice cream cones

2   (16-ounce) cans chocolate frosting
    Red, yellow, and orange decorating icing

PARTY HAT:

12 waffle or sugar ice cream cones

2   (12-ounce) cans fluffy white frosting
    Neon food coloring, various colors
    Decorating icing and candy confetti

FOR THE CHICK-A-DEE:

12 large marshmallows

2   (12-ounce) cans fluffy white frosting
    Yellow food coloring, sanding sugar, and
    spice drops

24 vanilla wafer cookies

FOR THE PETITE FLOWER GARDEN:

12 large marshmallows

2   (12-ounce) cans fluffy white frosting
    Food coloring
    Sugar flowers

1. Preheat oven to 350°F. Lightly spray 12 large muffin cups with baking spray.

2. For the cake, combine cake mix, eggs, oil, and juice in a large mixing bowl. Beat together on low speed for 30 seconds; scrape down the sides of the bowl, then beat for 2 minutes on medium speed. Divide batter evenly among the baking cups. Bake in preheated oven for 20 to 25 minutes or until a tester inserted in the cupcakes comes away clean. Let cool for 5 minutes in the pans before transferring to a wire cooling rack to cool completely.

3. For the marshmallow filling, melt butter in a large microwave-safe bowl for 20 seconds on 100 percent power. Stir in marshmallow cream and cherry extract, and microwave for 1 minute on 50 percent power. Remove and cool for 2 minutes. Beat with an electric mixer until smooth.

4. Level the tops of the cupcakes and turn upside-down—the bottom is now the top. Make a ½-inch slit in the top center of each cupcake. Place marshmallow filling in a pastry bag and pipe filling into each cupcake center gently, so the filling doesn't come through the bottom. Set cakes on mini foil pie pan pedestals and decorate.

5. *Volcano*: Frost cupcakes and snip off the tip of the cone for the crater. Frost cone and set on top of cupcake. Use colored decorating icing to create the lava flow.

6. *Party Hats*: Color each can of frosting with a different shade of food coloring. Frost cupcakes one color and cones the other. Set the cones on the cakes and decorate with decorating icing and candy confetti.

7. *Chick-a-dee*: Color the frosting yellow and frost the cakes. Set a marshmallow on top of each cake and, using a piping bag, swirl the frosting around and over the marshmallow. Smooth frosting and sprinkle with sanding sugar. Trim and smash small pieces of white and purple spice drops for the eyes and trim orange spice drops for beaks. Insert vanilla wafer cookies into the side for wings and frost.

8. *Petite Flower Garden*: Color the frosting light green and frost the cakes. Set a marshmallow on top of each cake and, using a piping bag, swirl the frosting around and over the marshmallow. Decorate with sugar flowers.

SANDY'S ICED CUTOUT COOKIES

MAKES: 36 cookies **BAKE:** 11 minutes

FOR THE COOKIES:

 (17.25-ounce) package sugar cookie mix

½ cup all-purpose flour

4 tablespoons butter, softened

¼ cup cream cheese, softened

1 egg

1 teaspoon lemon extract

 Flour, for dusting board

FOR THE ICING:

1 pound powdered sugar

¼ cup pasteurized egg whites

1 teaspoon lemon extract

 Food coloring

1. Preheat oven to 375°F. Line baking sheets with kitchen parchment.
2. Whisk together cookie mix and flour in a large mixing bowl. With a wooden spoon, stir in softened butter and cream cheese, egg, and extract until a soft dough forms.
3. Split dough in half and shape each half into a disk. Roll out on a lightly floured surface to ¼-inch thick. Cut out desired shapes and place on baking sheets. Repeat with remaining dough. Chill cutout cookies in refrigerator for 15 minutes before baking. Bake in preheated oven for 9 to 11 minutes or until edges are just golden. Cool on baking sheets for 2 minutes before transferring to wire cooling racks. Scraps can be gathered up and rerolled once with good results.
4. For the icing, combine ingredients in a medium mixing bowl. Beat on low speed until incorporated, then beat on medium speed until medium peaks form. If icing is too thin, add more powdered sugar; thin with a few drops of water if too stiff. Color icing if desired. Use immediately to frost or pipe onto cookies.

SWEDISH PANCAKE DELIGHT

MAKES: 8 servings   **COOK:** 15 minutes

FOR THE PANCAKES:

2   cups milk

2   large eggs

4   tablespoons melted butter, divided use

½   teaspoon vanilla

1   cup all-purpose flour

¼   cup sugar

1   pinch salt

FOR THE FILLINGS:

1   (15-ounce) can cherry pie filling, divided use

1   (8-ounce) container whipped cream cheese

2   bananas, sliced

½   cup chocolate and hazelnut spread
    Powdered sugar, for garnish

1. For the batter, whisk together milk, eggs, 2 tablespoons melted butter, and vanilla in a large bowl. In another bowl, whisk together flour, sugar, and salt. Combine the dry ingredients into the wet ingredients, whisking out any lumps. Let the batter rest for a few minutes while you prepare the fillings.

2. For the fillings, mix together 1 cup cherry pie filling and cream cheese. Cover and refrigerate until ready to serve. Put the remaining cherry pie filling into a serving bowl.

3. For the pancakes, grease the pan with a bit of melted butter. Pour ¼ cup of batter into the pan, swirling to coat the pan evenly. When the top looks dry and bubbles and the edges are lightly browned, about 1 minute, flip the pancake over and cook for an additional 20 seconds. Place the pancake onto a plate and continue cooking remaining batter in ¼-cup increments, brushing the pan with melted butter as needed. Stack the pancakes on top of each other and set aside, covered with foil, until ready to serve.

4. To serve, put the pancakes out along with bowls of the remaining cherry pie filling, sliced bananas, and chocolate spread. Fill a pancake with a dollop of one of the fillings. Fold it in half and roll it up like a cigar. Garnish with a dollop of the remaining cherry pie filling, or sprinkle with a little powdered sugar.

FEBRUARY

BRIE AND MERLOT MUSHROOM BITES

MAKES: 15 pieces **COOK:** 20 minutes

1 package mini phyllo shells

2 tablespoons butter

1 shallot, finely diced

2 cloves garlic, finely diced

4 ounces mixed oyster mushrooms, sliced

4 ounces shiitake mushrooms, stems removed and sliced

½ cup Merlot wine

2 teaspoons fresh thyme leaves

¼ pound Brie cheese

4 chives, sliced, for garnish

Salt and pepper, to taste

1. Preheat oven to 350°F. Bake the shells according to package directions. Let cool while you make the filling.

2. Heat a skillet over medium heat and add the butter. When the butter is melted, add the shallot and garlic and cook until soft, about 5 minutes. Add the mushrooms and season with salt and pepper. When the mushrooms have released their liquid, add the Merlot and cook until most of the liquid has evaporated, about 10 minutes. Stir in the thyme leaves.

3. Cut the Brie into 15 small pieces. Divide the mushroom mixture among the shells. Top each with a piece of cheese. Return the shells to the oven and bake until the cheese has melted, about 5 minutes. Serve warm. Garnish with sliced chives.

CHAMPAGNE ARTICHOKE HEARTS

MAKES: 6 servings   **COOK:** 12 minutes

- 2 tablespoons butter
- 1 tablespoon crushed garlic
- ¼ cup frozen chopped onions, thawed
- 2 (9-ounce) boxes frozen artichoke hearts, thawed
- 1 cup vegetable broth
- 1 cup sparkling wine
- 1 teaspoon salt
- ½ teaspoon ground black pepper

1. In a large pot over medium heat, combine butter, garlic, and onions, and sweat for 5 minutes until onions are soft and translucent. Stir in artichoke hearts, vegetable broth, and sparkling wine. Season with salt and pepper. Simmer over medium heat for 6 to 7 minutes. To serve, ladle the artichokes into a bowl.

CHARDONNAY RICE WITH GOLDEN RAISINS

MAKES: 4 servings   **COOK:** 25 minutes

- 1½ cups dry white wine
- ½ cup golden raisins
- 2 cups water
- 1 tablespoon butter
- 1 pinch salt
- 1½ cups long grain rice
- ½ cup sliced almonds
- 1 tablespoon chopped fresh parsley, for garnish

1. In a small pot over medium heat, warm ½ cup of wine. Take the pot off the heat, add the raisins, and let sit until cooled and raisins plump up.
2. In a medium pot over high heat, bring water, remaining wine, butter, and salt to a boil. Stir in the rice, reduce the heat to low, cover, and cook until the rice is tender, about 20 minutes. Strain the raisins and scatter them over the top of the rice. Cover and let rest for about 10 minutes. Fluff the rice with a fork, stir in the almonds, garnish with parsley, and serve.

ICEBERG WEDGE SALAD WITH WARM BACON DRESSING

MAKES: 4 servings   **COOK:** 12 minutes

1   head iceberg lettuce
4   slices bacon
2   teaspoons brown sugar
¼   cup red wine vinegar
1   hard-boiled egg, finely chopped
    Salt and pepper, to taste

1. Remove core from lettuce and cut into 4 quarters. Set aside.
2. In a skillet, sauté bacon until crisp. Remove from skillet to a plate lined with a paper bag. Once cooled, chop into small pieces. Add brown sugar, vinegar, and salt and pepper to skillet. Whisk together until combined and sugar is completely dissolved. Stir in egg and bacon and season with salt and pepper. Pour over top of iceberg wedges and serve immediately.

PORK CABBAGE WRAPS

MAKES: 4 rolls   **COOK:** 1 minute

4   cabbage leaves
¼   carrot, grated
¼   small cucumber, julienned
¼   cup shredded cabbage
1   tablespoon freshly chopped cilantro
1   teaspoon chopped garlic
1   tablespoon chopped ginger
1   tablespoon white vinegar
3   tablespoons soy sauce
1   tablespoon canola oil
1   pork chop, precooked, from deli counter

1. Make a V-shaped cut in the bottom of each cabbage leaf to remove the tough part of the stem. In a large pot of salted boiling water, blanch cabbage leaves for 30 seconds. Remove from pot and stop cooking by shocking in an ice bath.
2. In a large bowl, mix together grated carrot, julienned cucumber, shredded cabbage, and cilantro.
3. In another bowl, whisk together garlic, ginger, white vinegar, soy sauce, and oil. Pour over vegetables and toss to coat. Dice pork chop into bite-size pieces, add to the vegetables, and toss.
4. Remove cabbage leaves and pat dry. Place a quarter of the filling onto the lower third of one of the cabbage leaves. Roll up the leaf halfway. Fold the sides of the leaf in toward the center, and finish rolling it up from the bottom. Repeat with remaining ingredients.

SAUTÉED MUSHROOMS AND ONIONS

MAKES: 4 servings   **COOK:** 15 to 20 minutes

4   tablespoons butter
1   (8-ounce) package sliced shiitake mushrooms
1   (8-ounce) package sliced baby portobello mushrooms
1   cup frozen onions, thawed
¼   cup Canadian whisky
2   sprigs fresh thyme leaves, chopped
1   cup heavy cream
    Salt and pepper, to taste

1. In a large skillet over medium heat, add the butter. When the butter has melted, add the mushrooms and onions, and season with salt and pepper. Cook until they begin to soften and the mushrooms release their juices, about 7 minutes. Take the pan off the heat and add the whisky. Place back on the heat, add thyme, and cook until the moisture has evaporated and the pan is almost dry, about 3 minutes. Add the cream and bring to a simmer. Cook until the cream thickens a bit, about 4 to 5 minutes. Taste and adjust the seasoning with salt and pepper. Transfer to a serving bowl and serve with Rib Eye Steaks.

ZUCCHINI AL FORMAGGIO

MAKES: 4 servings   **COOK:** 7 minutes

2   tablespoons olive oil
4   medium zucchini, sliced ¼-inch thick
2   tablespoons butter, room temperature
1   teaspoon Italian seasoning
½   cup grated Parmesan cheese
2   tablespoons finely chopped fresh parsley
    Shaved Parmesan cheese, for garnish
    Salt and pepper, to taste

1. Heat olive oil in a large sauté pan over high heat. Add zucchini slices and sauté for 5 minutes until slightly brown and tender. Add butter, Italian seasoning, grated Parmesan, parsley, salt, and pepper, and toss to combine.
2. Remove to a serving bowl with a slotted spoon. Top with shaved Parmesan. Serve hot.

CHICKEN CHERRY BAGUETTE BURGERS

MAKES: 4 Servings **COOK:** 40 minutes

FOR THE BURGERS:

- 1 (11-ounce) roll refrigerated French bread dough
- 1 pound ground chicken
- 1 cup frozen cherries, thawed and minced
- 1 tablespoon minced sweet cherry peppers
- 1 teaspoon minced fresh rosemary
- ½ teaspoon salt
- ¼ teaspoon pepper

  Nonstick cooking spray

FOR THE CHERRY MAYO:

- 2 tablespoons black cherry jam, divided use
- ⅔ cup mayonnaise

FOR THE GARNISH:

- 1 large, ripe tomato, thinly sliced
- 8 pieces leaf lettuce

1. Preheat oven to 350°F.
2. Bake bread according to package directions, then cool. Cut loaf horizontally.
3. Combine ground chicken, cherries, cherry peppers, rosemary, and salt and pepper in a large bowl. Stir well to combine. Shape into 4 patties. Mist a large nonstick frying pan with cooking spray and place over medium heat until hot. Cook burgers for about 5 minutes per side, or until cooked through.
4. Stir jam into mayonnaise in a small bowl. Spread mixture on cut sides of bread. Cut the loaf into 4 equal sections. Top the bottom of each section with burger, then tomato slices and 2 pieces lettuce. Place bread top on lettuce and serve.

CRISPY EGGPLANT PARMESAN

MAKES: 4 servings **COOK:** 30 minutes

2 tablespoons canola oil

1 medium onion, chopped

1 tablespoon chopped garlic

½ teaspoon red pepper flakes

2 teaspoons Italian seasoning

1 (28-ounce) can crushed tomatoes

½ cup all-purpose flour (plus extra for dredging)

2 eggs

½ cup water

1 cup dried Italian bread crumbs

½ cup cornmeal

¼ cup grated Parmesan, divided

2 eggplants

1 cup shredded mozzarella cheese

2 tablespoons chopped parsley leaves, for garnish

Salt and pepper, to taste

1. In a large pot over medium-high heat, add the canola oil. Add the onion and cook until softened, about 5 minutes. Add the garlic and red pepper flakes and cook for 1 minute. Add the Italian seasoning and tomatoes, and season with salt and pepper, to taste. Bring to a simmer and let cook for 10 minutes.

2. Preheat oven to 375°F.

3. Set up a breading station using 3 baking dishes. In the first dish, add the flour and season with salt and pepper, to taste. In the second dish, whisk the eggs with the water. In the third dish, combine the bread crumbs, cornmeal, and 2 tablespoons Parmesan, and season with salt and pepper, to taste. Slice the eggplants into ¾-inch slices. Dredge them in flour, then in the egg wash, and then in the bread crumbs. Arrange the eggplant on 2 sheet trays fitted with racks and bake in oven until crispy, about 20 to 25 minutes. Reserve 4 slices of eggplant for the online round 2 recipe Eggplant and Pasta.

4. Turn the oven to broil. Put the eggplant slices, overlapping, into a baking dish in 2 rows. Cover each row with about a cup of sauce and sprinkle with the mozzarella cheese and remaining 2 tablespoons of Parmesan. Put under the broiler until the cheese is melted and bubbling, about 3 to 4 minutes. Garnish with parsley and serve.

FLAT IRON STEAK WITH CABERNET SAUCE

MAKES: 4 Servings   **COOK:** 20 minutes

1   (1½-pound) flat iron steak
1   cup beef broth
1   cup Cabernet Sauvignon wine
1   tablespoon grill seasoning
3   tablespoons canola oil
1   shallot, chopped
4   tablespoons butter

1. Take the steak out of the refrigerator 25 minutes before you are ready to cook it. This will help it cook more evenly.
2. In a small pot over high heat, add the broth and wine and simmer until reduced by half, about 10 minutes.
3. Heat oil in a cast-iron skillet over medium-high heat until it is very hot. Season the steak with the grill seasoning and place it in the skillet. Cook about 3 minutes per side for medium rare. Remove steak from skillet, cover it with foil, and let it rest for 10 minutes while you finish the sauce.
4. Reduce the heat under the skillet to medium and add the shallot. Cook until it begins to soften, about 3 to 4 minutes. Add the reduced broth-and-wine mixture and cook for about 5 minutes, until thickened. Remove from the heat and swirl in the butter.
5. Slice the steak against the grain into thin slices, place on a serving platter, and serve with the sauce on the side or poured over the top.

FARM HENS WITH TRUFFLED CREAM

MAKES: 4 servings   **COOK:** 1 hour 40 minutes

4   Cornish game hens
4   tablespoons butter, softened
2   teaspoons chopped garlic
1   tablespoon herbes de Provence
1   cup chicken broth
½   cup white wine
1   (10.5-ounce) can white sauce
¼   teaspoon truffle oil
    Salt and pepper, to taste

1. Preheat oven to 375°F.
2. Remove giblets from hens, rinse hens with cold water, and pat dry inside and out. Mix together the butter, garlic, and herbes in a small bowl. Loosen skin on the breast of each hen. Using half the butter mixture, spread under skin of each hen. Rub skin with remaining butter, and season with salt and pepper. Place hens on a rack in a shallow roasting pan.
3. Roast hens 1 to 1½ hours; internal temperature should be 180°F at the thigh. Add broth to the pan after 20 minutes and baste twice during cooking time. Transfer hens to a platter.
4. Place roasting pan directly on top of burner over medium heat. Add wine, scrape up browned bits, and boil until reduced to ¼ cup. Whisk in white sauce until smooth. Strain sauce and stir in truffle oil. Season with salt and pepper. Spoon sauce over hens.

FRAGRANT ORANGE ROASTED PORK LOIN

MAKES: 8 servings   **COOK:** 1 hour 40 minutes

½ cup plus 2 tablespoons frozen orange juice concentrate, divided use

2 tablespoons Dijon mustard

1 tablespoon chopped garlic

1 tablespoon ground bay leaves

1 teaspoon salt

1 teaspoon black pepper

1 (3-pound) boneless pork loin roast

2 tablespoons olive oil

½ cup water

1 cup dry white wine

1 (0.9-ounce) packet béarnaise sauce mix

¼ cup heavy cream

1. Preheat oven to 350°F.
2. Mix ½ cup orange juice concentrate, mustard, garlic, bay leaves, salt, and pepper, to make a paste.
3. Rinse pork under cold water and pat dry with paper towels. Place in a roasting pan and rub with paste. Drizzle with olive oil.
4. Roast the pork, turning and basting with pan liquids. After 30 minutes add ½ cup of water to pan to prevent basting liquid from burning. Continue basting. After 1 hour, if basting liquid begins to burn, add another ½ cup water to pan. Cook for 1½ hours or until meat thermometer reads 155°F. Remove roast from pan onto a serving platter.
5. Deglaze pan with wine, and then pour off liquid from pan into a small saucepan. Heat over medium-high heat for 3 minutes. Combine sauce mix and heavy cream. Whisk remaining 2 tablespoons orange juice concentrate and cream mixture into sauce. Bring to a boil for additional 2 minutes. Serve with roast.

MEDITERRANEAN CASSEROLE

MAKES: 6 servings   **COOK:** 40 minutes

1   (24-ounce) bag Steam n' Mash Cut Russet
    Potatoes—Ore-Ida®

½   cup evaporated milk

1   tablespoon butter

1¼ pounds ground lamb

1   teaspoon garlic and herb seasoning

4   teaspoons Greek seasoning, divided use

6   ounces cream cheese, softened

¼   cup plain Greek yogurt

1   egg, lightly beaten

2   teaspoons lemon juice

2   packages frozen spinach, thawed

¼   cup pitted Kalamata olives, chopped

1   (4-ounce) container crumbled feta cheese
    Salt and pepper, to taste

1. Preheat oven to 350°F.

2. Microwave potatoes according to package
   directions. In a medium bowl, mash cooked
   potatoes, evaporated milk, and butter. Season
   to taste with salt and pepper, then press into
   the bottom of a 9 × 9-inch baking pan. Set
   aside.

3. Brown the lamb in a large skillet over medium
   heat, seasoning with garlic and herb seasoning
   and 2 teaspoons of Greek seasoning. Transfer
   with a slotted spoon to top the potatoes.

4. In a medium bowl, stir together cream cheese,
   yogurt, egg, and lemon juice until smooth.
   Squeeze excess moisture from spinach, add it
   to cream cheese mixture, then stir in remaining
   Greek seasoning and olives. Spoon evenly
   over top of lamb and then sprinkle with feta
   cheese.

5. Bake in preheated oven for 30 to 35 minutes.
   Serve hot.

OSSO BUCO

MAKES: 4 servings **COOK:** 8 to 10 hours

- 4 center-cut veal shanks
- ½ cup all-purpose flour
- 3 tablespoons olive oil
- 2 cups chopped turnips
- 1 cup diced celery
- 2 cups frozen sliced carrots
- 1 cup frozen pearl onions
- 1 (14.5-ounce) can diced tomatoes
- 1½ cups chicken stock
- ½ cup white wine
- 2 teaspoons Italian seasoning
  - Salt and pepper, to taste

1. Rinse veal under cold water and pat dry with paper towels. Use kitchen twine to tie the veal shanks around the circumference and season with salt and pepper. Dredge them in the flour and shake off any excess.
2. Heat a large sauté pan with 3 tablespoons olive oil over high heat. Add the floured shanks and brown on both sides, about 4 minutes per side. Remove to a plate.
3. Combine turnips, celery, carrots, pearl onions, and tomatoes in the bottom of a preheated 5-quart slow cooker. Place veal shanks on top of vegetables.
4. In a small bowl, stir together the chicken stock, wine, and Italian seasoning. Pour into slow cooker over veal shanks. Cover and cook on low setting for 8 to 10 hours. Strain, and remove fat from cooking liquid. Serve as sauce on the side.

PAPRIKA PORK CHOPS OVER SAFFRON COUSCOUS

MAKES: 6 servings **COOK:** 20 minutes

FOR THE PORK:
- 6 center-cut pork loin chops
- 1 tablespoon paprika
- 1 tablespoon steak seasoning
- 2 tablespoons vegetable oil

FOR THE COUSCOUS:
- 2 cups less-sodium chicken broth
- 1 pinch saffron threads
- ½ teaspoon salt
- 1 (10-ounce) box instant couscous
- ½ cup slivered almonds
- ⅓ cup dried apricots, chopped
- ⅓ cup currants
- 4 ounces goat cheese, crumbled
- ½ cup Niçoise olives, pitted
- ¼ cup finely chopped fresh parsley

1. Preheat oven to 350°F.
2. Rinse chops with water and pat dry. Combine paprika and steak seasoning and season chops. Heat oil in a large ovenproof skillet. Sauté for 1 minute per side until golden, then transfer skillet to the oven. Bake chops for 15 minutes or until cooked through. Transfer chops to a plate.
3. Meanwhile, in a saucepan, bring broth, saffron, and salt to a boil. Remove from heat and stir in couscous. Cover and set aside for 5 minutes. Transfer couscous to a bowl. Add remaining ingredients and toss.

RIB EYE STEAKS WITH SAVORY CHOCOLATE SAUCE

MAKES: 4 servings   **COOK:** 15 minutes

4   rib eye steaks (about 1½ to 2 pounds)

2   tablespoons canola oil

2   shallots, finely chopped

1   (14.5-ounce) can beef broth

1   tablespoon Worcestershire sauce

1   tablespoon brown gravy mix

2   tablespoons water

¼   cup grated dark chocolate

2   tablespoons cold butter, cut into cubes

2   tablespoons chopped fresh parsley, for garnish

Salt and pepper, to taste

1. Let the steaks sit out for 30 minutes before cooking to come to room temperature. Heat canola oil in a cast-iron skillet over medium-high heat. Season the steaks with salt and pepper. Sear them in the hot pan for about 3 minutes per side for medium rare. Remove the steaks from the pan, cover them loosely with foil, and let them rest for 5 minutes before slicing, while you make the sauce.

2. Turn the temperature of the skillet down to medium. Add the shallots, and cook until they soften a bit, about 2 minutes. Pour in the broth and Worcestershire sauce and bring to a simmer.

3. While broth comes to a simmer, combine the gravy mix and water in a small bowl. Add to the broth, stir, and simmer until thickened. Stir in the chocolate and cold butter to thicken the sauce. Taste and adjust the seasoning with salt and pepper.

4. Place the steaks onto a serving platter, pour sauce over top or serve on the side, and garnish with parsley.

RIGATONI WITH EGGPLANT SAUCE

MAKES: 4 servings   **COOK:** 25 minutes

- ½ (1-pound) package rigatoni
- 1 baby Italian eggplant, sliced in ½-inch-thick disks
- 1 tablespoon olive oil
- 4 cups chunky tomato sauce

FOR THE GARNISH:

- ¼ cup grated Parmesan cheese
- 1 tablespoon chopped fresh parsley

Salt and pepper, to taste

1. Bring a large pot of water to a boil. Add salt and cook pasta according to package directions.
2. Lightly brush all sides of eggplant with olive oil and season with salt and pepper. Place on the grill or grill pan, and grill for 3 minutes per side. Transfer to a cutting board and cut all the vegetables into bite-size pieces.
3. In a large skillet over medium heat, add the tomato sauce. When the pasta is cooked, drain it and add it to the skillet. Add eggplant and stir to completely coat the pasta with the sauce. Serve immediately, garnished with Parmesan cheese and parsley.

SMOTHERED PORK CHOPS

MAKES: 4 servings   **COOK:** 15 minutes

- 4 end-cut pork chops, about 1 ¼ pounds
- 2 tablespoons canola oil
- 1 medium onion, chopped
- 1 cup sliced mushrooms
- ¼ cup all-purpose flour
- 1 teaspoon cumin
- 1 (14.5-ounce) can chicken broth
- 2 tablespoons spicy mustard
- 2 tablespoons chopped fresh parsley, for garnish

Salt and pepper, to taste

1. Preheat an ovenproof skillet over high heat.
2. Rinse pork chops under cold water and pat dry with paper towels. Season pork chops with salt and pepper. Add 1 tablespoon canola oil to the pan. Sear pork chops on both sides until golden brown. Remove from skillet and set aside.
3. Heat remaining tablespoon of canola oil in same skillet over medium heat, add onions and mushrooms, and sauté until slightly softened. Add flour and cumin and cook until lightly golden in color. Mix in chicken broth and mustard and bring to a boil. Reduce to a simmer and return pork to skillet. Season with salt and pepper and spoon gravy over pork chops. Simmer for 5 minutes or until pork chops are cooked through. Garnish with parsley.

STUFFED CHICKEN BREAST WITH TOMATO BÉARNAISE SAUCE

MAKES: 4 servings   **COOK:** 16 minutes

FOR THE CHICKEN:

- 4 boneless, skinless chicken breasts, rinsed and patted dry
- 1 (3-ounce) package sliced prosciutto
- 4 ounces (4 to 6 sticks) mozzarella string cheese
- 2 teaspoons chicken seasoning
- 1 tablespoon olive oil
- 1 tablespoon butter

FOR THE SAUCE:

- 1 cup milk
- 1 tablespoon tomato paste
- 1 (0.9-ounce) packet béarnaise sauce mix

1. Rinse chicken under cold water and pat dry with paper towels. With a thin boning knife, carefully make a pocket in each chicken breast by inserting knife into the thick end and working the knife through the meat to the small end. The point of the knife should stop about 1 inch short of the thin end of the chicken breast.

2. At this point, you've just made a long, narrow hole. Insert a round wooden spoon handle to make the pocket as large as you need to accommodate the stuffing.

3. Divide the prosciutto slices and wrap them snugly around each cheese stick. Insert a wrapped cheese stick into the pocket of each breast, twisting slightly to hold the prosciutto around the cheese. Seal the open end (and any holes) securely with a toothpick. Sprinkle with chicken seasoning.

4. Heat the olive oil and butter in a medium skillet over medium-high heat. Sauté the stuffed breasts for 6 to 7 minutes. Turn often to sear the meat quickly. When lightly browned, turn the heat to medium and continue to cook for 6 to 8 minutes until golden brown and temperature registers 160°F. Do not put the thermometer in the cheese; try to keep it in the meat. Remove breasts from skillet and let them rest for 10 minutes, covered with foil.

5. In the same skillet, whisk in the milk, tomato paste, and sauce mix. Stirring constantly, cook for about 1 minute or until thickened. Serve chicken sliced and topped with sauce.

WEST COAST WHITE PIZZA

MAKES: 4 servings **BAKE:** 18 minutes

Nonstick cooking spray

1 (13.8-ounce) can refrigerated pizza crust dough

½ cup roasted garlic Alfredo pasta sauce

2 cups shredded mozzarella cheese

½ sweet onion, thinly sliced

1 (4-ounce) jar sliced mushrooms, drained

1½ cups shredded rotisserie chicken

¼ cup grated Parmesan cheese

2 teaspoons Italian seasoning

1. Adjust oven rack to lowest position and preheat oven to 425°F. Lightly spray a baking sheet with cooking spray.

2. Unroll dough and spread it into a 10 × 13-inch rectangle. Spread sauce over dough. Top with mozzarella cheese, onion, mushrooms, and chicken. Combine Parmesan and Italian seasoning, and sprinkle over pizza. Bake in preheated oven for 13 to 18 minutes or until crust is golden brown and cheese is bubbling. Slice and serve hot.

WHOLE SNAPPER WITH LEMON AND OREGANO

MAKES: 4 servings   **COOK:** 14 minutes

2 whole (1¼- to 1½-pound) red snappers, cleaned and scaled

¼ cup fresh lemon juice

2 tablespoons extra-virgin olive oil

1 tablespoon dried oregano, crushed

2 teaspoons chili powder

1 tablespoon crushed garlic

Canola oil cooking spray

12 corn tortillas, warm, for serving

1 lemon, cut into wedges, for serving

Salt

1. Rinse fish inside and out with cold water, then pat dry with paper towels, including the cavity. Lightly score each side of both fish in a crisscross pattern, at about 1-inch intervals; set fish aside in a baking dish. Whisk together lemon juice, olive oil, oregano, chili powder, and garlic, and pour over fish.

2. Rub marinade over and in the cavity of each fish, making sure marinade gets into the score marks as well. Let cure for 30 minutes.

3. Set up the grill for direct cooking over medium heat. Brush and oil grate before cooking. Pat the surface of the fish dry with paper towels. Spray both sides of fish with cooking spray and season well with salt. Place fish in a grill basket or onto a very clean grill. Cook 7 minutes per side. Remove fish carefully so it doesn't stick. Transfer fish to a platter. Run a knife between the flesh and the bones and lift off the fillet. Turn the fish over and remove bottom fillet. Repeat with the other fish. Serve hot with warm tortillas and lemon wedges.

WRAPPED FILET MIGNON WITH BURGUNDY MUSHROOM SAUCE

MAKES: 4 servings   **COOK:** 45 minutes

FOR THE FILETS:

   Nonstick cooking spray

4 (8-ounce) beef tenderloin filets

2 whole portobello mushrooms, divided use

2 tablespoons extra-virgin olive oil

2 (10.1-ounce) packages Big & Flaky crescent rolls—Pillsbury®

4 slices whole milk mozzarella cheese, sliced ¼-inch thick

4 whole pieces jarred roasted sweet red bell pepper, patted dry

2 tablespoons pesto sauce, divided use

1 teaspoon chopped garlic

1 teaspoon water

FOR THE SAUCE:

¾ cup dry red wine

¼ cup finishing sauce for beef

1 teaspoon beef bouillon paste

   Salt and pepper

1. Preheat oven to 500°F. Line a baking sheet with aluminum foil and spray with cooking spray.

2. Place meat and mushrooms on baking sheet, drizzle with oil, and season with salt and pepper. Bake for 10 minutes, turning beef to brown on all sides. Remove meat from oven, and continue to cook mushrooms for another 10 minutes. Wipe the baking sheet clean and spray again with cooking spray.

3. Turn oven down to 375°F. Cut filets in half horizontally. Slice mushrooms thinly. Unroll crescent dough and keep 2 triangles together for each filet. Pinch together at seams and smooth with a rolling pin. Lay the top of each tenderloin top-side down on the center of each crust. Divide the sliced mozzarella, bell pepper, and half the sliced mushrooms and place over each tenderloin.

4. In a small bowl, mix 1 teaspoon of pesto with garlic and water. Set aside. Divide remaining pesto over the top of each stack, then top with the bottom piece of tenderloin. Fold dough over meat as if wrapping a present. Pinch seams and trim excess dough. Place on baking sheet seam-side down. Brush lightly with the pesto-garlic mixture. Cut a ¼-inch vent in the center of each package. Bake at 375°F for 18 to 25 minutes or until crust is golden brown. Let rest for 5 minutes before serving.

5. Meanwhile, roughly chop remaining mushroom slices. Add wine to a small saucepan, bring to a boil, and reduce by half. Stir in the finishing sauce, beef paste, and chopped portobello. Simmer 3 to 4 minutes or until thickened. Keep warm. To serve, place the filet on a serving plate and spoon sauce on the side.

BLACKBERRY-MERLOT CHOCOLATE CAKE

MAKES: 12 servings   **BAKE:** 40 minutes

Nonstick cooking spray

1 (19.5-ounce) box dark chocolate cake mix

1 cup Merlot wine

½ cup vegetable oil

3 eggs

1 cup plus 6 tablespoons blackberry preserves, divided use

1 cup heavy cream

1 (11.5-ounce) bag bittersweet chocolate chips

Fresh blackberries, for garnish

1. Preheat oven to 350°F. Spray three 8-inch cake pans with cooking spray and set aside.

2. Beat cake mix, Merlot, oil, eggs, and ½ cup preserves in a large bowl with an electric mixer on low speed for 30 seconds. Scrape down sides of bowl and beat for 2 minutes on medium speed. Pour batter into prepared cake pans.

3. Bake in preheated oven for 35 to 40 minutes or until a tester inserted in the cake comes out clean. Remove and cool completely.

4. To make a ganache, heat cream and ½ cup preserves in a small saucepan over medium heat until just below a boil. Pour over chocolate chips in a medium bowl and stir with a rubber spatula until completely smooth.

5. To assemble, place one cake layer on a serving plate. Spread with ¼ cup of ganache and 3 tablespoons of preserves, then repeat with second cake layer. Add third layer and frost entire cake with remaining ganache. Garnish with fresh blackberries.

LONE STAR SOUR

MAKES: 4 servings

2 cups Blood Orange Martini mix—Stirrings
2 tablespoons fresh lemon juice
2 tablespoons fresh lime juice
4 tablespoons store-bought simple syrup
6 ounces bourbon
Blood orange slices, for garnish

1. Mix together the martini mix, lemon juice, lime juice, and simple syrup, and chill.
2. When ready to serve, pour the mixture into small chilled rocks glasses and top with 1 shot of bourbon. Garnish with a slice of blood orange.

MOCHA MOUSSE

MAKES: 4 servings

1 (3.9-ounce) package instant chocolate pudding mix
1 cup cold milk
¼ cup strong brewed coffee, chilled
1 cup heavy whipping cream
3 tablespoons powdered sugar
½ teaspoon vanilla extract
2 tablespoons chocolate chips, for garnish

1. In a large bowl, stir together the pudding mix, milk, and coffee until very thick.
2. In another large bowl, using an electric hand mixer, beat the heavy cream, powdered sugar, and vanilla until soft peaks form. Reserve ¼ cup for topping.
3. Stir ⅓ of the whipped cream into the pudding to lighten it. Gently fold pudding mixture into whipped cream. Spoon into dessert glasses and refrigerate for at least 30 minutes. To serve, top each with a small dollop of reserved whipped cream and sprinkle with chocolate chips.

O' CHOCO CAFÉ CAKE

MAKES: 6 to 8 servings

- 1 pint chocolate ice cream, softened
- 1 pint coffee ice cream, softened
- 1 pint vanilla ice cream, softened
- 20 chocolate creme sandwich cookies
- 1 stick (½ cup) butter, softened
  Nonstick cooking spray

1. Set ice cream out on counter for about 30 to 45 minutes to soften but not melt.
2. Crush cookies in food processor with butter.
3. Spray a 9 × 5-inch loaf pan with cooking spray. Line pan with enough waxed paper to cover sides and extend up over the top of the pan. Press the crushed cookie mixture in the bottom of the pan to make a thick base layer. Do not allow the cookies to go up the sides.
4. Layer the ice cream in the order you prefer. Spread and smooth out each layer before adding in the next flavor of ice cream, to make a level surface for the next layer. Fill the pan with the last layer so that the ice cream is level with the top of the pan.
5. Cover with plastic wrap and place in freezer for 5 to 6 hours or until ice cream is solid.
6. Once ice cream is firm and solid, remove plastic wrap. Dip pan in warm water to make it easier to remove the cake, but do not let water get inside pan. Invert pan onto a decorative plate and, using the waxed paper, ease the cake out of the pan. Remove waxed paper and serve.

TIRAMISU

MAKES: 4 servings

- 1 cup heavy cream, divided use
- ¾ cup sugar, divided use
- 1 (8-ounce) package cream cheese, at room temperature
- 1 teaspoon vanilla extract
- 2 (7-ounce) packages ladyfingers
- 1 cup strong black coffee
- 1 teaspoon cocoa powder

1. Have four 8-ounce wine glasses ready.
2. In a chilled bowl, combine ¾ cup heavy cream and ¼ cup sugar. Whip with a hand mixer until soft peaks form. Set aside in refrigerator.
3. In a large bowl, combine the cream cheese, ¼ cup heavy cream, vanilla, and ½ cup sugar. Whip with a hand mixer until light and fluffy.
4. Take 1 ladyfinger, snap or cut it in half, dip the halves quickly into the coffee, and drop them into the bottom of a wine glass. Repeat with the other 3 glasses. Put a heaping tablespoon of the cream cheese mixture on top of the ladyfingers. Add another layer of ladyfingers dipped in coffee, another of the cream cheese mixture, then one more layer of ladyfingers. Top with remaining filling and dollop with the whipped cream. Break 4 ladyfingers in half and insert 2 halves into the top of each glass.
5. Put the cocoa powder into a small sieve and tap it gently over each glass to dust the tops. Refrigerate for at least 1 hour before serving.

VALENTINE'S DAY CUPCAKE PARADE

MAKES: 24 cupcakes   **BAKE:** 22 minutes

1   (18.25-ounce) box white cake mix

3   egg whites

⅓   cup vegetable oil

1¼   cups white grape juice

1½   teaspoons strawberry extract, divided use

3   (16-ounce) cans white frosting
    Red food coloring

3   tablespoons pink and red candy confetti

1. Preheat oven to 350°F. Line regular muffin pans with 24 baking cups.
2. Combine cake mix, egg whites, oil, juice, and 1 teaspoon extract in a large mixing bowl. Beat together on low speed for 30 seconds. Scrape down the sides of the bowl, then beat for 2 minutes on medium speed. Divide batter evenly among the baking cups (about two-thirds full). Bake in preheated oven for 18 to 22 minutes or until a tester inserted into center comes out clean. Let cool for 5 minutes in the pans before transferring to a wire cooling rack to cool completely. Group cooled cupcakes together in a heart shape.
3. Color the frosting pink, and frost collectively as you would a cake.
4. Use pink and red candy confetti to decorate.

WHITE CHOCOLATE MOUSSE WITH CRANBERRY SAUCE

MAKES: 4 servings   **COOK:** 10 minutes

½ cup cranberry juice

1 (8-ounce) can jellied cranberry sauce

½ cup whole milk

1 (12-ounce) bag white chocolate chips

1 cup heavy whipping cream

1. Heat cranberry juice in a small saucepan over high heat. Whisk in cranberry sauce and heat until sauce is completely melted and a pourable consistency is reached. Remove from heat and allow to cool to room temperature.

2. In a small saucepan over medium-low heat, bring milk to just below a simmer. Put white chocolate chips in a bowl and pour hot milk over them. Let sit for 1 minute, then whisk until smooth. Place in refrigerator until chilled but not set. The mixture should have a thick but pourable consistency.

3. In a chilled medium bowl, beat cream until stiff peaks form.

4. To make the mousse, add the white chocolate mixture to the whipped cream, and gently fold together until completely incorporated.

5. Spoon about 1 tablespoon of cranberry sauce into the bottom of 4 dessert glasses. Put mousse into a resealable zip-top bag and snip off one corner. Use bag to pipe mousse filling into the 4 glasses. Chill for a minimum of 2 hours and up to overnight. Just before serving, top with a drizzle of the remaining cranberry sauce.

MARCH

ASPARAGUS MUSHROOM CUPS

MAKES: 6 servings   **COOK:** 35 minutes

- 1 box puff pastry shells, thawed
- 1 (10.75-ounce) can condensed cream of asparagus soup
- 2 tablespoons salt-free lemon pepper blend
- 1 (14.5-ounce) can asparagus spears, drained
- 1 (4.5-ounce) jar sliced mushrooms, drained
- ¼ cup shredded Parmesan cheese
- 3 tablespoons milk
-    Salt, to taste

1. Preheat oven to 400°F.
2. Evenly space puff pastry shells on a baking sheet. Bake in preheated oven for 20 to 25 minutes until puffed and golden brown. Remove from oven and carefully take tops off with a fork. Return bottoms to oven and bake for 5 to 8 minutes. Remove and cool for 10 minutes.
3. Heat ¾ cup soup (right from can) and lemon pepper blend in a medium saucepan over medium-high heat for 5 minutes. Add asparagus and mushrooms and heat for 2 minutes. Stir in cheese and heat for 1 minute. Remove from heat and season to taste with salt.
4. Heat remaining soup and milk in a small microwave-safe bowl for 90 seconds, stirring every 30 seconds.
5. To serve, scoop ¼ cup of asparagus mixture into each puff pastry bottom shell and replace shell top. Spoon heated sauce over the top.

BLT WEDGE WITH CREAMY TOMATO DRESSING

MAKES: 4 servings

- ¼ cup mayonnaise
- ¼ cup spicy cocktail sauce
- 1 tablespoon sweet pickle relish
- ¼ cup canola oil
- 1 head iceberg lettuce, cored and quartered
- 16 teardrop cherry tomatoes, halved
- ¼ cup crumbled bacon—Hormel
-    Salt and pepper, to taste

1. In a medium bowl, combine mayonnaise, cocktail sauce, sweet pickle relish, and canola oil. Season with salt and pepper. Spoon dressing over iceberg wedges and garnish with halved tomatoes, bacon, and freshly ground black pepper.

BUTTERY ALE ASPARAGUS

MAKES: 4 servings   **COOK:** 9 minutes

1   tablespoon butter

1   teaspoon chopped garlic

½   cup English ale

1   tablespoon spicy brown mustard

2   (10.5-ounce) bags frozen asparagus spears, thawed

Salt and pepper, to taste

1. Melt butter in a large skillet over medium heat. Add garlic and sauté for 1 minute. Add ale and cook until ale has reduced by half. Whisk in mustard and mix until incorporated. Add asparagus and season with salt and pepper to taste. Cook for another 3 minutes until asparagus is heated through. Transfer to a serving bowl and serve immediately.

CORNBREAD RINGS

MAKES: 4 servings   **COOK:** 15 minutes

Canola oil (about 2 cups), for frying

1   (8.5-ounce) box corn muffin mix

½   teaspoon chili powder

1   egg

1   cup milk

1   tablespoon hot sauce

1   medium yellow onion, cut into ½-inch-wide rings

1   red bell pepper, cut into ½-inch-wide rings

1   green bell pepper, cut into ½-inch-wide rings

1   cup all-purpose flour

Salt and pepper, to taste

1. In a large skillet, heat enough oil over medium-high heat to come halfway up the side (about 2 cups).

2. In a large bowl, mix corn muffin mix with chili powder and salt and pepper to taste. Whisk in egg, milk, and hot sauce until combined.

3. When oil is hot (around 350°F), toss onion and pepper rings with flour. Shake off excess flour and dip rings into cornbread batter, allowing excess to drip off before placing carefully into the hot oil. Fry in batches, for 2 to 3 minutes, until golden brown and batter is cooked through. Remove from oil and drain on a paper-towel–lined sheet tray or wire cooling rack. Sprinkle with salt and pepper to taste, and serve.

LEMONY RICE

MAKES: 4 servings   **COOK:** 30 minutes

2 cups low-sodium chicken broth

2 tablespoons olive oil

zest of ½ lemon and juice of 1 lemon

2 (3.8-ounce) boxes Chicken & Herb Classico Whole Grain Blends—Rice-A-Roni®

½ cup white wine

1. In a large saucepan over low heat, combine the chicken broth and olive oil and bring to a simmer. Add zest, lemon juice, rice, one seasoning packet from Whole Grain Blends boxes, and wine. Cover and cook until rice is tender and liquid is absorbed, about 25 to 30 minutes.

CRISPY RED ONION RINGS

MAKES: 4 servings   **COOK:** 18 minutes

3 medium yellow onions, sliced into ¼-inch slices

½ cup buttermilk

½ cup all-purpose flour

½ cup cornmeal

1 teaspoon cayenne pepper

1 teaspoon salt

1 teaspoon pepper

2 cups canola oil

Salt and pepper, to taste

1. Combine sliced onions and buttermilk in a large bowl. Let soak for 5 minutes.

2. Pour oil into a large saucepan to a depth of 1½ inches, and heat to 375°F.

3. Mix flour, cornmeal, cayenne, salt, and pepper in a baking dish. Drain onion rings. Working in batches, add a few onion rings to flour mixture and turn to coat. Carefully add to oil and fry until golden brown, about 2 minutes. Drain on paper towels. Sprinkle with salt and pepper to taste, and serve.

THAI CHICKEN SPRING ROLLS

MAKES: 8 spring rolls   **COOK:** 15 minutes

¼   cup rotisserie carved chicken breast, shredded
¼   cup carrots, grated
¼   cup cucumber, julienned
½   cup cabbage, shredded
8   spring roll wrappers
1 to 2   cups canola oil
¼   cup peanut dressing

1. In a medium bowl, toss together the shredded chicken and vegetables. Put a wrapper onto a clean work surface with the corners of the wrapper facing North, South, East, and West. Spoon about 2 to 3 tablespoons of the filling onto the bottom third of the wrapper. Dampen the edges of the wrapper with some water to seal. Fold the bottom edge of the wrapper up over the filling and roll up halfway. Fold the 2 side corners in toward the middle and continue to roll, pulling back slightly as you do so, to ensure a tightly wrapped roll. Repeat with the remaining wrappers. Cover with a damp towel to keep from drying out.

2. In a high-sided skillet heated over medium-high heat to 350°F, add canola oil. Place spring rolls, 3 to 4 at a time, in the hot oil. Fry on all sides until crispy and golden brown, about 2 to 3 minutes per side. Transfer the rolls to a platter and serve with the peanut dressing, for dipping.

THAI CHICKEN WRAPS

MAKES: 4 servings   **COOK:** 15 minutes

2   pounds bone-in chicken thighs, about 5 pieces
3   tablespoons soy sauce
½   cup peanut butter, chunky style
2   tablespoons lime juice
2   teaspoons sugar
1   teaspoon chopped garlic
½   teaspoon red pepper flakes
⅓   cup water
4   large flour tortillas
2   carrots, grated
1   small cucumber, julienned
2   cups shredded cabbage
¼   cup chopped fresh cilantro

1. Rinse chicken under cold water and pat dry. In a saucepan over medium heat, bring to a boil 2 cups of water and the soy sauce. Reduce to a simmer and add chicken thighs. Simmer until cooked through, about 15 minutes. Remove chicken from pan. When cool, remove skin and shred meat from the bone.

2. In a bowl, combine the peanut butter, lime juice, sugar, garlic, and red pepper flakes. Whisk in about ⅓ cup of water until a thick but pourable consistency is reached.

3. Warm tortillas in a microwave, wrapped in a slightly damp towel, for about 45 seconds. Assemble wraps by layering chicken, dressing, and vegetables and top with more dressing before rolling up. Secure with toothpicks and slice in half.

ZESTY RICE SALAD

MAKES: 4 servings **COOK:** 20 minutes

1 tablespoon canola oil

1 tablespoon chopped garlic

1½ cups long grain rice

2¼ cups water

1 tablespoon chili seasoning

1 tablespoon white vinegar

1 (14.5-ounce) can red beans, drained and rinsed

½ medium red onion, diced

1 yellow pepper, diced

1 tablespoon fresh cilantro, chopped

1. Heat oil over medium heat in a medium saucepot. Add garlic and rice and sauté for 1 minute until rice is toasted. Add water and chili seasoning and bring to a boil. Cover, reduce heat to low, and simmer for 15 minutes. The rice should be slightly undercooked. Remove to a baking sheet and let cool.
2. In a large bowl, combine rice and vinegar. Let cool for 5 minutes, then add beans, onion, yellow pepper, and cilantro. Mix well and serve.

ANDOUILLE CREOLE

MAKES: 6 servings   Cook: 55 minutes

¼ cup vegetable oil

¼ cup all-purpose flour

1½ cups chopped onions

1 tablespoon chopped garlic

1 large green pepper, chopped

½ cup chopped celery

¾ cup sliced scallions

1 (14.5-ounce) can diced tomatoes

1 (8-ounce) can tomato sauce

1 (6-ounce) can tomato paste

½ teaspoon red pepper flakes

1½ teaspoons seasoning salt

2 bay leaves

1 cup water

1 teaspoon hot sauce

1 tablespoon lemon juice

2 teaspoons Worcestershire sauce

1½ pounds andouille sausage, sliced

1 tablespoon chopped fresh parsley

1. Combine oil and flour in a Dutch oven and cook over medium heat, stirring, until mixture is golden colored, about 10 minutes. Add onion, garlic, green pepper, celery, and scallions. Cook 10 minutes, stirring often.
2. Stir in tomatoes, tomato sauce and paste, red pepper flakes, seasoning, bay leaves, water, hot sauce, lemon juice, Worcestershire sauce, and sausage. Bring to a simmer, cover, and reduce heat. Simmer for 30 minutes, stirring occasionally. Remove bay leaves. Garnish with parsley.

BURRITO ENCHILADAS

MAKES: 4 servings   **COOK:** 25 minutes

1½   cups rice, cooked

½   cup grilled chicken breast, cut into strips

1   cup shredded Monterey Jack cheese

1   (10-ounce) can enchilada sauce

1   teaspoon chili seasoning

2   tablespoons fresh cilantro, chopped

8   corn tortillas, warmed

½   cup sour cream, optional, for serving

Salt and pepper, to taste

1. Preheat oven to 350°F.

2. Cook rice according to package directions.

3. In a medium bowl, combine cooked rice, chicken, half the cheese, 2 tablespoons enchilada sauce, chili seasoning, and 1 tablespoon cilantro. Evenly distribute the mixture among 8 tortillas and roll each one up. Cover the bottom of an ovenproof baking dish with a layer of the enchilada sauce. Place rolled enchiladas in a single layer on top of the sauce, and top with the remainder of the sauce and cheese. Bake in oven until cheese melts and enchiladas are heated through, about 15 minutes.

4. Remove from oven and top with cilantro and sour cream, if desired. Serve immediately.

CHICKEN SCALOPPINI

MAKES: 4 Servings   **COOK:** 30 minutes

2   boneless, skinless chicken breasts

1   teaspoon poultry seasoning

½   cup all-purpose flour

2   tablespoons canola oil

2   tablespoons butter

1   (14.5-ounce) can chicken broth

2   tablespoons lemon juice

1   tablespoon chopped fresh parsley

1   tablespoon chopped fresh basil

Salt and pepper, to taste

1. Rinse chicken under cold water and pat dry with paper towels. Slice the breasts in half lengthwise to make thin cutlets. Pound each of the 4 cutlets between sheets of plastic wrap to flatten them evenly, about ¼-inch thick. Season with salt, pepper, and poultry seasoning. Coat the chicken with the flour, shaking off any excess.

2. In a large skillet over medium-high heat, melt the oil and butter. Working in batches, cook the chicken until it is golden brown, about 4 to 6 minutes per side. Remove the chicken and cover to keep warm. Add the chicken broth to the pan and cook it over high heat until it reduces by half and thickens slightly, about 5 minutes. Stir in the lemon juice, parsley, and basil, and taste, adjusting the seasoning with salt and pepper. Pour the sauce over the cooked chicken and serve.

CORNED BEEF AND CABBAGE WITH HERB BUTTERED POTATOES

MAKES: 4 servings   **COOK:** 8 hours

FOR THE CORNED BEEF:

- 2 carrots, cut into 2-inch pieces
- 2 medium onions, chopped
- 3 pounds corned beef brisket, with spice packet
- 1 small head green cabbage, cored and roughly chopped
- 2 cups apple juice
- 1 cup water

FOR THE POTATOES:

- 1½ pounds baby red potatoes, sliced in half
- ½ stick (4 tablespoons) butter, softened
- 1 tablespoon chopped garlic
- 2 tablespoons chopped fresh parsley
- Salt and pepper, to taste

1. For the corned beef, place carrots and onions on bottom of a slow cooker, and place corned beef on top. Arrange chopped cabbage around beef. Add apple juice and water to the cooker along with spice packet. Cook on low for 6 to 8 hours until beef is tender.

2. For the potatoes, in a pot of boiling salted water, cook potatoes until tender, about 12 to 15 minutes, drain, and return to pot. Add butter, garlic, parsley, salt, and pepper. Gently mix until all the potatoes are evenly coated. Serve potatoes with corned beef and vegetables from the slow cooker.

DEEP-FRIED CHICKEN WITH CHEDDAR CHEESE GRITS

MAKES: 4 servings   **COOK:** 15 minutes

FOR THE CHICKEN:

- 3   cups canola oil
- 1   egg
- ½   cup buttermilk
- 2   tablespoons hot sauce
- 1   (10-ounce) box fish fry mix
- 2   tablespoons Cajun seasoning
- 1   pound boneless, skinless chicken breasts, thinly sliced

FOR THE GRITS:

- 2   cups milk
- 3   tablespoons butter
- 1   cup instant grits
- ½   cup cheddar cheese plus ¼ cup, grated, divided use

1. Fill a large heavy-bottomed high-sided skillet with enough oil to come one-third of the way up the sides. Place over medium heat.

2. Set up a breading station by whisking together eggs, buttermilk, and hot sauce in one pie plate or baking dish and stir together the fish fry mix and Cajun seasoning in another. Dip each chicken breast in egg mixture, then press into cornmeal mixture, making sure the chicken gets completely coated. Set aside while oil is heating.

3. When oil reaches around 365°F, carefully place the chicken into oil. Fry in batches of 2 so that the pot does not get overcrowded. Fry until just cooked through, about 6 to 8 minutes. Remove from oil and drain onto a tray lined with paper towels.

4. For the grits, heat milk to a simmer in a medium pot over medium heat. Whisk in butter until melted. Add grits and continue to whisk until thickened. Mix in ½ cup cheese and stir until cheese is melted and incorporated. Remove from heat and serve along with fried chicken. Sprinkle each serving with 1 tablespoon of the remaining cheddar cheese.

DEMI-GLAZE HERB ROAST

MAKES: 8 servings   **COOK:** 1 hour 5 minutes

1 (3-pound) bottom round beef rump roast

1 tablespoon minced fresh rosemary

1 tablespoon minced fresh parsley

1 tablespoon minced fresh thyme leaves

1 tablespoon chopped garlic

1 tablespoon extra-virgin olive oil

2 (1-ounce) packets demi-glace mix

2 cups water

¼ cup dry sherry

Salt and pepper, to taste

1. Rinse beef with cold water and pat dry with paper towels. Season well with salt and pepper. Mix together rosemary, parsley, thyme, garlic, and oil. Cut small slits on surface of roast and rub herb mixture completely over it, making sure to work mixture into slits. Place in a flameproof roasting pan fat-side up. Let roast come to room temperature, about 30 minutes.

2. Put oven rack in middle position and preheat oven to 500°F.

3. Roast the beef for 15 minutes, then reduce oven temperature to 325°F. Continue to roast until a thermometer inserted into center of meat registers 140°F for medium rare, about 35 to 45 minutes more. Transfer roast to a cutting board and let it stand, uncovered, for 15 minutes.

4. While roast stands, drain fat from roasting pan. Place pan directly on stovetop over medium heat. Add water and deglaze pan, scraping up the browned bits. Remove from heat and transfer liquid to a small saucepan. Add demi-glace mix and sherry, then bring to a boil, stirring constantly. Simmer 1 to 2 minutes.

5. Thinly slice meat across the grain and serve with sauce.

GLAZED SCALLOPS WITH GRAPEFRUIT SAUCE AND SNOW PEAS

MAKES: 4 servings   **COOK:** 15 minutes

12   extra-large dry-packed sea scallops

2   teaspoons salt

½   teaspoon black pepper

3   tablespoons butter

1   tablespoon olive oil

¼   cup natural cane turbinado sugar

1   tablespoon lemon juice

1   tablespoon ginger puree

1   teaspoon vanilla

1   (15-ounce) jar pink grapefruit, juice reserved

2   (8-ounce) boxes frozen sugar snap peas
    Red lettuce leaves, for garnish

1. Preheat oven to 425°F.

2. Lightly rinse and pat the scallops dry with paper towels. Rub the scallops with salt and pepper.

3. In a skillet large enough to hold all the scallops in a single layer without crowding, heat 1 tablespoon butter and olive oil over medium-high heat. When hot, add the scallops and sear them until golden brown on both sides, about 2 minutes per side. Remove the scallops and set aside. Add sugar and lemon juice to pan and cook until sugar melts and starts to caramelize. Remove pan from heat and return scallops to pan. Turn each scallop over so sugar-coated side is facing up. Add ginger puree, vanilla, ¼ cup reserved grapefruit juice, and remaining 2 tablespoons butter. Place in oven until scallops are firm, about 5 minutes.

4. Place peas in a large microwave-safe dish. Cover and microwave on high for 4 minutes, stirring halfway through cooking.

5. To serve, place lettuce leaves on serving plates and arrange scallops on lettuce leaves. Add grapefruit sections to the pan and heat until warmed through. Divide sauce and grapefruit sections over the scallops. Place sugar snap peas on the side.

GRILLED CHEESE WITH TOMATO SOUP

MAKES: 4 servings   **COOK:** 45 minutes

FOR THE TOMATO SOUP:

- 1 tablespoon canola oil
- ½ medium onion, diced
- 3 stalks celery, diced
- 2 teaspoons minced garlic
- ½ teaspoon red pepper flakes
- 1 (28-ounce) can crushed tomatoes
- 2 (14.5-ounce) cans vegetable broth
  Salt and pepper, to taste

FOR THE GRILLED CHEESE:

- 4 tablespoons butter
- 8 slices whole wheat bread
- 8 deli slices American cheese
- ½ cup grated cheddar cheese

1. For the tomato soup, heat canola oil in a medium pot over medium heat. Add onions and celery and cook until onions are soft and translucent, about 5 minutes. Add garlic, red pepper flakes, salt and pepper to taste, and sauté an additional 2 minutes. Add crushed tomatoes and vegetable broth. Bring to a boil and reduce to a simmer. Cook, covered, for 30 minutes. In a blender, puree soup until smooth, then return to pot. You may need to do this in 2 batches. Adjust seasoning with salt and pepper, if necessary.

2. For the grilled cheese, heat a large grill pan over medium-high heat. Butter one side of all 8 slices of bread. Lay 4 slices of bread butter-side down in the pan. Place a slice of American cheese on each of the 4 slices, then sprinkle 2 tablespoons of cheddar cheese on top of each one. Add another slice of American cheese on top of the cheddar, and finally cover with the remaining bread slices, butter-side up. Grill until golden brown on both sides and cheese is melted, about 3 minutes per side. Cut into triangles and serve with tomato soup.

ITALIAN FRIED CHICKEN

MAKES: 6 pieces **COOK:** 30 minutes

2 large eggs

½ cup milk

1 cup cornmeal

¼ cup Parmesan cheese

2 tablespoons Italian seasoning

2 each chicken legs, thighs, and wings

2 cups canola oil, for frying

Salt and pepper, to taste

1. Preheat oven to 350°F.

2. Break the eggs into a shallow dish and beat them well with the milk. In another shallow dish, mix together the corn meal, Parmesan cheese, and Italian seasoning. Rinse chicken under cold water and pat dry with paper towels. Season the chicken with salt and pepper, to taste. Dip the chicken pieces in the egg-and-milk mixture. Dredge them in the cornmeal mixture, coating generously, and put them on a large plate.

3. In a large skillet, heat the oil over medium-high heat to 360°F. Fry the chicken until golden brown, about 4 to 5 minutes per side. Place the chicken pieces onto a plate lined with a brown bag to soak up excess oil. Transfer to a baking sheet and finish cooking them in the oven, about 20 minutes. Arrange on a serving platter and serve.

MINT MARINATED LEG OF LAMB WITH RHUBARB CHUTNEY

MAKES: 6 servings   **COOK:** 1 hour

FOR THE LAMB:

3½ pounds boneless butterflied leg of lamb

1½ cups plain yogurt

3 tablespoons lemon juice

2 teaspoons pumpkin pie spice

1 tablespoon spicy steak seasoning

1 cup chopped fresh mint

2 teaspoons minced ginger

1 teaspoon crushed garlic

FOR THE CHUTNEY:

2 pounds frozen or fresh rhubarb, chopped

2 cups chopped sweet onion

1 cup cider vinegar

1½ cups brown sugar

2 teaspoons pumpkin pie spice

2 teaspoons salt

1. Remove boneless leg of lamb from netting. Rinse with cold water and pat dry with paper towels. Place lamb in a shallow baking pan and set aside.

2. In a large bowl, combine remaining ingredients and stir until smooth. Pour over lamb and make sure it is thoroughly coated. Cover with plastic wrap and refrigerate at least 4 to 6 hours, preferably overnight.

3. For the chutney, combine all the ingredients in a large saucepan. Bring to a boil over medium heat and cook until thickened, stirring frequently, for about 30 minutes.

4. Set up grill for indirect cooking over medium-high heat. Remove lamb from refrigerator and crisscross metal skewers through meat. Let lamb sit at room temperature for 30 minutes. Oil grate when ready to start cooking.

5. Cook lamb covered over a drip pan for 50 to 60 minutes or until internal temperature reaches 150°F for medium. Let stand 5 to 10 minutes before slicing. Serve hot with chutney alongside.

PEANUT CURRY CHICKEN THIGHS

MAKES: 4 servings   **COOK:** 30 minutes

8 skinless chicken thighs

1 (11.5-ounce) bottle Thai peanut sauce

1 tablespoon lime juice

2 tablespoons chili-garlic sauce

1 teaspoon Thai seasoning

1 tablespoon sesame seeds, toasted, for garnish

2 scallions, thinly sliced on the diagonal, for garnish

1. For the chicken, rinse under cold water, then pat dry with paper towels. Place chicken in a zip-top bag. Stir together the peanut sauce, lime juice, chili-garlic sauce, and Thai seasoning in a bowl. Pour into bag with the chicken. Squeeze air from bag and seal. Marinate in refrigerator for at least 2 hours, or as long as overnight.

2. Set up grill for direct cooking over medium heat. Oil grate when ready to start cooking.

Let chicken stand at room temperature for 20 to 30 minutes before grilling.

3. Remove chicken from bag and discard marinade. Place on hot, oiled grill and cook for 18 to 22 minutes per side or until no longer pink at the bone and the juices run clear (180 degrees F). Transfer chicken to a platter and let rest for 5 minutes before serving. Serve hot garnished with sesame seeds and sliced scallions.

4. *Indoor Method*: Preheat oven to 425°F. Remove chicken from marinade and discard marinade. Place chicken on a foil-lined baking sheet and roast for 30 minutes or until no longer pink at the bone, the juices run clear, and an inserted thermometer reads 180°F. Transfer chicken to a platter and let rest for 5 minutes before serving.

ROAD HOUSE T-BONE

MAKES: 4 servings **COOK:** 10 minutes

4   T-bone steaks, ¾ to 1-inch thick

3   tablespoons chili sauce

3   tablespoons steak sauce

2   teaspoons crushed garlic

2   tablespoons brown sugar

2   tablespoons chili powder

1   teaspoon salt

1. Rinse steaks under cold water and pat dry with paper towels. Stir to combine remaining ingredients in a small bowl. Coat steaks with chili rub and place in a zip-top bag. Squeeze air from bag and seal. Marinate in refrigerator for at least 4 hours.

2. Preheat broiler. Place steaks on a foil-lined baking sheet or broiler pan. Broil 6 to 8 inches from heat source for 4 to 5 minutes per side for medium (160°F). Transfer steaks to a platter and let rest for 5 minutes before serving hot.

SAUTÉED BALSAMIC CHICKEN BREASTS

MAKES: 4 servings **COOK:** 15 minutes

4   boneless, skinless chicken breasts

1   tablespoon Italian seasoning

½   teaspoon crushed celery seed

3   tablespoons extra-virgin olive oil

¾   cup less-sodium chicken broth

1   tablespoon garlic puree

½   cup balsamic vinegar

1   teaspoon brown sugar

½   teaspoon black pepper

1. Preheat oven to low, about 175°F.

2. Rinse chicken under cold water and pat dry with paper towels. Season chicken breasts with Italian seasoning and celery seed. Heat oil in a large skillet over medium-high heat. Sauté chicken breasts until they are lightly browned on one side, about 4 minutes. Turn breasts over and sauté for another 4 minutes. At this point, the meat is just about done and will be firm to the touch. Remove pan from heat, transfer breasts to a plate, cover with foil, and keep warm in the oven on low.

3. Deglaze the pan with half of the chicken broth, scraping up the brown bits. Add garlic and cook for 1 minute. Add the rest of the broth, balsamic vinegar, brown sugar, and black pepper. Turn the heat to high and cook until the sauce is reduced by half, about 5 to 6 minutes, stirring occasionally. To serve, pour the sauce over the breasts.

SEARED SALMON WITH MIXED FRUIT AND SPRING GREENS

MAKES: 4 servings   Cook: 8 minutes

4   (6-ounce) skinless center-cut salmon fillets
1   cup oil-and-vinegar salad dressing
2   tablespoons orange juice concentrate
2   teaspoons fines herbes
2   tablespoons extra-virgin olive oil
8   cups spring mix greens
2   cups fresh strawberries, quartered
1   (11-ounce) can mandarin oranges, drained
½   pint fresh blueberries
    Salt and pepper, to taste

1. Rinse salmon under cold water and pat dry with paper towels. Place in a zip-top bag and set aside.

2. Whisk together salad dressing, orange juice concentrate, and fines herbes. Pour half of the dressing into the bag with the fish. Squeeze air from bag and seal. Marinate in refrigerator for up to 2 hours.

3. Remove fish from marinade and discard marinade; pat fillets dry with paper towels and season with salt and pepper. Heat oil in a large skillet over medium-high heat. Place salmon in skillet skinned-side down and sear for 4 minutes. Carefully turn fish and reduce heat to medium. Cook for another 3 to 4 minutes or until just cooked through.

4. Meanwhile, add salad mix and fruit to a large mixing bowl and toss with remaining salad dressing until well combined. Divide salad among 4 plates. Carefully transfer fish to plates with a metal fish spatula and serve.

STUFFED CHICKEN THIGHS WITH SMASHED POTATOES

MAKES: 4 servings   **COOK:** 30 minutes

2   tablespoons butter

½   medium onion, diced

1   Granny Smith apple, cored, peeled, and diced

1½   teaspoons brown sugar

1   tablespoon chopped fresh rosemary leaves

1   tablespoon chopped fresh parsley leaves

2   slices whole wheat bread, toasted and diced

2   pounds boneless and skinless chicken thighs

2   tablespoons canola oil

Kosher salt and freshly ground black pepper

FOR THE SMASHED POTATOES:

1½   pounds Yukon gold potatoes, cubed

1   tablespoon kosher salt, plus more for seasoning

½   cup milk

2   tablespoons unsalted butter

2   teaspoons chopped garlic

1   whole sprig rosemary

Freshly ground black pepper

1. In a medium skillet over medium-high heat, melt the butter and add the onion and diced apple. Add brown sugar and cook for 2 to 3 minutes, until onion begins to soften, stirring frequently. Add chopped fresh rosemary and parsley and mix to combine. Remove from heat. Stir in diced bread and season with salt and pepper, to taste.

2. Lay the chicken thighs out flat on a work surface. Cover with plastic wrap and pound with a meat mallet or rolling pin until about ¼-inch thick. Spoon some of the apple filling into each thigh, making sure not to overstuff so you don't lose the filling while cooking. Roll up each thigh and secure with toothpicks.

3. Heat 2 tablespoons canola oil in a large skillet over high heat. Generously salt and pepper each side of the thighs. Place thighs in the skillet and cook for 5 minutes on each side. Remove chicken from the pan to a serving platter and let rest for a few minutes before serving.

4. For the potatoes, add potatoes to a large pot and cover with cold water. Add 1 tablespoon of salt and bring to a boil over medium heat. Reduce heat and cook until the potatoes are tender, about 15 to 20 minutes. In the meantime, add milk, butter, garlic, and rosemary sprig to a small saucepan and warm over low heat. Drain potatoes and return to the pot. Use a potato masher or large fork to mash the potatoes. Remove rosemary sprig from milk mixture and discard. Add the hot milk to the mashed potatoes. Mix to combine and season with kosher salt and freshly ground black pepper. Transfer to a serving bowl and serve with the chicken.

STEAK CERVEZA

MAKES: 4 servings   **COOK:** 25 minutes

1½   pounds top round steak
2   tablespoons chili seasoning
½   medium onion, diced
1   tablespoon chopped garlic
1   (12-ounce) bottle beer
2   tablespoons lemon juice
2   tablespoons white vinegar

1. Rinse steak under cold water and pat dry with paper towels. Rub chili seasoning into both sides of steak. Place in a zip-top bag. Add onions, garlic, beer, lemon juice, and vinegar. Squeeze air from bag and seal. Marinate in refrigerator for at least 4 hours or overnight.
2. Set up grill for direct cooking over high heat. Let steak stand at room temperature for 20 to 30 minutes before grilling. Oil grate when ready to start cooking. Remove steak from bag and reserve marinade. Grill steak for 4 minutes per side for medium rare (145°F). Transfer steaks to a platter and let rest for 5 minutes before slicing.
3. Pour the marinade into a large skillet over medium heat. Reduce by half or until thickened, about 10 to 15 minutes.
4. Slice steak thinly across the grain and serve with reduced marinade.

TUSCAN SPRING CHICKEN

MAKES: 6 servings   **COOK:** 2 hours

1   large roasting chicken
2   tablespoons extra-virgin olive oil
1   tablespoon chicken seasoning
1   lemon, sliced
5   whole garlic cloves, smashed
⅓   cup pesto
    Shaved Parmesan cheese, for garnish

1. Preheat oven to 350°F.
2. Rinse chicken inside and out with cold water and pat dry with paper towels. Rub chicken with oil, season well with chicken seasoning, and place on a rack in a roasting pan. Stuff chicken with lemon and garlic.
3. Roast for about 1½ to 2 hours or until the juices run clear and the internal temperature of the thigh reads 180°F. During the last half hour of roasting, brush chicken liberally with pesto.
4. Let rest 10 minutes before carving. Garnish with the Parmesan cheese shavings.

GLAZED IRISH CAKE

MAKES: 10 servings **BAKE:** 35 minutes

Nonstick cooking spray

1   (18.3-ounce) box fudge brownie mix

2   tablespoons espresso powder

3   eggs

1   stick (½ cup) butter, melted

¼   cup Irish whiskey

½   cup heavy cream

½   cup Irish cream liqueur

1   tablespoon corn syrup

1¼   cups bittersweet chocolate chips

Fresh mint leaves, for garnish

1. Preheat oven to 350°F. Spray a 9-inch cake pan with cooking spray and set aside.

2. Stir together brownie mix, espresso powder, eggs, butter, and whiskey in a large bowl with a wooden spoon until well combined. Pour batter into prepared cake pan.

3. Bake in preheated oven for 30 to 35 minutes or until just set. Remove and cool completely.

4. To make glaze, heat cream, cream liqueur, and corn syrup in a small saucepan over medium heat until just below a boil. Pour over chocolate chips in a medium bowl and stir with a rubber spatula until completely smooth. Cool to room temperature.

5. Place cake on a serving plate. Pour glaze over top of cake and spread down sides with a knife. Garnish with fresh mint leaves. Slice and serve.

LEMON DAFFODIL CAKE

MAKES: 12 servings

FOR THE CAKE:

- 1 store-bought pound cake ring
- 1 (10-ounce) jar lemon curd
- 2 cups whipped topping, divided use

FOR THE ICING:

- 3 cups powdered sugar, sifted
- ½ cup frozen lemonade concentrate, thawed
- 1 tablespoon lemon-flavored gelatin powder
- ¼ cup whipped topping
   Fresh mixed berries, for serving
   nosegay of roses or other edible flowers
      placed in center of cake, for decorating

1. For the cake, level the wider end of the cake with a serrated knife; this will become the bottom. Slice off the top inch of cake. Set aside, taking care not to break. Scoop out a trench in the bottom layer of the cake for the filling. Set aside.

2. In a bowl, combine lemon curd and 1 cup of whipped topping. Carefully fold in remaining cup of whipped topping until just combined. Do not overstir. Fill center trench with filling and return the top of the cake to its place.

3. To make the icing, place powdered sugar, lemonade concentrate, gelatin powder, and whipped topping in a bowl and stir to combine, making sure that all lumps are dissolved. Drizzle icing over cake and serve with fresh berries. Pound cake ring can also be decorated with a beautiful nosegay of roses or other edible flowers placed in the center hole.

PEACH MUG PIE WITH CARAMEL SAUCE

MAKES: 4 servings   **COOK:** 15 minutes

FOR THE CARAMEL SAUCE:

- 1   cup sugar
- ¼   cup water
- 1   teaspoon lemon juice
- ½   cup heavy cream

FOR THE CAKE:

- 1   (21-ounce) can peach pie filling
- 1   cup heavy cream
- 3   tablespoons powdered sugar
- 1   pint vanilla ice cream
- 8   graham crackers, crumbled

1. For the caramel sauce, bring the sugar, water, and lemon juice to a boil over medium heat. Once boiling, reduce to a simmer, cooking until the sugar turns a golden brown color, about 7 minutes. Watch the sugar, as it can burn very quickly. Remove from heat and pour in ½ cup heavy cream. Using a wooden spoon, stir the cream into the sugar until completely combined. Be careful when adding cream, as the mixture will bubble intensely—just stir and let cool a bit. Set aside.

2. Heat peach pie filling in a small saucepan over medium heat, stirring until warmed through, about 3 minutes.

3. In a chilled mixing bowl, whip 1 cup heavy cream until soft peaks form. Add the powdered sugar and whip until stiff.

4. Begin assembling peach pies in clear glass mugs. Place a layer of graham crackers at the bottom of mug, then a big spoonful of peach pie filling. Top with a scoop of vanilla ice cream, a dollop of whipped topping, and more crushed graham crackers. Drizzle caramel sauce generously over top.

PASTEL CUPCAKES

MAKES: 24 cupcakes **BAKE:** 30 minutes

1 (18.25-ounce) package butter-recipe yellow cake mix

1¾ cups plus 2 tablespoons buttermilk

1 stick (½ cup) butter, softened

3 eggs

2 (12-ounce) cans vanilla frosting

Food coloring

1. Preheat oven to 350°F.
2. Line twenty-four 2½-inch muffin cups with paper baking cups and set aside. In a large bowl, combine cake mix, 1¾ cups buttermilk, butter, and eggs. Beat with an electric mixer on low speed for 30 seconds. Using a rubber spatula, scrape down sides of bowl and beat on medium speed for 2 minutes more. Stir in chocolate chips. Spoon batter into prepared muffin cups, filling each ⅔ full.
3. Bake in preheated oven for 25 to 30 minutes or until toothpick inserted in centers comes out clean. Remove from muffin cups and cool on wire racks.
4. In 4 small mixing bowls, place 6 ounces of frosting in each. For pastel shades, add a couple drops of yellow, blue, green, and red coloring to each. Mix well. Frost cooled cupcakes with colored frosting.

APRIL

- Asparagus are good sources of Iron, Magnesium, Zinc, and dietary fiber

- Broccoli is packed with fiber and vitamins A and C

- Spinach is filled with vitamins A and C, folic acid, and Magnesium, which may help control cancer

ARTICHOKE BOTTOMS WITH TOMATOES, MOZZARELLA, AND PESTO

MAKES: 15 pieces   **COOK:** 3 hours 10 minutes

8 Roma tomatoes, cored and sliced lengthwise

3 tablespoons balsamic vinaigrette

3 (14-ounce) cans artichoke bottoms, rinsed and drained

2 tablespoons lemon juice

15 fresh mozzarella balls, cherry tomato–size

¼ cup pesto

Salt and pepper, to taste

1. Preheat oven to 250°F. Line a baking sheet with parchment paper.
2. Carefully remove seeds from tomatoes that have been cored and sliced lengthwise. Put in a bowl and toss with the balsamic vinaigrette. Season with salt and pepper. Place tomatoes cut-side up on the baking sheet. Roast in preheated oven for 3 hours. Transfer tomatoes to a plate to cool.
3. Preheat oven to 400°F. Line baking sheet with parchment paper again.
4. Trim bottoms of rinsed and drained artichoke bottoms so that they will sit flat. Place in a bowl and toss with lemon juice. Let sit for 5 minutes, then rinse with cold water and pat dry. Arrange on the parchment-lined baking sheet.
5. Top each artichoke bottom with an oven-roasted tomato and a mozzarella ball. Spoon over a dab of pesto. Bake for 10 minutes. Remove from oven and serve immediately.

BARCELONA POTATOES

MAKES: 4 servings   **COOK:** 15 minutes

½ cup mayonnaise

2 tablespoons tomato paste

2 teaspoons hot sauce

½ teaspoon red pepper flakes

1 teaspoon paprika

Pinch salt and freshly ground black pepper

3 large russet potatoes

2 cups canola oil

1 teaspoon salt

1. In a small bowl mix together the mayonnaise, tomato paste, hot sauce, red pepper flakes, paprika, salt, and pepper until well combined. Set aside.

2. Peel and cut the potatoes into ½-inch cubes. Add the potatoes and and teaspoon of salt to a large pot of cold water over medium heat. Bring to a boil, then cook for 5 minutes. Remove from the heat and drain in a colander. Let sit out on the counter for 20 minutes to allow to dry thoroughly.

3. Heat the oil in a high-sided skillet over medium-high heat to about 350°F. Fry the potatoes until golden brown on all sides. Transfer the potatoes to a serving bowl and serve with the spicy dipping sauce.

BROCCOLI PIE

MAKES: 4 servings   **COOK:** 5 minutes

2 heads broccoli

¼ teaspoon salt

1 cup plain Greek yogurt

8 ounces low-fat or light cream cheese, room temperature

1 tablespoon onion soup mix

12 small cherry tomatoes, for garnish

1. Bring a large pot of water to a boil over high heat. Fill a large bowl with ice water.

2. Trim the broccoli into florets. When the water boils, add the florets and salt. Cook until the broccoli is just tender, about 3 minutes. Drain and plunge the florets into the ice water to stop the cooking. When they are thoroughly chilled, drain and spread florets out on a towel-lined sheet pan to dry.

3. Mix together the yogurt, cream cheese, and onion soup mix. Transfer the yogurt mixture to a large resealable plastic bag. Arrange the broccoli on a serving platter, cut-sides down, so that they form a domed pie-like appearance. Cut the tip off a corner of the bag and pipe a latticework design over the broccoli. Garnish with the cherry tomatoes and serve.

CAESAR PASTA SALAD

MAKES: 4 servings   **COOK:** 8 minutes

½   (16-ounce) box rotini pasta
½   cup creamy Caesar salad dressing
     Zest and juice of 1 lemon
3   tablespoons chopped fresh parsley
¼   cup Parmesan cheese, grated
1   cup garlic croutons
     Salt and pepper, to taste

1. Bring a large pot of salted water to a boil. Add pasta and stir gently. Boil pasta uncovered, stirring occasionally, for 8 minutes or until al dente. Remove from heat. Drain well and rinse with cold water.

2. In a large bowl, combine the Caesar dressing, lemon zest and juice, and parsley, and stir together. Add the pasta and the remaining ingredients. Toss to combine.

CHEESY GRILLED POLENTA SQUARES

MAKES: 8 servings   **COOK:** 10 minutes

     Olive oil cooking spray
2   cups evaporated milk
2   cups less-sodium chicken broth
1   teaspoon garlic salt
1   cup instant polenta
1   cup shredded cheddar cheese

1. Spray an 8 × 8-inch baking dish with cooking spray and set aside. Combine milk, broth, and garlic salt in a medium saucepan and bring to a boil over medium heat. Slowly whisk in polenta. Cook, stirring constantly, for 5 minutes or until thickened. Remove from heat and stir in cheese. Transfer to the prepared baking dish and smooth top. Refrigerate for 3 hours or until firm.

2. Heat a grill pan over medium-high heat. Brush or spray with oil and cook polenta for 2 to 3 minutes per side. Cut into 16 small squares. Serve warm.

FRIED OKRA WITH TOMATOES

MAKES: 4 servings **COOK:** 12 minutes

1   cup buttermilk
1   (16-ounce) bag frozen okra, thawed
2   cups peanut oil
1   (8.5-ounce) box corn muffin mix
1   (10-ounce) can diced tomatoes and green chilies
2   tablespoons tomato paste
1   tablespoon Cajun seasoning
2   tablespoons heavy cream
    Salt and pepper, to taste

1. In a large bowl, combine buttermilk and okra and let sit for 5 minutes.
2. In a large cast-iron skillet, heat peanut oil over high heat to 375°F.
3. In a large bowl, add the corn muffin mix. Using a slotted spoon, remove the okra from the buttermilk and place it in the bowl with the corn muffin mix. Gently toss, making sure all the okra is coated with corn muffin mix.
4. Carefully add half the coated okra to skillet and fry for about 6 minutes or until golden brown. Use a slotted spoon to remove okra to a paper towel–lined plate. Fry remaining okra.
5. Combine diced tomatoes and chilies, tomato paste, and Cajun seasoning in a large saucepan. Heat through over medium heat. Stir in heavy cream, season with salt and pepper, and bring to a simmer. Remove to a shallow-sided plate and top with fried okra. Serve immediately.

SPANISH DIP

MAKES: 2 servings

1½ cups white beans, drained and rinsed
¼   cup frozen chopped spinach, thawed
1   teaspoon minced garlic
½   teaspoon cumin
1   tablespoon lemon juice
¼   cup olive oil
4   pita pockets
    Salt and pepper, to taste

1. In the bowl of a food processor, combine the white beans, spinach, garlic, cumin, and lemon juice and season with salt and pepper. Pulse until almost smooth. With machine running, drizzle in the olive oil until completely incorporated.
2. Cut the pita pockets into quarters, place on a baking sheet, and then toast in oven at 400°F for approximately 8 minutes until crisp. Remove from oven to cool. Serve with the dip.

SPANISH TORTILLA

MAKES: 4 servings   **COOK:** 25 minutes

1   large russet potato

2⅔ cup canola oil

5   eggs

½   cup milk

1   tablespoon canola oil, divided use

Salt and pepper, to taste

FOR THE TOPPING:

2   plum tomatoes, diced

2   tablespoons fresh basil, chopped

1   tablespoon olive oil

1. Peel and chop potato into ½-inch cubes. Add the potato and 1 teaspoon salt to a large pot of cold water, and bring to a boil. Parboil potato for 5 minutes. Remove and drain. Let sit out on the counter for 20 minutes to allow to thoroughly dry.

2. Heat ⅔ cup oil in a high-sided skillet over medium-high heat to about 350°F. Fry potato until golden brown on all sides. Remove from pan.

3. In a large bowl, beat together the eggs with milk. Season with salt and pepper to taste.

4. Preheat oven to 350°F.

5. In an 8-inch nonstick ovenproof skillet over medium heat, add canola oil. Add the potatoes and then the egg mixture. Reduce heat to medium low. Allow to cook undisturbed for 3 minutes or until almost completely set. Place in oven for 5 to 8 minutes until set and slightly puffed up. Let cool for 5 minutes, remove from pan, and cut into wedges.

6. For tomato topping, mix together tomatoes, basil, olive oil, and salt and pepper to taste in a small bowl and serve alongside tortilla wedges.

SPICY SPINACH STEW

MAKES: 4 servings **COOK:** 10 minutes

1   tablespoon canola oil

1   medium onion, chopped

2   teaspoons minced garlic

1   teaspoon paprika

½   teaspoon red pepper flakes

1   (15-ounce) can diced tomatoes

3   (15-ounce) cans white beans, drained and
    rinsed

1   (10-ounce) box frozen chopped spinach,
    thawed
    Salt and pepper, to taste

1. Heat canola oil in a large sauté pan over
   medium heat. Add onion and sauté until
   slightly tender, about 3 minutes. Add garlic
   and season with salt, pepper, paprika, and red
   pepper flakes. Sauté for 1 more minute, then
   add the tomatoes, white beans, and spinach.
   Mix together and cook for 6 minutes, stirring
   every couple of minutes until heated through.
   Serve warm or at room temperature.

SWEET AND SOUR CHORIZO

MAKES: 6 servings **COOK:** 10 minutes

1   pound cured chorizo sausage

2   tablespoons canola oil

1   medium onion, sliced

2   teaspoons chopped garlic

1   cup raisins

¼   cup red wine vinegar

2   tablespoons brown sugar

1. Slice chorizo into half-inch-thick rounds. Add
   canola oil to a large skillet over medium heat.
   Add onion, chorizo, and garlic and cook for 2
   minutes. Add raisins, red wine vinegar, brown
   sugar, and ½ cup water. Cook for 10 minutes,
   until chorizo is heated through and liquid has
   reduced slightly, about 10 minutes. Transfer to
   a serving dish and serve.

SWEET CARROT SALAD

MAKES: 10 servings

2 (8-ounce) packages pre-shredded carrots
1 cup golden raisins
1 (8-ounce) can crushed pineapple
1 cup miniature marshmallows
⅓ cup mayonnaise
¼ cup whipped topping
1 teaspoon honey

1. In a medium bowl, mix together all ingredients until thoroughly combined.
2. Cover and chill in refrigerator for at least 1 hour. Serve chilled.

BEEF AND BROCCOLI STUFFED PEPPERS

MAKES: 6 servings   **COOK:** 30 minutes

6 red bell peppers
1 pound ground beef
1 teaspoon Italian seasoning
1 teaspoon garlic salt
1 (24-ounce) bag Steam n' Mash Cut Russet Potatoes
⅔ cup evaporated milk
3 tablespoons butter, divided use
¼ cups frozen chopped broccoli, cooked according to microwave directions
1 cup shredded cheddar jack cheese
½ cup French fried onions, divided use

1. Preheat oven to 375°F.
2. Cut bell peppers in half lengthwise. Remove and discard seeds and membranes. Rinse, pat dry.
3. In a large skillet, brown ground beef with Italian seasoning and garlic salt. Set aside.
4. Microwave potatoes according to package directions. In a medium bowl, mash cooked potatoes, milk, and 1 tablespoon butter. Microwave broccoli according to package directions. Add to bowl with potatoes and stir in ground beef and cheese. Spoon potato mixture evenly into bell pepper halves. Cut remaining butter into small pieces and dot the tops of potato mixture, then sprinkle with fried onions.
5. Bake in preheated oven for 25 to 30 minutes or until heated through and onions are lightly browned. Serve immediately.

BREAKFAST-FOR-DINNER CAKES

MAKES: 4 servings **COOK:** 25 minutes

FOR THE JELLY SYRUP:

1   cup grape jelly

2   teaspoons cornstarch

2   tablespoons water

FOR THE PANCAKES:

1½   cups milk

¾   cup peanut butter

2½   cups baking mix—Bisquick®

2   eggs

Canola oil cooking spray

1. To make syrup, heat grape jelly in a small saucepan over medium-high heat. Stir in cornstarch dissolved in water. Simmer for 5 to 10 minutes until a syrupy consistency is reached.

2. To make the pancakes, warm milk in a small saucepan. Whisk in peanut butter until completely smooth. Remove from heat. In a large mixing bowl, add baking mix and stir in eggs and milk mixture until just incorporated.

3. Place a large cast-iron or nonstick skillet over medium heat. Spray with cooking spray. For each pancake, pour ¼ cup of pancake batter in center of skillet and cook for 1 to 2 minutes per side or until golden brown. You will know when to flip pancakes when bubbles in the center have deflated. Store on a sheet tray in a 200°F oven to keep warm while finishing the rest of the pancakes. Serve pancakes with warm grape syrup.

CHICKEN FRANÇAISE

MAKES: 4 servings   **COOK:** 40 minutes

4   boneless, skinless chicken breasts

2   eggs

¼   cup plus 2 tablespoons less-sodium chicken broth, divided use

1¼ cups all-purpose flour

1   tablespoon chicken seasoning

½   cup vegetable oil

1   cup dry white wine

1   (0.9-ounce) package hollandaise sauce mix—Knorr

4   tablespoons butter, cut into 4 pieces

1   tablespoon lemon juice

½   teaspoon dried thyme

1   lemon, sliced, for garnish

1. Preheat oven to 150°F.

2. Rinse chicken under cold water and pat dry with paper towels. Place a chicken breast between 2 sheets of plastic wrap and gently pound with flat side of a meat pounder or with a rolling pin until no more than ¼-inch thick. Repeat with remaining breasts.

3. Lightly beat eggs with 2 tablespoons chicken broth in a shallow bowl. Stir together flour and chicken seasoning in another shallow bowl. Dip each chicken breast in egg mixture, then dredge in flour mixture, shaking off excess. Set aside on a platter.

4. Heat oil in a medium-heavy skillet over medium heat until hot but not smoking. When oil is hot, lay one chicken breast in the pan and fry, turning over once, until golden brown and just cooked through, about 4 minutes. Transfer to a plate lined with paper towels and keep warm in oven, loosely covered with foil. Fry remaining chicken in same manner.

5. Slowly pour off oil, leaving brown bits behind in pan. Add wine and bring to a boil, stirring to bring up the brown bits. Reduce heat to medium and simmer for 3 minutes. Whisk hollandaise sauce mix with remaining ¼ cup broth in a small bowl until smooth, and add to simmering wine. Stir in butter until melted, then add lemon juice and thyme.

6. Spoon sauce over chicken and garnish with lemon slices.

CHILI RUBBED TRI-TIP

MAKES: 4 servings   **COOK:** 1 hour 10 minutes

1   (1.25-ounce) packet Tex-Mex Chili Seasoning Mix
1   (1-ounce) packet Au Jus gravy mix
2   tablespoons chili powder
1   (2.5-pound) beef tri-tip steak

1. In a small bowl, stir together chili seasoning, gravy mix, and chili powder. Rub mixture into tri-tip steak. Wrap in plastic wrap and let cure in refrigerator for 2 to 4 hours.
2. Set up a grill for indirect cooking over medium-high heat, so that no direct heat source will be under meat. Let steak stand at room temperature for 30 minutes. Oil grate when ready to start cooking. Unwrap steak and place on hot, oiled grill. Cover grill and cook for 30 to 35 minutes per side for medium (150°F).
3. Transfer to a platter and let stand for 5 to 10 minutes before thinly slicing across the grain. Serve hot or at room temperature.

DRUNKEN PORK

MAKES: 4 servings   **COOK:** 8 hours

1   Vidalia onion, sliced
2   medium carrots, sliced
1   (5-pound) bone-in pork shoulder
1   cup spiced rum
1   (20-ounce) can pineapple slices in juice
1   cup Hawaiian marinade
¼   cup light brown sugar
    Freshly ground black pepper

1. Spread the onion and carrots on the bottom of a slow cooker. Put the pork, fat-side up, on top of the vegetables. Pour over the rum, juice from the pineapple (reserve the rings), and Hawaiian marinade. Cover and cook on low for 6 to 8 hours or on high for 4 to 6 hours—until fork-tender. Remove the meat from the pot and set aside to cool a bit. Drain the braising liquid, discarding the solids. Skim any excess fat from the top and pour the liquid into a medium saucepan. Put over medium-high heat and reduce by half.
2. Shred the pork, set aside, and keep warm. When ready to serve, heat the broiler.
3. Line a baking sheet with aluminum foil. Place the pineapple rings on the prepared baking sheet. Sprinkle with brown sugar and a few grindings of black pepper. Put under the broiler and cook until the sugar is melted and the pineapple rings are lightly browned, about 1 to 2 minutes.
4. Put 2 pineapple rings onto each plate. Top each ring with about ⅓ cup shredded pork. Spoon over a little warm sauce and serve.

FENNEL MARINATED VEAL CHOPS

MAKES: 4 servings **COOK:** 12 minutes

4 8-ounce veal loin chops, 1-inch thick

2 large fennel bulbs, with fronds attached

1 cup balsamic vinaigrette

1 tablespoon Sambuca

1 teaspoon fennel seeds, crushed

2 tablespoons extra-virgin olive oil

2 tablespoons lemon juice

1 teaspoon crushed garlic

3 teaspoons steak seasoning, divided use

1. Rinse chops under cold water, pat dry with paper towels, and place in a large zip-top bag. Set aside. Remove stalks and fronds from fennel and reserve bulbs. Chop stalks and fronds into small pieces and place them along with vinaigrette, Sambuca, and crushed fennel seeds in a blender to puree. Pour into bag with chops. Squeeze air from bag and seal. Gently massage bag to coat chops. Marinate in refrigerator at least 4 hours or as long as overnight.

2. Cut each fennel bulb lengthwise into ½-inch-wide slices through the narrow side. Place in a medium bowl and toss with oil, lemon juice, garlic, and 1 teaspoon steak seasoning. Cover and marinate in refrigerator until ready to grill.

3. Set up a grill for direct cooking over medium-high heat. Let chops sit at room temperature for 30 minutes. Remove chops from marinade and discard marinade. Season meat with remaining 2 teaspoons steak seasoning. Oil grate when ready to start cooking. Place chops on hot, oiled grill and cook for 5 to 6 minutes per side for medium (160°F). Meanwhile, place fennel on grill and cook for as long as you cook the chops. Save any lemon-and-oil marinade left in bowl. Serve hot and drizzle fennel with remaining marinade.

LAMB CHOPS WITH RHUBARB RELISH

MAKES: 4 servings **COOK:** 25 minutes

Nonstick cooking spray

¾ teaspoon garam masala, divided use

¼ teaspoon ground cumin

½ teaspoon salt

½ teaspoon black pepper

2 tablespoons plus 1 teaspoon dark brown sugar, divided use

2 frenched racks of lamb

2½ cups frozen rhubarb, thawed

½ cup pre-diced onions

1 teaspoon chopped garlic

1 tablespoon red wine vinegar

¼ cup seedless strawberry preserves

1 tablespoon canned diced jalapeños

1. Preheat oven to 425°F. Line a baking sheet with foil, spray with cooking spray, and set aside.

2. Stir together ½ teaspoon garam masala, cumin, salt, pepper, and 1 teaspoon brown sugar in a small bowl. Pat mixture over all sides of lamb. Place on prepared baking sheet, meat-side up. Roast in preheated oven for 20 to 25 minutes or until internal temperature reaches 130°F.

3. Meanwhile, heat rhubarb, onions, garlic, vinegar, strawberry preserves, and jalapeños, remaining ¼ teaspoon garam masala, and remaining 2 tablespoons brown sugar in a large skillet over medium-high heat. Bring to a boil, cover, and reduce heat. Simmer for 10 minutes. Remove lid, stir, and simmer for 5 more minutes or until rhubarb is soft and relish is heated through.

4. Remove lamb rack from oven and tent with foil. Let rest for 5 minutes before slicing. To serve, put a large spoonful of relish on serving plate and place 3 lamb chops on top.

LEMON-TARRAGON BRINED PORK LOIN

MAKES: 6 servings   **COOK:** 1 hour 30 minutes

- 1 (3-pound) pork loin
- ½ cup water
- 3 tablespoons salt
- 2 tablespoons sugar
- 1½ cups lemonade
- 1 teaspoon crushed garlic
- 1 tablespoon dried tarragon

1. Rinse roast with cold water, pat dry with paper towels, then place in a large zip-top bag and set aside. In a small pan, combine water, salt, and sugar. Bring to a boil and reduce heat. Simmer until sugar and salt have dissolved. Remove from heat and stir in remaining ingredients. Let marinade cool, and pour over roast in bag. Squeeze air from bag and seal. Marinate in refrigerator for 6 to 8 hours.

2. *Outdoor Method*: Set up a grill for indirect cooking over medium heat, so that no direct heat source will be under meat. Let roast sit at room temperature for 30 to 40 minutes. Oil grate when ready to start cooking. Remove roast from brine and pat dry with paper towels. Discard brine. Place roast on hot, oiled grill over a drip pan. Cover grill. Cook for 1 to 1½ hours or until meat is slightly pink in the center and juices run clear (150°F). If using charcoal, add 10 briquettes to each pile of coals after 1 hour. Remove from grill and let stand 10 minutes before slicing. Serve hot.

Indoor Method: Prepare roast as directed above. Preheat oven to 450°F. Remove roast from brine, pat dry, and discard brine. Place on a wire rack in a roasting pan. Place in oven and immediately reduce temperature to 325°F. Roast for 1¼ to 1½ hours (about 25 minutes per pound) or until slightly pink in the center and juices run clear (150°F). Remove from oven and let stand 10 minutes before slicing. Serve hot.

MATZO BALL BRISKET

MAKES: 4 servings   **COOK:** 4 hours 20 minutes

FOR THE BRISKET:

1   (3-pound) beef brisket

1   cup dry red wine

1   (1-ounce) packet onion soup mix

1   (14-ounce) bag frozen pearl onions

1   (16-ounce) bag baby carrots

FOR THE MATZO BALLS:

2   eggs

2   tablespoons vegetable oil

½   (5-ounce) box matzo ball mix

2   tablespoons finely chopped chives

2   (14-ounce) cans beef broth

2   cups water

1   (1-ounce) packet onion soup mix

1. Rinse brisket under cold water and pat dry with paper towels. Place in zip-top bag. In a bowl, stir together wine and soup mix, then pour into bag with brisket. Squeeze air from bag and seal. Marinate in refrigerator for at least 4 hours, or as long as overnight.

2. Preheat oven to 325°F.

3. Remove brisket from refrigerator and let stand at room temperature for 30 minutes. Place brisket and marinade in a 9 × 13-inch glass baking dish. Add onions and carrots. Cover tightly with foil and bake in preheated oven for 3 to 4 hours or until fork-tender.

4. One hour before brisket is finished, beat together eggs and oil. Stir in matzo ball mix and chives until well combined. Let rest in refrigerator for 15 minutes. In a 4-quart pot, bring beef broth, water, and onion soup mix to a boil. With wet hands, shape matzo dough into twelve 1-inch balls. Carefully drop matzo balls into boiling water. Cover pot, reduce heat, and simmer for 20 minutes. Serve brisket hot with matzo balls and vegetables on the side.

MARVELOUS SKIRT STEAK TAMPIQUEÑA

MAKES: 4 servings **COOK:** 8 minutes

1½ pounds skirt steak

2 teaspoons steak seasoning

1 tablespoon Mexican seasoning

1 (10-ounce) can Mexican-style tomatoes—Rotel, drained

1 (7-ounce) can whole green chilies, cut into strips

4 slices pepper jack cheese

8 Corn tortillas, for serving

1 (16-ounce) can refried beans, heated

1 pouch (8.8-ounce) precooked ready rice, Spanish style—Uncle Ben's, prepared according to package directions

1. Rinse steak under cold water and pat dry with paper towels. Lightly score both sides of the steak with a sharp knife in a diamond pattern. Cut into 4 servings and sprinkle with steak seasoning and Mexican seasoning.

2. Set up grill for direct cooking over high heat. Oil grate when ready to start cooking. Place steaks on hot, oiled grill and cook for 4 minutes. Turn and top each steak with tomatoes, chili strips, and a slice of cheese. Close grill cover and cook 3 to 4 minutes more for medium (160°F), until cheese is melted. Transfer steaks to a platter and let rest for 5 minutes. Serve hot with tortillas, beans, and rice.

MOJO MARINATED CARNITAS

MAKES: 6 servings   **COOK:** 4 to 6 hours

1 (3 ½-pound) pork shoulder roast

2 cups pineapple soda

½ cup lime juice

2 tablespoons orange juice concentrate

2 tablespoons crushed garlic

2 tablespoons Jamaican jerk seasoning

¼ cup Mexican seasoning, divided use

1 tablespoon salt

¼ cup paprika

12 flour tortillas, for serving

1 white onion, chopped, for serving

½ bunch chopped fresh cilantro, for serving

2 fresh tomatoes, chopped, for serving

1. Rinse pork roast with cold water, pat dry with paper towels, and place in a large zip-top bag. In a bowl, stir together pineapple soda, lime juice, orange juice concentrate, garlic, jerk seasoning, and 2 tablespoons Mexican seasoning. Pour into bag with pork. Squeeze air from bag and seal. Let marinate in refrigerator at least 4 hours, preferably overnight.

2. Remove pork from refrigerator and let stand at room temperature for 30 to 40 minutes. Remove meat from bag but do not discard marinade. Pat pork dry with paper towels. Combine remaining Mexican seasoning, salt, and paprika, then rub into pork until all seasoning is used. Let cure for 15 minutes before grilling.

3. Pour marinade into a saucepan and bring to a boil for 5 minutes. Remove from heat and set aside.

4. *Outdoor Method*: Set up a grill for indirect cooking over medium heat, so that no direct heat source will be under meat. Oil grate when ready to start cooking. Place roast over a drip pan on heated grill. Cook covered for 4 to 6 hours or until internal temperature reaches 180°–190°F. If using charcoal, add 10 briquettes to each pile of coals every hour. Brush pork with sauce every hour and every 15 minutes during the last hour or so of cooking.

5. Remove from grill and chop meat. Place on a serving platter and pour over any remaining sauce. Serve with warm tortillas, chopped onions, cilantro, and tomatoes.

6. *Indoor Method*: Prepare pork shoulder and sauce as directed for outdoor method. Place pork in a 5-quart slow cooker. Pour 2 cups of marinade over roast. Cover and cook on high for 3 to 4 hours or on low for 7 to 8 hours. Meat should fall apart easily. Serve as directed.

MOLASSES GLAZED HAM

MAKES: 20 servings   **COOK:** 2 hours 30 minutes

1   (7- to 8-pound) fully cooked ham

½   cup molasses

½   cup dark brown sugar

¼   cup bourbon

1½ teaspoons Worcestershire sauce

½   teaspoon dried mustard

½   teaspoon black pepper

1. Preheat oven to 325°F. Line a roasting pan with aluminum foil and set aside.

2. Cut the thick layer of fat and skin from ham and discard. Score the ham in a diamond pattern. Place in roasting pan and roast in preheated oven for 1 hour.

3. Meanwhile, combine remaining ingredients in a medium saucepan. Bring to a boil, reduce heat, and simmer, stirring constantly until sugar is dissolved. Remove from heat.

4. After ham has roasted for 1 hour, baste with glaze and continue roasting. Baste ham every 15 minutes until the internal temperature of the ham reaches 130°–140°F, about another 1½ hours.

5. To serve, slice half of the ham, brush slices with any remaining glaze, and rest slices against the unsliced portion on a large platter.

SOUTHWESTERN PORK CHOPS WITH SWEET POTATO GRATIN

MAKES: 6 servings   **COOK:** 1 hour 10 minutes

Nonstick cooking spray

6 thick center-cut pork loin chops

1 (1.25-ounce) packet chili seasoning mix

1 (24-ounce) bag Steam n' Mash Sweet Potatoes

1 cup evaporated milk

1 (1.6-ounce) packet Garlic & Herb sauce mix

¼ cup honey

2 teaspoons crushed garlic

1 (7-ounce) can chipotle peppers in adobo sauce, finely chopped

1 cup grated hot-pepper Monterey Jack cheese

Salt and pepper, to taste

1. Preheat oven to 350°F. Line a small baking sheet with aluminum foil and lightly spray a 6-cup soufflé dish with cooking spray. Set both aside.

2. Season chops with chili seasoning and set aside.

3. Microwave Steam n' Mash Cut Sweet Potatoes according to package directions, but do not mash. In a small saucepan, whisk together the milk and sauce mix. Bring to a boil, reduce to a simmer, and stir in honey, garlic, and chipotle peppers. Simmer for 3 minutes more, stirring frequently. Remove from the heat and let steep until cooled, about 15 to 20 minutes. Puree in a blender. Layer one-third of the sweet potatoes in the prepared dish. Lightly season with salt and pepper. Ladle one-third of the milk mixture over the potatoes and sprinkle with one-third of the cheese. Repeat layering two more times. Set aside.

4. Rinse pork chops under cold water and pat dry with paper towels. Place chops on foil-lined baking sheet and bake in preheated oven for 15 minutes, then put sweet potato gratin in oven and continue baking both for another 45 minutes or until chops are cooked through and gratin is brown and bubbling. Serve hot.

STEAK BORDELAISE WITH ROASTED SHALLOTS AND MUSHROOMS

MAKES: 4 servings **COOK:** 1 hour 30 minutes

8   large shallots, unpeeled

7   tablespoons extra-virgin olive oil, divided use

1   small shallot, peeled and chopped

2   (8-ounce) packages sliced cremini mushrooms

1   (12-ounce) jar beef gravy

1½ cups dry red wine

1   tablespoon red wine vinegar

1   tablespoon cold butter

4   boneless strip steaks, about ½-inch thick

2   tablespoons coarsely chopped flat-leaf parsley

    Salt and pepper, divided use

1. Preheat oven to 375°F. Line a pie plate with foil, leaving a 5-inch edge of foil all the way around.

2. Remove excess peel from the 8 large shallots, leaving one or two layers of peel on the shallots. Place the shallots in the pie plate, drizzle with 2 tablespoons olive oil, and season with salt and pepper. Fold the foil over the shallots. Place in oven and bake for 1 hour, or until the shallots are fully roasted and soft.

Remove the last layers of peel, and using a serrated knife, cut the shallots in half and set aside.

3. In a medium saucepan over high heat, combine 3 tablespoons olive oil and chopped small shallot. When shallot becomes aromatic, add the mushrooms and cook until mushrooms start to turn color, about 4 minutes. Add the gravy and wine and bring to a boil. Simmer over moderately high heat until reduced to 1½ cups, about 15 minutes. Whisk in the vinegar and butter over low heat and season with salt and pepper. Keep warm.

4. In 2 large skillets over high heat, heat the remaining 2 tablespoons olive oil until almost smoking. Season the steaks with salt and pepper and put 2 steaks in each skillet. Cook over high heat until richly browned on the bottom, about 3 minutes. Turn and cook the steaks for about 2 minutes for medium rare, 5 minutes for medium.

5. Transfer the steaks to plates. Spoon ¼ cup of the sauce over each steak and place the shallots alongside the steaks. Sprinkle with the parsley and serve.

STUFFED BAKED SOLE

MAKES: 4 servings **BAKE:** 20 minutes

Nonstick cooking spray

8 (4-ounce) fillets of sole

1 (8-ounce) package spinach, cheese, and
   artichoke dip, thawed

1 lemon, ½ cut into wedges and ½ juiced
   Salt and pepper, to taste

1. Preheat oven to 350°F. Spray the bottom of a
   9 × 9-inch casserole dish with non-stick
   cooking spray.

2. Lay fillets out on a clean work surface. Evenly
   divide spinach and artichoke dip, about 2
   tablespoons each, among the fillets and
   spread it over the length of the fillets. Roll
   each fillet up and place seam-side down in
   prepared casserole dish. Place the lemon
   wedges down the center of the casserole dish
   between the rolls, and drizzle with the lemon
   juice. Season generously with salt and pepper.

3. Bake for 20 minutes until fish is opaque and
   cooked through.

TURKEY BREAST FAJITAS WITH MANGO SALSA

MAKES: 6 servings **COOK:** 8 minutes

FOR THE MANGO SALSA:

- 8 ounces frozen mango chunks, diced small
- 1 cup chunky salsa
- ¼ cup chopped fresh cilantro
- 2 tablespoons lime juice

FOR THE FAJITAS:

- 1 (2-pound) boneless, skinless turkey breast half
- 1½ cups premade margarita
- 2 teaspoons crushed garlic
- 3 tablespoons frozen limeade concentrate
- ⅓ cup chopped fresh cilantro
- 1 teaspoon salt
- 1 tablespoon salt-free fajita seasoning— The Spice Hunter
- 1 tablespoon canola oil
- 2 red onions, cut into thick rings
- 2 bell peppers, seeded and cut into 1-inch strips
- 6 flour tortillas

1. For the mango salsa, stir to combine diced mango, salsa, cilantro, and lime juice. Cover and refrigerate until ready to serve.

2. To make the turkey, rinse turkey breast under cold water, pat dry with paper towels, then place in a zip-top bag and set aside. In a bowl, stir together margarita, garlic, limeade concentrate, and cilantro. Pour into bag with turkey. Squeeze air from bag and seal. Marinate in refrigerator 2 to 4 hours.

3. Remove turkey from marinade and discard marinade. Slice turkey into ¼-inch strips and season with salt and fajita seasoning. Heat canola oil in a 12-inch skillet over medium-high heat. Add the turkey, turning pieces as they cook (5 to 8 minutes). Remove the turkey to a dish to keep warm. Add the onions and peppers to the pan and toss as they cook. Cook the vegetables until done. Transfer turkey and vegetables to a platter and let rest for 5 minutes before slicing. Serve hot with mango salsa and tortillas.

WHITE WINE BRINED PORK TENDERLOIN WITH APRICOT CHUTNEY

MAKES: 6 servings   **COOK :** 35 minutes

1½   pounds pork tenderloin

½   cup water

2   tablespoons salt

2   tablespoons sugar

1½   cups dry white wine

1   teaspoon crushed garlic

1   tablespoon pickling spice

FOR THE CHUTNEY:

¾   cup apricot jam

½   cup dried apricots, finely chopped

½   cup rice vinegar

2   tablespoons mustard seed

1   tablespoon minced ginger

1. Rinse tenderloin with cold water, pat dry with paper towels, then place in a large zip-top bag and set aside. In a small pan, combine water, salt, and sugar. Bring to a boil, reduce heat, and simmer until sugar and salt have dissolved. Remove from heat. Stir in wine, garlic, and pickling spice. Allow the mixture to cool, and then pour over tenderloin in bag. Squeeze air from bag and seal. Marinate in refrigerator 3 to 6 hours.

2. For the chutney, combine jam, apricots, vinegar, mustard seed, and ginger in a small saucepan. Bring to a boil, stirring often, and continue boiling until reduced to 1¼ cups. Set aside to cool. Cover and hold in the refrigerator until ready to serve.

3. Preheat oven to 375°F. Remove tenderloin from bag and discard brine. Roast for 20 to 25 minutes or until slightly pink in the center and juices run clear (155°F). Transfer to a platter and allow the meat to rest for 10 minutes before carving. Serve hot with apricot chutney.

CARROT CAKE WHOOPIE PIES

MAKES: 12 pies   **BAKE:** 10 minutes

1   (18-ounce) box carrot cake mix

1   stick (½ cup) butter, softened

3   eggs

1   carrot, grated

½   cup raisins

FOR THE FILLING:

1   pound cream cheese

1   stick (½ cup) unsalted butter, softened

2   cups powdered sugar

2   teaspoons vanilla extract

1   cup walnuts, finely chopped

1. Preheat oven to 375°F.
2. In a large bowl, beat together cake mix with butter, slowly add the eggs, and mix until incorporated. Stir in the grated carrot and raisins. Refrigerate for at least 30 minutes and up to 2 hours. Remove from the refrigerator and, using a small ice cream scoop, drop batter onto a parchment-lined cookie sheet in mounds about 2 tablespoons each, spacing them about 2 inches apart. Bake 10 to 12 minutes or until golden brown, rotating pans halfway through. Remove from oven and cool 5 minutes on pan before moving to a wire rack to cool completely.
3. In a mixing bowl, beat together the cream cheese, butter, powdered sugar, and vanilla with a hand mixer until well combined, light, and fluffy.
4. To assemble whoopie pies, put filling into a zip-top bag and snip off one corner. Place chopped walnuts into a shallow dish or pie plate. Flip over one carrot cake cookie and pipe about ¼ cup of frosting onto center of flat side. Top with another cookie, flat-side down, and press gently to distribute frosting to edges. Roll edges of pie in the chopped walnuts and set aside. Repeat with remaining cookies and frosting.

EASTER GARDEN CAKE

MAKES: 12 servings   **BAKE:** 32 minutes

Nonstick cooking spray

1 (18-ounce) box carrot cake mix

½ cup pineapple juice

½ cup vegetable oil

3 eggs

1 cup pre-shredded carrots, chopped

1 (8-ounce) can crushed pineapple

½ cup chopped walnuts

1 (12-ounce) can whipped cream-cheese frosting

Green food coloring

¾ cup sweetened shredded coconut

1 (9-ounce) box chocolate wafer cookies, crushed

12 marshmallow bunnies and chicks—Peeps

1 (4-to 6-inch) white chocolate bunny

Gumdrops

1 (4.25-ounce) tube white decorating icing

1 (1.5-ounce) package mini chocolate eggs—Cadbury

1. Preheat oven to 350°F. Spray a 9 × 13-inch baking pan with cooking spray and set aside.

2. Beat cake mix, pineapple juice, oil, and eggs in a large bowl with mixer on low speed for 30 seconds. Scrape down the sides of the bowl and beat on medium-high speed for 2 minutes. Add carrots, crushed pineapple, and walnuts, and beat on low speed until combined. Pour into prepared pan.

3. Bake in preheated oven for 25 to 30 minutes or until a tester inserted in cake comes out clean. Remove and cool completely.

4. Stir green food coloring into cream cheese frosting until desired shade is reached and coloring is well combined; set aside. Pour shredded coconut into a pie plate. Add enough green food coloring and toss with a gloved hand until coconut is desired shade of green.

5. To decorate, frost top and sides of cake with green cream-cheese frosting. Sprinkle green coconut to make a rectangular 9 x 13 border on top of cake. Fill the center of coconut border with crushed chocolate wafers to look like "dirt." Press marshmallow bunnies and chicks into sides of cake. Stand white chocolate bunny in center of cake.

6. For the flowers, cut a gumdrop 5 times with scissors and fan out the sticky centers to look like petals. Pipe icing in the centers of gumdrop flowers. Scatter flowers and mini eggs around bunnies in "garden."

MAY

BROCCOLI PASTA SALAD

MAKES: 10 servings

- 3 cups packaged broccoli florets
- 2 tablespoons water
- ¾ cup sour cream
- ¼ cup mayonnaise
- ¼ cup Caesar salad dressing
- 2 teaspoons Italian seasoning
- 8 ounces mini penne pasta, cooked according to package directions
- 1 cup roasted red peppers, chopped
- 1 (2.25-ounce) can sliced black olives
- 1 (4.5-ounce) jar sliced mushrooms
- 3 scallions, sliced
- 1 tablespoon oil-packed sundried tomatoes, drained and julienned

1. Place broccoli florets and water in a large microwave-safe bowl. Cover and heat in microwave for 4 to 5 minutes or until broccoli is steamed. Drain broccoli well and set aside to cool.
2. Stir together sour cream, mayonnaise, salad dressing, and Italian seasoning in a small bowl.
3. Stir together all remaining ingredients and steamed broccoli in a large bowl. Pour dressing over top and toss until well combined.
4. Refrigerate for at least 1 hour. Serve chilled or at room temperature.

CRANBERRY AND ORANGE WILD RICE

MAKES: 4 servings   **COOK:** 25 minutes

- ½ cup dried cranberries
- 1 cup fresh orange juice
- 1¼ cups water
- 1 tablespoon unsalted butter
- 1 (8.8 ounce) package long grain and wild ready rice pouch—Uncle Ben's
  Zest of 1 orange
- ½ cup sliced almonds
  Finely chopped chives, for garnish

1. Cover the cranberries with hot water and set aside while you make the rice.
2. In a medium pot over high heat, bring the juice, water, and butter to a boil. Stir in the rice and its included seasoning packet and return to a boil. Turn the heat to low, cover, and cook until the rice is tender, about 20 to 25 minutes. Drain the cranberries and add them to the rice along with the orange zest and almonds. Gently stir them in, fluffing the rice. Cover and keep warm until ready to serve. Garnish with chives.

CREAMY CHICKEN SALAD TEA SANDWICHES

MAKES: 16 triangle sandwiches

- 1 (6-ounce) package grilled chicken-breast strips, finely chopped
- ⅓ cup baby spinach leaves, finely chopped
- ¼ cup pecan chips, toasted
- ¼ cup sweetened dried cranberries, finely chopped
- ½ teaspoon poultry seasoning
- ⅓ cup mayonnaise
- 16 slices thin-sliced wheat bread, crusts removed
   Salt and pepper, to taste

1. Stir together chopped chicken, spinach, pecans, cranberries, poultry seasoning, and mayonnaise in a large bowl until well combined. Season with salt and pepper to taste.
2. Scoop 3 tablespoons of chicken salad mixture onto a slice of crustless bread and top with another slice of bread. Cut horizontally to make 2 triangle sandwiches. Repeat with remaining ingredients to make 16 sandwiches.

EARLY SUMMER SOUP

MAKES: 6 servings

- 1 (2-ounce) can pineapple chunks, drained
- 1 cup pineapple coconut nectar
- 1 tablespoon pineapple gelatin mix
- 3 cups frozen sliced strawberries in sugar, thawed
- 3 tablespoons frozen lemonade concentrate, thawed
   Fresh blueberries, for garnish

1. Puree pineapple chunks and nectar in blender on high until smooth, about 30 seconds. Transfer to a 4-cup liquid measuring cup and stir in gelatin mix. Cover with plastic wrap and chill in refrigerator for 1 hour. Blend sliced strawberries and lemonade concentrate in blender on high until smooth, about 30 seconds. Leave in blender container, cover with lid, and chill in refrigerator until ready to use.
2. To serve, simultaneously pour ½ cup of each fruit mixture into serving bowl to create 2 colored sides. Marble with spoon if desired. Garnish with fresh blueberries and serve immediately.

ONION SHORTCAKE

MAKES: 9 servings   **COOK:** 50 minutes

    5   tablespoons butter, divided use
3 ½   cups diced red onions
    ¼   cup packed brown sugar
    ¼   cup red wine vinegar
2 ⅓   cups baking mix—Bisquick®
    1   tablespoon sugar
    1   cup shredded Monterey Jack cheese
    ½   cup milk
    1   egg, beaten
    1   cup sour cream, plus extra for serving

1. Preheat oven to 375°F. Heat 2 tablespoons butter in a large skillet. When butter has melted, add onions and sauté for 5 minutes. Turn heat to low, cover pan, and cook onions for 15 minutes or until soft and wilted. Remove lid and turn heat to medium. Stir in brown sugar and vinegar. Continue cooking until liquid has all but evaporated. Set aside to cool.

2. Melt remaining butter in microwave. In a large mixing bowl, stir together baking mix, sugar, cheese, and milk until soft dough forms. Shape into a ball and knead ten times on a surface sprinkled with baking mix. Press dough in ungreased 9 × 9-inch baking pan.

3. Spread cooled onion jam over shortcake dough. Stir together egg and sour cream and spread over jam.

4. Bake in preheated oven for 30 minutes or until set and shortcake has cooked through. Cool 10 minutes before serving. Serve with extra sour cream.

GRILLED ARTICHOKES WITH LEMONY PESTO AIOLI

MAKES: 4 servings   **COOK:** 8 minutes

    1   (8-ounce) box frozen artichokes, thawed
    1   (10-ounce) jar large garlic-stuffed green olives, drained
    1   cup mayonnaise
    ¼   cup pesto
    2   tablespoons lemon juice
    1   teaspoon crushed garlic

1. Soak 4 wooden skewers in water for at least an hour. Thread thawed artichokes and olives alternately on skewers and set aside. In a bowl, stir together remaining ingredients. Brush skewers with aioli mixture.

2. Set up a grill for direct cooking over medium heat. Oil grate when ready to start cooking. Place skewers on grill for 3 to 4 minutes per side, brushing with aioli with each turn. Serve hot with extra aioli.

SCALLOPED POTATOES

MAKES: 4 servings **COOK:** 30 minutes

- 2 cups milk
- 2 tablespoons butter
- 2 russet potatoes, washed and sliced into ¼-inch disks
- ¼ cup shredded cheddar cheese
   Salt and pepper, to taste

1. Preheat oven to 350°F.
2. In a small pot, heat milk and butter over low heat.
3. Layer the potato slices in a buttered 9-inch pie plate and season with salt and pepper. Add hot milk and butter. Top with cheese and bake in oven for 30 minutes.

BAKED FALAFEL WITH YOGURT SAUCE

MAKES: 8 pieces **BAKE:** 20 minutes

FOR THE FALAFEL:

- 1¾ cups canned chickpeas, drained and rinsed
- ½ teaspoon red pepper flakes
- ¼ red onion, diced
- ½ small green bell pepper, diced
- ⅛ cup lemon juice
- 1 tablespoon olive oil
- ¼ cup chopped fresh parsley
- ½ teaspoon ground cumin
- ¼ cup all-purpose flour
- 1 teaspoon baking powder
   Nonstick cooking spray

FOR THE YOGURT SAUCE:

- ½ cup plain yogurt
- 1 teaspoon hot sauce
- 1 tablespoon chopped fresh parsley
- ¼ teaspoon ground cumin

1. For the falafel, place a baking sheet in the oven and preheat oven to 400°F.
2. Combine all falafel ingredients in a food processor. Pulse until coarsely ground.
3. Form the falafel mixture into balls about the size of walnuts. Set aside. Remove the baking sheet from the oven and spray with nonstick cooking spray. Place the falafel on the baking sheet. Bake in oven for 15 to 20 minutes, turning halfway through to brown on both sides.
4. For the yogurt sauce, combine all ingredients in a small bowl and set aside.

CHIMICHURRI MARINATED CHICKEN HALVES

MAKES: 4 servings   **COOK:** 50 minutes

FOR THE CHIMICHURRI:

    1 bunch flat-leaf parsley, chopped
    ¼ cup fresh oregano leaves
    2 tablespoons fresh marjoram leaves
    2 tablespoons fresh thyme leaves
 1½ cups oil-and-vinegar salad dressing
    2 tablespoons crushed garlic
    ½ teaspoon salt

FOR THE CHICKEN:

    1 (4-pound) whole roasting chicken
       Garlic salt and pepper, to taste

1. For the chimichurri, place herbs in a food processor fitted with a blade attachment and pulse until finely chopped. Transfer to a bowl and stir in salad dressing, garlic, and salt. Set aside.

2. For the chicken, cut chicken in half with kitchen shears, removing backbone. Remove excess skin and rinse chicken halves under cold water, then pat dry with paper towels. Place chicken in a large zip-top bag. Pour half of the chimichurri sauce into bag with chicken, reserving the remaining chimichurri for basting. Squeeze air from bag and seal. Marinate in refrigerator for 2 to 4 hours.

3. Preheat oven to 375°F.

4. Remove chicken halves from marinade and discard marinade. Place chicken on a foil-lined baking sheet and roast for 40 to 50 minutes or until no longer pink at the bone and the juices run clear (180°F at the thigh). Transfer chicken to a platter and let rest for 5 minutes before serving. Serve hot.

CHURRASCO BEEF WITH AVOCADO-CORN SALSA

MAKES: 4 servings   **COOK:** 8 minutes

FOR THE STEAK:

1½ pounds center-cut beef tenderloin, trimmed of fat and silver skin

3 tablespoons steak rub

2 tablespoons Mexican seasoning

FOR THE SALSA:

1 Hass avocado, diced

1 (11-ounce) can Mexicorn, drained

1 (10-ounce) can diced tomatoes with lime and cilantro (suggested: Rotel), drained

2 teaspoons lime juice

½ teaspoon salt

1. Place tenderloin on a cutting board. Holding your knife parallel to cutting board, cut tenderloin lengthwise into ½-inch-thick, flat, even slices. Place each slice between 2 pieces of plastic wrap and pound with a meat mallet to ¼-inch thick. In a small bowl, combine steak rub and Mexican seasoning. Rub seasoning into both sides of beef slices. Set aside for 15 to 30 minutes for meat to cure.

2. For avocado-corn salsa, stir together remaining ingredients in a medium bowl. Set aside until ready to serve.

3. *Outdoor Method*: Set up a grill for direct cooking over high heat. Oil grate when ready to start cooking. Arrange the beef slices diagonally on hot, oiled grill and cook for 3 to 4 minutes per side for medium (160°F). Serve hot with avocado-corn salsa.

Indoor Method: Prepare steaks and marinade as directed above. Preheat broiler. Place steaks on a foil-lined baking sheet or broiler pan. Broil 6 to 8 inches from heat source for 3 to 4 minutes per side for medium (160°F). Serve hot with avocado-corn salsa.

COUSCOUS STUFFED FLANK STEAK

MAKES: 4 servings   **COOK:** 1 hour 25 minutes

1 (1½-pound) flank steak

1 (1.07-ounce) packet zesty herb marinade mix—McCormick Grill Mates

¼ cup red wine vinegar

¼ cup plus 2 tablespoons vegetable oil, divided use

1 (8-ounce) package sliced mushrooms, finely chopped

1¼ cups water

1 (5.8-ounce) box couscous with roasted garlic and olive oil—Near East®

Nonstick cooking spray

1. Pound flank steak to ½-inch thick with a meat mallet. Lightly score one side of meat in a diamond pattern. Place in a large zip-top bag. Stir together marinade mix, vinegar, and ¼ cup oil in a small bowl. Pour into bag with meat. Squeeze air from bag and seal. Marinate in refrigerator for at least 1 hour, or as long as overnight.

2. Preheat oven to 350°F. Remove meat from refrigerator and set aside.

3. Heat remaining 2 tablespoons oil in a medium saucepan. Add chopped mushrooms and sauté until liquid released from mushrooms has evaporated, about 10 minutes. Add 1¼ cups water and spice packet from the couscous. Bring to a boil and stir in couscous. Cover, remove from heat, and let sit for 5 minutes. Remove lid and fluff with a fork.

4. Remove meat from marinade and discard marinade. Spray a large piece of aluminum foil lightly with cooking spray and lay on meat, scored-side down, with a longer side toward you. Spread couscous over the surface of the meat, leaving a 2-inch border at the opposite long side. Starting with the side nearest you, roll meat up tightly and tie with string. Wrap with aluminum foil, twisting ends of foil to secure. Place on a rimmed baking sheet and roast in preheated oven for 1 ¼ hours.

5. Let rest for 10 minutes before removing string and slicing. Serve hot.

CRISPY CRUNCHY FISH AND CHIPS

MAKES: 4 servings **COOK:** 40 minutes

3   small russet potatoes, washed

3   cups plus 2 teaspoons canola oil, divided use

    Nonstick cooking spray

4   tilapia fillets, each sliced in half

2½ cups all-purpose flour, divided use

2   teaspoons baking powder

2   cups seltzer water

FOR THE TARTAR SAUCE:

1   cup mayonnaise

2   teaspoons lemon juice

2   teaspoon seafood seasoning

2   tablespoons pickle relish

    Salt and pepper, to taste

1. Preheat oven to 400° F. Place a baking sheet in the oven to preheat.

2. Using the slicing attachment on a food processor or a knife, slice the potatoes into thin discs about ¼-inch thick. Place in a large bowl with 2 teaspoons canola oil, salt, and pepper, and toss to coat. Remove the baking sheet from the oven and spray with nonstick cooking spray. Transfer the potatoes to the baking sheet and bake for 10 minutes, flip each chip, and bake for another 10 minutes. In a medium pot heat 3 cups of canola oil to 360°F.

3. In a large bowl, combine 2 cups flour with baking powder and season with salt and pepper. Whisk in seltzer water. Place the remaining ½ cup flour on a pie dish and season with salt and pepper. Dredge the tilapia in flour, shake off the excess, then dip into batter. Carefully place the battered fish into the hot oil. Working in batches, so as not to crowd the pot, fry for 6 minutes until golden brown. Remove to a plate lined with paper towels. Repeat with remaining fillets. While frying remaining fish, hold the finished fillets in a 250°F oven.

4. For tartar sauce, combine all ingredients in a small bowl and mix until well blended.

5. Serve fish immediately with chips and tartar sauce on the side.

FARM STAND PIZZA WITH CHICKPEA SALAD

MAKES: 4 servings **BAKE:** 28 minutes

16 ounces fresh or frozen pizza dough, thawed if necessary
Nonstick cooking spray
1 cup jarred or canned tomato sauce
½ cup mushrooms, sliced
½ cup broccoli florets, chopped
1 bell pepper, chopped
½ medium onion, sliced
10 basil leaves, torn
1 cup mozzarella cheese, shredded
2 tablespoons olive oil
Salt and pepper, to taste

FOR THE SALAD:

2 (15-ounce) cans chickpeas, drained and rinsed
1 carrot, grated
½ red onion, sliced
1 small green bell pepper, diced
¼ cup chopped fresh parsley
¼ cup lemon juice
2 tablespoons olive oil
Salt and pepper, to taste

1. Preheat oven to 400°F. Place a baking sheet in the oven.
2. Roll out or stretch pizza dough into a long rectangle and place on a 13 × 18-inch sheet pan. Remove baking sheet from oven and spray with nonstick cooking spray. Place dough onto baking sheet. Using a fork, dot holes all over crust and brush with olive oil. Bake in oven for 8 minutes.
3. Remove pizza crust from oven and top with sauce, vegetables, and basil. Sprinkle cheese, drizzle with olive oil, and season with salt and pepper. Bake pizza for 20 minutes or until crust is golden brown and cheese is melted and bubbly.
4. For chickpea salad, add all ingredients to a bowl and toss to combine. Season with salt and pepper to taste.

FLAT IRON STEAK WITH TANGO SAUCE

MAKES: 6 servings   **COOK:** 8 minutes

1   pound flat iron steak or top blade steak
1   teaspoon paprika
1   teaspoon salt
1   teaspoon pepper

FOR THE SAUCE:
½   cup chopped fresh cilantro
¾   cup chopped fresh parsley leaves
2   tablespoons minced garlic
¼   cup red wine vinegar
2   tablespoons lemon juice
⅓   cup olive oil

1. Take the steak out of the refrigerator about 20 minutes before you cook so it can come to room temperature. This will help the steak cook more evenly. Preheat a grill pan or prepare an outdoor grill over medium-high heat.
2. In a small bowl, combine paprika, salt, and pepper. Generously season the steak with spice mix. Place on grill and cook 4 minutes per side or until medium rare. Remove from grill and allow to rest for 5 minutes. Slice against the grain into ½-inch-thick strips. Serve topped with tango sauce.
3. For the tango sauce, place all ingredients except olive oil in the bowl of a food processor or blender and pulse to combine. With machine running, stream in the olive oil until well incorporated. Serve with steak.

GRILLED CHICKEN WITH CREAMY CAPER SAUCE

MAKES: 4 servings   **COOK:** 12 minutes

4   boneless, skinless chicken breasts, thinly sliced
2   teaspoons lemon pepper seasoning
3   tablespoons olive oil
1   shallot, diced
1   tablespoon chopped garlic
1   cup white wine or chicken stock
2   tablespoons capers
1   tablespoon Dijon mustard
2   tablespoons chopped fresh parsley
2   tablespoons sour cream
    Salt and pepper, to taste

1. Preheat a grill pan or prepare an outdoor grill over medium-high heat. Brush the grate of the grill with canola oil just before you put the chicken on. Rinse chicken under cold water and pat dry with paper towels. Season the chicken with lemon pepper and place on hot, oiled grill. Grill 4 to 5 minutes per side.
2. Heat olive oil in a medium skillet over medium heat. Add shallot and garlic and sauté for 2 minutes. Add white wine and capers and reduce by half. Whisk in mustard and parsley. Season with salt and pepper to taste. Let simmer for 1 minute. Remove from heat and whisk in sour cream.
3. Place the grilled chicken on a platter and dollop with the creamy sauce.

HERBED LAMB BURGERS

MAKES: 4 servings   **COOK:** 13 minutes

FOR THE TAPENADE DRESSING:

1 (10-ounce) jar olive bruschetta—DeLallo, drained

½ cup mayonnaise

1 teaspoon lemon juice

1 teaspoon Dijon mustard

FOR THE BURGERS:

1 tablespoon extra-virgin olive oil

2 shallots, minced

1 teaspoon crushed garlic

1½ pounds ground lamb

2 tablespoons finely chopped mint

2 tablespoons finely chopped fresh parsley

2 teaspoons Dijon mustard

4 rustic burger rolls

Butterleaf lettuce, for serving

Sliced tomatoes, for serving

1. For the tapenade dressing, stir together bruschetta, mayonnaise, lemon juice, and mustard in a small bowl. Cover and refrigerate.

2. For the burgers, heat oil in a medium skillet over medium heat. Sauté shallots and garlic until soft, about 5 minutes. Set aside to cool. Once cooled, combine shallots and garlic with lamb, mint, parsley, and mustard. Form into 4 patties slightly larger than rolls.

3. Preheat broiler. Place patties on a wire rack over a foil-lined baking sheet. Broil 6 to 8 inches from heat source for 3 to 4 minutes per side for medium (160°F). Serve hot on rolls with lettuce, tomatoes, and tapenade dressing.

JAMAICAN DUCK BREAST WITH MANGO MINT SALSA

MAKES: 4 servings   **COOK:** 18 to 24 minutes

FOR THE SALSA:

- 1   (16-ounce) bag frozen mango chunks, diced small
- 2   teaspoons canned diced jalapeños
- ¼   cup fresh mint leaves, torn into small pieces
- 2   tablespoons lime juice
- 1   teaspoon Jamaican jerk seasoning—McCormick

   Salt and pepper, to taste

FOR THE DUCK:

- 4   Muscovy duck breasts
- 2   tablespoons Jamaican jerk seasoning—McCormick

   Salt and pepper, to taste

1. Set up a grill for direct cooking over medium heat.

2. For mango mint salsa, toss together diced mango chunks, jalapeños, mint leaves, lime juice, and jerk seasoning. Adjust seasoning with salt and pepper. Set aside until ready to serve.

3. For the duck breasts, rinse under cold water and pat dry with paper towels. Score skin several times with a sharp knife; be careful not to cut through to the meat. Season with salt and pepper and rub completely with jerk seasoning. Let cure for 15 minutes.

4. *Outdoor Method*: Set up a grill for direct cooking over high heat. Oil grate when ready to start cooking. Place duck breasts, skin-side down, on hot, oiled grill. Cook for 10 minutes, watching for flare-ups. Turn and cook an additional 6 to 8 minutes or until internal temperature reaches 155°F. Remove from grill and let stand 5 minutes before slicing. Serve hot with mango mint salsa.

Indoor Method: Prepare salsa and duck breasts as directed above. Place duck, skin-side down, in a hot, unoiled skillet over medium-low heat for 10 to 12 minutes as fat renders from breasts. Increase heat to medium and turn duck. Continue cooking for 10 to 12 more minutes for medium. Let stand 5 minutes before slicing. Serve hot with mango mint salsa.

MAGIC MOLE TAMALES

MAKES: 6 servings   **COOK:** 60 minutes

2 (8.8-ounce) bags Spanish Style Ready Rice—Uncle Ben's

1 teaspoon Mexican seasoning—The Spice Hunter

1 cup seasoning blend—PictSweet

1 (10-ounce) can diced tomatoes and green chilies—Rotel, drained

1 (11-ounce) can Mexicorn—Green Giant, drained

½ cup mole sauce

1 (14.5-ounce) can low-sodium beef broth

½ teaspoon cinnamon

1 (3-ounce) package 6 beef tamales (suggested: XLNT®), thawed if frozen

¼ cup canned whole green chilies, cut into thin strips

1. Preheat oven to 350°F.
2. Heat rice in microwave according to package directions; empty contents into a bowl. Stir in Mexican seasoning, seasoning blend, drained tomatoes, and corn. Transfer to a 9 × 13-inch baking dish and set aside.
3. In a small saucepan, combine mole sauce, broth, and cinnamon. Bring to a simmer, whisking until smooth and thickened, about 6 to 8 minutes.
4. Place tamales on rice and spoon over mole. Top with strips of green chilies. Cover with foil and bake in preheated oven 45 to 50 minutes or until tamales are heated through. Serve hot.

MONTE CRISTO DOG WITH SWEET MUSTARD SAUCE

MAKES: 8 servings   **COOK:** 10 minutes

FOR THE SAUCE:

1 cup frozen blackberries

½ cup spicy brown mustard

3 tablespoons blackberry preserves

FOR THE SANDWICHES:

8 bun-length franks, butterflied

8 French rolls, split horizontally

1 (10-ounce) package deli-shaved honey-roasted turkey

16 slices Gouda cheese, thinly sliced, from deli

1. Combine all sauce ingredients in a blender and puree until smooth. Transfer to an airtight container and store in refrigerator until ready to use.
2. Set up a grill for direct cooking over medium heat. Oil grate when ready to start cooking. Place butterflied franks on hot, oiled grill and cook for 8 to 10 minutes or until heated through, turning once. Toast rolls lightly while franks are cooking.
3. Slather sweet mustard sauce on both halves of French rolls and divide turkey, franks, and cheese to build sandwiches.

MOUSSAKA STACKS

MAKES: 6 servings   **COOK:** 40 minutes

1   large eggplant, sliced ⅓-inch thick

1   tablespoon salt

1   pound ground lamb

2   tablespoons Greek seasoning—McCormick, divided use

1   tablespoon tomato paste

½   cup red wine

½   cup egg substitute

1   cup bread crumbs
    Nonstick cooking spray

¼   cup olive oil

1   pinch nutmeg

⅓   cup white sauce—Aunt Penny's

2   cups homestyle mashed potatoes

¾   cup Petite-Cut diced tomatoes

¼   cup shredded Parmesan cheese

1. Preheat oven to 375°F. Line a baking sheet with a layer of paper towels.

2. Place sliced eggplant on towels and sprinkle salt over the top. Cover with more paper towels. Let sit for 30 minutes for salt to draw out bitterness of eggplant.

3. Meanwhile, brown lamb in a large skillet with 1 tablespoon Greek seasoning. Drain off grease and stir in tomato paste and red wine. Simmer until thickened. Set aside.

4. Place 2 pie plates next to each other. Pour egg substitute into the first pie plate. Pour bread crumbs and remaining Greek seasoning into the second pie plate and stir together. Pat dry eggplant with paper towels. Dip each eggplant slice into egg mixture, then dredge in bread crumbs until well coated on both sides. Place on baking sheet. Repeat until all slices are coated.

5. Heat oil in a large skillet over medium-high heat. Place as many eggplant slices as will fit comfortably in the skillet and fry 2 minutes per side—do not overcrowd pan. Remove paper towels from original baking sheet, spray with cooking spray, and use to lay out fried eggplant slices. Repeat until all slices are fried.

6. Stir nutmeg into white sauce. Spread a thin layer of mashed potato on each fried eggplant slice. Top with lamb mixture, white sauce, and diced tomatoes. Sprinkle Parmesan cheese over the top of each. Bake in preheated oven for 15 to 20 minutes or until eggplant is cooked through but not mushy. Serve immediately.

PESTO PORK WITH CUCUMBER AND SNAP PEAS

MAKES: 6 servings   **COOK:** 25 minutes

- 1   (8-ounce) bag stringless sugar snap peas, chopped
- 1   large hothouse cucumber, seeded and diced
- ½   cup pesto sauce, divided use
- ¼   cup plain yogurt
- 2   tablespoons red wine vinegar
- ¼   teaspoon celery salt—McCormick
- ¼   teaspoon ground black pepper
- 2   pounds pork tenderloin
- 1   tablespoon Dijon mustard
- 1   cup panko bread crumbs

1. Preheat oven to 425°F.
2. Mix together chopped snap peas and chopped cucumber in a large bowl. Stir together 3 tablespoons pesto, yogurt, vinegar, celery salt, and pepper in a small bowl until well combined. Pour over vegetables and toss to coat. Refrigerate for at least 30 minutes.
3. While salad chills, stir together remaining pesto and mustard in a small bowl. Rinse pork tenderloin under cold water and pat dry with paper towels. Brush mixture on pork and coat with bread crumbs. Roast in middle of oven until a thermometer inserted diagonally 2 inches into meat registers 155°F, about 20 to 25 minutes. (Check after 15 minutes to see if crumbs are getting too dark; if they are, tent loosely with foil.) Transfer to a cutting board, tent with foil, and let stand 10 minutes before slicing.

PORK CHOP SALAD WITH SPINACH AND STRAWBERRIES

MAKES: 4 servings   **COOK:** 12 minutes

FOR THE CHOPS:

4	(6-ounce) bone-in pork chops
2	eggs
2	tablespoons water
1¼	cups all-purpose flour
2	tablespoons chicken seasoning

FOR THE SALAD:

¾	cup balsamic dressing
1	tablespoon coarse-grain mustard
1	(6-ounce) bag baby spinach
1	pint strawberries, hulled and quartered
1	large shallot, finely minced
1	handful oil-cured olives, pitted

1. Preheat oven to 425°F. Line 2 rimmed baking sheets with foil and spray with cooking oil.

2. Rinse pork chops under cold water and pat dry with paper towels. Place each pork chop between 2 sheets of plastic wrap and gently pound with flat side of a meat pounder until ¼-inch thick or less.

3. Lightly beat eggs and water in a shallow bowl. Stir together flour and chicken seasoning in another shallow bowl. Holding by the bone, lightly dip each chop in the egg mixture and then dredge in flour mixture, shaking off excess. Set on baking sheets, 2 chops per sheet, spray well with cooking oil, flip, and spray again.

4. Bake the chops for 3 minutes. Flip over and cook another 3 minutes, then turn and cook 3 minutes more, before turning again and cooking an additional 3 minutes. Remove from oven and let sit for 10 minutes.

5. In a small bowl, whisk the mustard into the dressing. In a large salad bowl, toss the spinach and strawberries with ½ cup of dressing.

6. To serve, place a chop on the center of a plate or large shallow soup bowl. Divide the salad among the 4 plates, place on chops, and sprinkle with shallot and olives. Drizzle with the balance of dressing if necessary.

RED SNAPPER WITH MANGO CREAM

MAKES: 4 servings   **COOK:** 20 minutes

Nonstick cooking spray

4   (6-ounce) red snapper fillets

1   (14-ounce) can lite coconut milk

1   cup mango nectar—Kern's

1   tablespoon garlic puree

2   teaspoons ginger puree—Gourmet Garden

Hot white rice, cooked

Green onions, sliced, for garnish

Mango wedges, for garnish

Salt and black pepper, to taste

1. **Preheat oven to 425°F. Spray a 9 × 13-inch glass baking dish with cooking spray.**

2. Rinse snapper and pat dry with paper towels. Season with salt and pepper and place in baking dish. Cover with foil and bake for about 15 minutes or until fish flakes easily. Remove from oven and preheat broiler. Place pan under broiler for 2 to 3 minutes or until fillets are lightly browned.

3. Combine coconut milk, mango nectar, garlic, and ginger in a medium saucepan over medium-high heat. Bring to a boil, reduce heat to medium, and continue to reduce sauce for 10 to 15 minutes or until thickened.

4. To serve, place a large spoonful of rice in center of a plate and arrange a fillet slightly off-center on the rice. Spoon some of the sauce over the top and garnish with a couple of mango wedges and a sprinkling of green onion.

RUM MARINATED GRILLED FRUIT CREPES WITH MINTED YOGURT SAUCE

MAKES: 8 servings **COOK:** 7 minutes

- 4   peaches, cut in half and pit removed
- 4   plums, cut in half and pit removed
- 2   tablespoons sugar
- ½   cup mint leaves, divided use
- 1   cup white rum
- 1½   cups nonfat plain yogurt
- 4   tablespoons instant vanilla pudding mix
- 1   tablespoon vanilla extract
-     Nonstick cooking spray
- 8   store-bought crepes

1. Cut each peach and plum half into 4 wedges and place in a zip-top bag. Place sugar and ¼ cup of mint into a bowl. With the back of a spoon, mash the mint leaves into the sugar until well bruised. Stir in the rum and pour the mixture into the bag with the fruit. Squeeze air from the bag and seal. Marinate in the refrigerator for 30 minutes to 4 hours.

2. Set up a grill for direct cooking over medium heat. Remove fruit from marinade and drain on paper towels; reserve ½ cup of the marinade. Finely chop remaining mint and place in a medium bowl. Add yogurt, pudding mix, vanilla, and the reserved marinade. Stir until well combined. Set aside in refrigerator until ready to serve.

3. Pat fruit dry and spray both sides with cooking spray. Brush and oil grate before cooking. Place fruit on hot, oiled grill and cook for 2 to 3 minutes per side or until warmed and has visible grill marks. Place crepes on the grill for 30 seconds per side.

4. Divide fruit among crepes and roll. Serve topped with minted yogurt sauce.

SAVORY BREAKFAST CASSEROLE WITH A TRIO OF TOPPINGS

MAKES: 8 servings   **COOK:** 50 minutes

FOR THE CASSEROLE:

Nonstick cooking spray

10   large eggs

3   cups milk

2   (5-ounce) bags large cut croutons

1   (10.7-ounce) can cream of mushroom soup

1   (8-ounce) package diced ham

2   cups shredded cheddar cheese

2   tablespoons chopped fresh parsley

Salt and pepper, to taste

FOR THE ONION AND MUSHROOM JAM:

3   tablespoons extra-virgin olive oil

2   (12-ounce) bags frozen chopped onions, thawed

2   (8-ounce) packages sliced mushrooms

1   tablespoon sugar

1   tablespoon apple cider vinegar

Salt and pepper, to taste

FOR THE TOMATO AND PESTO TOPPING:

1   (15-ounce) can diced tomatoes, drained

½   cup pesto

1   tablespoon red wine vinegar

Salt and pepper, to taste

FOR THE AVOCADO AND BLACK BEAN SALSA:

1   pint guacamole

1   (15-ounce) can black beans, drained

1   canned jalapeño, finely chopped

1   tablespoon lime juice

1. To make the casserole, preheat oven to 350°F. Spray a 9 × 13-inch baking dish with cooking spray.

2. In a large bowl, whisk together eggs and milk until well blended. Add croutons and toss until well coated. Add remaining ingredients and mix. Pour into prepared baking dish and bake for 45 to 50 minutes until browned and puffy. Let rest 5 minutes before serving.

3. For the onion and mushroom jam, add the olive oil to a large skillet over medium heat. When the oil is hot, add the onions, mushrooms, sugar, vinegar, and salt and pepper to taste. Mix everything together and cook for 5 minutes. Turn the heat to low and cook, stirring often to prevent burning, until the onions are caramelized, about 20 to 25 minutes. Taste and season with salt and pepper. Remove from the pan and let cool. Cover and refrigerate until you are ready to serve.

4. For the tomato and pesto topping, combine all ingredients in a medium bowl and stir. Cover and refrigerate until ready to serve.

5. For the avocado and black bean salsa, mix all the ingredients together in a bowl. Cover and refrigerate until ready to serve.

SOUTHWESTERN CHICKEN ROLL-UPS

MAKES: 4 servings **BAKE:** 1 hour

Nonstick cooking spray

4 whole boneless, skinless chicken breasts, butterflied

½ cup lime juice

4 ounces cream cheese, room temperature

1 (4-ounce) can whole green chilies, slit on one side and spread open

2½ cups Mexican-blend shredded cheese, divided use

1 cup medium chunky salsa, drained

½ teaspoon ground cumin seed

½ (16-ounce) bag yellow corn tortilla chips, crushed

Black pepper, to taste

1. Preheat oven to 350°F. Spray a 9 × 13-inch baking pan with cooking spray.

2. Rinse chicken under cold water and pat dry with paper towels. Place a breast between 2 sheets of plastic wrap and gently pound with flat side of a meat pounder to a thickness of ¼-inch. Repeat with all chicken breasts. When done, put all the breasts in a zip-top bag and add lime juice. Seal and refrigerate for 2 to 4 hours.

3. Remove butterflied breasts from the bag, lay out flat, and pat dry with paper towels. Season lightly with black pepper top and bottom. Spread 2 tablespoons cream cheese evenly over each chicken breast, leaving a border of about 1 inch. Lay a whole chili on the breast, pressing in lightly. Sprinkle each breast with ¼ cup cheddar, ¼ cup salsa, and cumin.

4. Roll each chicken breast up lengthwise, spray with cooking oil, and roll in chips. Place in baking dish. Top with any remaining chips and spray with oil again. Sprinkle the remaining 1½ cups cheese over all. Bake for 50 minutes to 1 hour.

SPRING CHICKEN SALAD WITH CREAMY RASPBERRY VINAIGRETTE

MAKES: 4 servings

FOR THE SALAD:

- 8 cups spring mix salad
- 1 (16-ounce) package precut fruit medley—Ready Pac
- 2 (6-ounce) packages grilled chicken strips

FOR THE VINAIGRETTE:

- ⅓ cup Italian dressing
- ½ cup plain low-fat yogurt
- ½ cup frozen raspberries, thawed
- ¼ cup slivered almonds, for garnish

1. For the salad, arrange salad mix on a serving platter. Cut fruit into bite-size portions, if necessary, and arrange on top of salad greens. Add chicken.

2. For the vinaigrette, puree Italian dressing, yogurt, and raspberries in a blender until smooth. Spoon vinaigrette over salad and garnish with slivered almonds.

STEAK ARRACHERA WITH LEMONY ONION RINGS

MAKES: 4 servings **COOK:** 16 minutes

FOR THE STEAKS:

1½	pounds beef skirt steak
1	tablespoon steak seasoning
2	tablespoons Mexican seasoning—The Spice Hunter
2	tablespoons chili powder
1	(12-ounce) bottle Mexican beer
2	tablespoons lemon juice

FOR THE ONIONS:

2	sweet onions, sliced into ¼-inch-thick rounds
¼	cup canola oil
¼	cup lemon juice
2	tablespoons chopped fresh cilantro
½	teaspoon salt

1. For the steak, rinse steak under cold water and pat dry with paper towels. In a small bowl, combine steak seasoning, Mexican seasoning, and chili powder. Rub all the spice mixture into both sides of steak. Place in a large zip-top bag. Pour in beer and lemon juice. Squeeze air from bag and seal. Marinate in refrigerator for at least 4 hours, but preferably overnight.

2. For the lemony onion rings, run a presoaked bamboo skewer through each of the onion slices. Snip off pointed ends of skewers, place in a zip-top bag, and set aside. In a small bowl, whisk together remaining ingredients. Pour into bag with onions and marinate for 30 minutes.

3. Set up a grill for direct cooking over high heat. Let steaks stand at room temperature for 20 to 30 minutes before grilling. Oil grate when ready to start cooking. Remove steak from bag and discard marinade. Place steak on hot, oiled grill and cook for 6 to 8 minutes per side for medium (160°F). Remove onions from marinade and grill alongside steak. Turn onions often and cook until well marked and beginning to soften. Transfer steaks to a platter and let rest for 5 minutes before slicing. Remove skewers from onions. Slice steak thinly across the grain and serve hot or at room temperature with onion rings.

APRICOT TART

MAKES: 1 dozen bars **BAKE:** 40 minutes

1½ cups apricot fruit spread
1 tablespoon lemon zest
½ teaspoon vanilla extract
1 package refrigerated pie dough
1 egg
2 tablespoons water
2 tablespoons raw cane sugar
Powdered sugar, for garnish

1. Preheat oven to 375°F.
2. In a medium bowl, mix together the apricot preserves, lemon zest, and vanilla extract, and set aside.
3. Unroll both rounds of pie dough and, using a rolling pin, roll out to ¼-inch thickness. Fit one round into a ¼-size sheet pan. Trim excess and use to fill in corners. Using a fluted pastry cutter, cut 1-inch strips from second round of pie dough.
4. Spread apricot mixture into pan in one even layer over dough. Place strips across top, alternating directions to create a basket weave pattern, and crimp edges to seal. Beat egg with water and, using a pastry brush, completely coat top and edges of tart. Sprinkle with raw sugar and bake for 35 to 40 minutes until crust is golden and jam is thickened and set.
5. Remove from oven and let cool to room temperature before slicing into bars. Dust lightly with powdered sugar before serving.

FRUIT SAUCE TOPPED ZEPPOLE

MAKES: 4 servings **COOK:** 10 minutes

1 (12-ounce) package frozen cherries
¼ cup plus 1 tablespoon sugar, divided use
1 tablespoon lemon juice
1 teaspoon ground cinnamon
3 cups canola oil, for frying, or as needed
2 cups baking mix—Bisquick®
½ cup milk
1 large egg
½ cup powdered sugar

1. In a saucepan over medium heat, add the thawed cherries with their liquid, 1 tablespoon of sugar, lemon juice, and cinnamon. Bring to a simmer and cook for 5 minutes. Remove from the heat.
2. In a cast-iron skillet, heat 1 inch of oil over medium-high heat until it reaches 350°F.
3. While the oil is heating, make the batter. In a bowl, whisk together the baking mix and ¼ cup sugar. In another bowl, whisk together the milk and egg. Pour the wet ingredients into the dry ingredients and whisk until the batter is smooth.
4. When the oil is hot, carefully drop the batter by the tablespoonful into the oil. Fry, turning once, until zeppole are golden brown, about 30 seconds on each side. Drain on paper towels while you fry the remainder of the batter. Dredge in the powdered sugar to coat lightly. Serve zeppole in small bowls topped with fruit sauce.

PEAR TART

MAKES: 8 servings   **BAKE:** 20 minutes

1   sheet frozen puff pastry
1   egg, lightly beaten
1   tablespoon plus 2 teaspoons water
1   (26-ounce) can pear halves, drained and
    thinly sliced lengthwise
1   tablespoon sugar
1   tablespoon pear brandy, optional
2   tablespoons butter
¼   cup apricot jam

1. Preheat oven to 400°F.
2. Thaw puff pastry at room temperature for 20 to 30 minutes. Unfold. If pastry does not unfold easily, thaw for an additional 5 to 10 minutes and retry.
3. On a lightly floured surface, roll out pastry to a 10 × 12-inch rectangle. Transfer to an ungreased baking sheet. With a dry pastry brush, brush away any excess flour.
4. In a small bowl, lightly beat together egg and 1 tablespoon water to create an egg wash. With a pastry brush, brush a ½-inch border of egg wash around pastry. Fold over edges to create a rim. With a fork, prick pastry inside the rim all over.
5. Arrange pear slices on pastry, sprinkle with sugar and pear brandy (optional), and dot with butter. Bake in preheated oven for 20 minutes or until puffed and golden brown.
6. While tart is baking, combine apricot jam and 2 teaspoons water in a microwave-safe bowl. Stir to combine. Microwave on high until jam has melted, stirring every 15 seconds. When jam has completely melted, push through a fine mesh strainer to remove any lumps or pieces of fruit. Set aside.
7. Once tart has finished baking, remove from oven. Brush apricot glaze over entire tart—both fruit and pastry. Cool to room temperature and serve.

JUNE

- *Steaming*: Place artichokes in a steamer basket above 1 inch of water. Cover and steam for 20 to 25 minutes or until petals near the center pull out easily

- *Boiling*: Bring a pot of lightly salted water to a boil and add artichokes. Reduce heat and simmer covered for 20 to 30 minutes until petals near the center pull out easily

ARMADILLO EGGS

MAKES: 12 servings   **BAKE:** 20 minutes

12   jalapeños
4   ounces cream cheese, softened
½   cup shredded pepper jack cheese
2   tablespoons bacon bits
1   pound sweet Italian sausage, removed from casing if links
½   cup seasoned bread crumbs, divided use

1. Cut off stem end of jalapeño peppers. Using a straight peeler, scrape out the seeds and ribs from the inside.
2. In a small bowl, mix together cream cheese, pepper jack cheese, and bacon bits. Place in a zip-top bag and snip off one corner. Pipe each pepper with the cheese mixture, taking care not to overstuff.
3. Preheat oven to 375°F.
4. In a medium bowl, mix together the ground sausage and ¼ cup bread crumbs. Using damp hands, take about 3 tablespoons sausage mixture and form into a long flat oval shape. Wrap around pepper, pressing gently to coat completely; seal edges. Repeat with remaining peppers. Place remaining bread crumbs on a plate or pie dish and roll sausage-covered peppers in bread crumbs to lightly coat, shaking off excess. Place on a parchment-lined sheet tray and bake in oven for 15 to 20 minutes or until sausage is cooked through. Remove and cool slightly before serving.

CHERRY VEGETABLE SALAD

MAKES: 4 servings   **COOK:** 4 minutes

2   cups frozen seasoned summer vegetables—PictSweet
4   tablespoons goat cheese
12   pitted dark sweet cherries; reserve 2½ tablespoons juice from can
1   tablespoon plus 1 teaspoon red wine vinegar
2   teaspoons Italian salad dressing mix—Good Seasons
5   tablespoons vegetable oil
4   cups 5-lettuce mix

1. Place frozen vegetables in a medium microwave-safe bowl and cover tightly. Microwave on 100 percent power for 3 to 4 minutes or until heated through. Remove cover carefully and drain accumulated water. Cool vegetables to room temperature.
2. Form each tablespoon of goat cheese into 6 small balls (½ teaspoon each) for a total of 24 balls; set aside. Cut each cherry in half and set aside. Pour 2½ tablespoons cherry juice from can into a large bowl. Whisk in vinegar and salad dressing mix. Pour vegetable oil, slowly, into bowl while whisking and continue until vinaigrette is emulsified, about 30 seconds.
3. Add salad mix to bowl and toss with tongs until well combined. Arrange servings of salad on chilled serving plates. Place a quarter of vegetables on top of each salad. Top each plate with 6 cherry halves and 6 balls of goat cheese.

CREAMY ARTICHOKE SOUP

MAKES: 4 servings   **COOK:** 28 minutes

2   tablespoons olive oil

1   cup frozen chopped onions, thawed

2   (14-ounce) cans artichoke hearts, coarsely chopped

1   (32-ounce) box low-sodium vegetable broth

1   cup low-fat yogurt plus ¼ cup for garnish

2   tablespoons pesto

1½   tablespoons lemon juice

Salt and pepper, to taste

1. In a large stockpot, heat oil over medium heat. Add onions and sauté for 3 minutes until soft and translucent. Add artichoke hearts, season with salt and pepper to taste, and sauté for another 5 minutes. Add broth, bring to a simmer, and cook 20 minutes, stirring occasionally. Puree until smooth with a hand blender, or in a stationary blender in small batches. Whisk in ¾ cup yogurt and season with salt and pepper to taste.

2. In a small bowl, stir together pesto and lemon juice. Ladle soup into bowls, top each with about 1 tablespoon of yogurt, and drizzle with the thinned pesto sauce.

FRESH AND CRISPY SLAW

MAKES: 4 servings

½   cup coleslaw dressing

2   tablespoons Dijon mustard

Zest and juice of ½ lemon

1   tablespoon honey

2   tablespoons poppy seeds

1   (14-ounce) package coleslaw mix

1   yellow pepper, thinly sliced

½   (0.75-ounce) bunch tarragon, leaves removed from stems

Salt and pepper, to taste

1. In a small bowl, combine coleslaw dressing, mustard, lemon zest and juice, honey, poppy seeds, and salt and pepper to taste. Mix together and set aside.

2. In a large bowl, combine the coleslaw mix, yellow pepper, and tarragon. Pour over the dressing and toss to coat.

FRIED SPINACH

MAKES: 4 servings **COOK:** 1 minute

1 (6-ounce) bag baby spinach

Vegetable oil, for frying

Salt, to taste

1. In a deep fryer or a Dutch oven filled about halfway with oil, bring the oil to 375°F over medium-high heat.

2. While the oil is heating, look through the spinach leaves and pick off any tough stems. Gently drop a small handful of leaves into the hot oil. Be careful, as the oil may splatter. Cook for about 30 seconds, turning once, and remove leaves to paper towel–lined plates to drain. Season with salt, to taste. Serve immediately.

APPLE AND CHERRY GLAZED PORK CHOPS WITH MUSTARD RICE

MAKES: 4 servings   **COOK:** 15 minutes

FOR THE CHOPS:

- 4 boneless pork loin chops, 1-inch thick (about 2 pounds)
- 2 teaspoons steak seasoning
- 1 tablespoon olive oil
- 2 cups unsweetened apple juice
- ¾ cup diced dried apples—Sun-Maid
- ¼ cup dried cherries
- ¼ cup sliced scallions, white part only
- 1 teaspoon black pepper
- 1 (0.87-ounce) packet pork gravy mix—McCormick

FOR THE RICE:

- 1 (14.8-ounce) bag precooked rice—Uncle Ben's Ready Rice
- 1 tablespoon stone-ground mustard
- 1 teaspoon salt

- ¼ cup sliced scallions, green part only, for garnish

1. Preheat oven to 150°F.

2. Rinse pork chops under cold water and pat dry with paper towels. Trim fat from pork chops. Sprinkle each chop with steak seasoning on both sides. Heat oil in a large skillet over medium-high heat. Add pork chops and cook over medium heat 5 to 7 minutes or until done, turning once. Remove chops from skillet and keep warm in oven.

3. Add apple juice, apples, cherries, white part of scallions, and pepper to skillet. Simmer uncovered 4 to 5 minutes, or until apples and scallions are tender. Add gravy mix to skillet and turn up heat; stir until mixture comes to a boil. Reduce heat and simmer for 3 minutes.

4. For the rice, squeeze pouch to separate rice. Tear to vent. Place in microwave and heat on high for 90 seconds. Pour into serving dish and stir in mustard and salt. Serve pork chops over rice, and drizzle sauce over all. Garnish with sliced green part of scallions.

CHICKEN AND WHITE CORN CHOWDER

MAKES: 4 servings   **COOK:** 30 minutes

3   strips bacon, roughly chopped

1   medium onion, diced

3   tablespoons all-purpose flour

1   (15-ounce) can chicken broth

3   cups milk

3   ears white corn, kernels removed and cobs reserved

2   sprigs fresh thyme

2½ cups shredded rotisserie chicken, store-bought

Salt and pepper, to taste

1. In a large pot over medium heat, add the bacon and cook until browned, about 5 minutes. Add the onions and cook until softened, about 5 minutes. Add the flour, stirring constantly for 1 minute, until just slightly golden. Slowly add the chicken broth, whisking constantly to avoid lumps. Whisk in the milk and add the corn cobs and thyme to the pot. Bring to a simmer and cook about 15 minutes, stirring occasionally to infuse the corn flavor into the soup. Remove the cobs and thyme from the pot. Stir in the corn kernels and shredded chicken. Bring back to a simmer, remove from the heat, ladle into bowls, and serve hot.

CHILI-LIME GRILLED SHRIMP TACOS

MAKES: 4 servings **COOK:** 6 minutes

1½ pounds frozen large shrimp, peeled and deveined, thawed

1 (12-ounce) bottle Mexican chili and lime marinade—Lawry's
Cooking oil, for grill

1 (8-ounce) container sour cream

1 chipotle pepper in adobo sauce, finely chopped

1 tablespoon adobo sauce

12 corn tortillas

1 (6-ounce) bag shredded red cabbage

½ cup frozen chopped onion, thawed

1 cup guacamole

1 lime, for garnish

1. Marinate the shrimp in the marinade for at least 5 minutes but no more than 30 minutes.

2. Preheat a grill or grill pan over medium-high heat.

3. Brush the grill with a paper towel that has been soaked in cooking oil. Remove the shrimp from the marinade, discarding marinade, and place on hot, oiled grill. Grill the shrimp until cooked through, 2 to 3 minutes per side.

4. Mix the sour cream with chipotle pepper and adobo sauce in a bowl and set aside.

5. Wrap the tortillas in a damp towel. Place on a plate and microwave for 45 seconds.

6. Build each taco with shrimp, cabbage, onion, and guacamole and top with the chipotle sour cream. Garnish with lime wedges.

CHOP HOUSE GRILLED NEW YORK STRIP

MAKES: 4 servings **COOK:** 16 minutes

FOR THE STEAKS:

- 4 New York beef strip steaks, 1-inch thick
- 1½ cups oil-and-vinegar salad dressing
- 2 tablespoons Worcestershire sauce
- 1 tablespoon steak seasoning
- ¼ cup chopped fresh parsley

FOR THE HERB SALSA VERDE:

- ½ cup oil-and-vinegar salad dressing
- 1 teaspoon crushed garlic
- 2 tablespoons chopped fresh parsley
- 2 tablespoons chopped fresh oregano
- 2 tablespoons chopped fresh thyme leaves
  Salt and pepper, to taste

1. Rinse steaks under cold water and pat dry. Place steaks in a large zip-top bag and set aside. Combine dressing, Worcestershire, seasoning, and parsley in a small bowl. Pour marinade into bag with steaks. Squeeze air from bag and seal. Marinate in refrigerator for at least 4 hours.

2. For the herb salsa verde, stir together dressing, garlic, and herbs. Add salt and pepper to taste.

3. Set up a grill for direct cooking over high heat. Let steaks stand at room temperature for 20 to 30 minutes. Oil grate when ready to start cooking. Remove steaks from bag and discard marinade. Place steaks on hot, oiled grill and cook for 6 to 8 minutes per side for medium (160°F). Transfer steaks to a platter. Serve with herb salsa verde.

CHORIZO GRINDERS WITH SPICY SALSA

MAKES: 4 servings **COOK:** 25 minutes

- 4 fresh chorizo sausages, about 1 pound
- 1 tablespoon extra-virgin olive oil
- 1 (16-ounce) bag frozen pepper stir-fry
- 1 (16-ounce) jar salsa
- 2 chipotles in adobo sauce, chopped
- 1 tablespoon adobo sauce
- 1 tablespoon lime juice
- 4 hero rolls
- 2 tablespoons chopped fresh cilantro, for garnish

1. Preheat grill over medium heat.

2. Place the sausages on the grill. Use tongs to turn links often, every 4 to 6 minutes. Cook until golden brown, about 25 minutes. Make sure to close the grill lid between turnings.

3. Add olive oil to a hot pan. Add peppers and stir-fry. Cook until the peppers are soft, about 6 to 7 minutes.

4. Put the salsa into a bowl. Stir in the chipotles, adobo sauce, and lime juice. Set aside.

5. Put a chorizo sausage onto each split roll and divide the pepper mixture evenly among the rolls. Top with spicy salsa, garnish with cilantro, and serve.

CROUTON CRUSHED CHICKEN TENDERS WITH ORANGE BARBEQUE SAUCE

MAKES: 4 servings **COOK:** 15 minutes

FOR THE CHICKEN TENDERS:

- 1 (6-ounce) bag garlic and butter croutons
- ½ cup all-purpose flour
- 1 teaspoon poultry seasoning
- ½ cup buttermilk
- 1 egg
- ⅓ cup plain bread crumbs
- 1½ pounds chicken tenders
  Salt and pepper, to taste

FOR THE SAUCE:

- ⅓ cup barbeque sauce
- 2 tablespoons orange marmalade
- 1 teaspoon hot sauce
- 1 tablespoon apple cider vinegar

1. Preheat oven to 375°F.
2. Cut a corner off the bag of croutons, opening just enough to let air escape. Place the bag onto a cutting board, cover with a kitchen towel, and beat with a rolling pin. Crush the croutons until coarse in texture.
3. Set up a breading station with 3 pie plates or baking dishes. In one dish, mix the flour, poultry seasoning, and a generous pinch of salt and pepper. In the second dish, mix together the buttermilk and egg. In the third, mix the crushed croutons and bread crumbs.
4. Dip each chicken tender into the flour and shake off any excess. Dip into the buttermilk, then into the bread crumb mixture, making sure to thoroughly coat the tenders. Place the tenders onto a baking sheet and bake for 15 minutes. Transfer to a platter and serve with orange barbeque sauce.
5. For the orange barbeque dipping sauce, combine all ingredients in a small bowl and whisk together.

GARLICKY BUTTER STEAKS WITH CREAMY BAKED GREEN BEANS

MAKES: 4 servings   **COOK:** 40 minutes

4   sirloin steaks, approx. 1 pound each and ½-inch thick

1   tablespoon steak seasoning

2   (12-ounce) bags steam-in-bag trimmed green beans

1   (15-ounce) jar whole onions—Aunt Nellie's Holland-style, drained

⅔   cup chunky blue cheese dressing

2   teaspoons garlic and herb seasoning

1   cup Ritz crackers, crushed

4   tablespoons butter, melted

1   teaspoon garlic powder

1   teaspoon crushed garlic

1. Preheat oven to 350°F.

2. Rinse steaks under cold water and pat dry with paper towels. Season with steak seasoning and set aside.

3. Cut a small hole in both bags of green beans. Place in microwave and heat on 100 percent power for 4 minutes. Open bag, carefully, and empty into a 2-quart casserole dish. Add onions, blue cheese dressing, and herb seasoning. Toss together until well combined. Sprinkle crushed crackers over the top. Bake in preheated oven for 20 to 25 minutes or until heated through.

4. Heat grill pan over medium-high heat for 5 minutes or until smoking hot. Stir together butter, garlic powder, and crushed garlic. Grill steaks 2 at a time, for 5 minutes, turn, and brush with garlic butter. Cook another 4 to 5 minutes for medium. Transfer steaks to a platter and brush liberally with garlic butter.

GRILLED VEGETABLE PANINI

MAKES: 4 servings **COOK:** 10 minutes

1   medium yellow squash, sliced on the bias into ¼-inch strips

1   green bell pepper, stemmed and seeded, sliced into 8 pieces

1   medium eggplant, sliced on the bias into ¼-inch strips

1   medium onion, peeled and sliced into ¼-inch rounds

1   tablespoon minced garlic

1   teaspoon Italian seasoning

¼   cup red wine vinegar

½   cup canola oil, divided use

¼   cup green olives, finely chopped

1   loaf Italian bread

½   cup shredded mozzarella cheese

Salt and pepper, to taste

1. Preheat a grill pan over medium heat.

2. Brush sliced vegetables with ¼ cup oil. Season with salt and pepper and place on grill. Cook about 3 minutes per side or until they are slightly charred and have softened slightly. Remove to a baking sheet

3. In a large bowl, whisk together the garlic, Italian seasoning, vinegar, ¼ cup canola oil, salt, and pepper. Drizzle half the dressing over the grilled vegetables. Stir the chopped olives into the remaining dressing.

4. Cut bread into 4 equal pieces and slice open. Spread the olive dressing evenly on 4 bottom pieces of the bread. Top with a single layer of each of the vegetables. Sprinkle cheese over each and top with second piece of bread. Place on a well-oiled grill. Using a heavy skillet on top of bread as a press, grill about 2 minutes per side until bread is well toasted.

HAM STEAKS WITH BLUEBERRY SAUCE

MAKES: 4 servings   **COOK:** 18 minutes

2   cups frozen blueberries

⅓   cup blueberry vodka

¼   cup blueberry jam

1   tablespoon cornstarch

¼   teaspoon orange zest

2   (1-pound) ham steaks, cut into 4 serving portions

1. Stir together all ingredients except ham steaks in a medium saucepan. Cook over medium heat for 3 to 6 minutes or until jam has dissolved and sauce has thickened.

2. Cook ham steaks in a large skillet over medium-high heat for 1 minute per side. Pour in blueberry sauce. Turn ham steaks several times to coat. Bring to a boil. Reduce heat and simmer for 8 to 10 minutes, turning ham steaks occasionally. Serve immediately with extra sauce.

HOT DOG MUFFULETTAS WITH CAJUN DRESSING

MAKES: 8 servings   **COOK:** 10 to 30 minutes

1   (10-ounce) jar olive bruschetta—DeLallo

½   cup mayonnaise

1   teaspoon Cajun seasoning

8   bun-length turkey franks, butterflied

8   French rolls, split horizontally

1   (9-ounce) package Deli-Fresh honey ham

1   8-ounce deli-style pepperoni, sliced

16   slices provolone cheese, thinly sliced, from deli

1. Stir together bruschetta, mayonnaise, and Cajun seasoning in a bowl. Set aside in refrigerator until ready to serve.

Indoor Method: Preheat oven to 325°F. Prepare olive aioli as directed. Build sandwiches as directed below, then wrap in aluminum foil and bake for 30 minutes. Serve hot.

Outdoor Method: Set up a grill for direct cooking over medium heat. Oil grate when ready to start cooking. Place butterflied franks on hot, oiled grill and cook for 8 to 10 minutes or until heated through, turning once. Toast rolls lightly while franks are cooking. Slather olive spread on both halves of rolls and divide ham, pepperoni, franks, and cheese among them to build sandwiches.

LOMI LOMI SALMON

MAKES: 4 servings

- 1 pound salmon fillet, cooked
- 2 ripe tomatoes, seeded and chopped
- 1 large Maui or Vidalia onion, finely chopped
- 4 scallions, finely sliced
- 1 jalapeño, seeded and finely chopped
  Zest and juice of 1 lime
- 2 teaspoons Hawaiian grill seasoning
- 1 head butter lettuce, leaves separated
- ¼ cup cilantro leaves

1. In a large bowl, flake the salmon. Add the tomatoes, onion, scallions, jalapeño, and lime zest and juice. Sprinkle over the seasoning and stir to combine all ingredients. Taste and add more seasoning, if needed. Refrigerate for 1 hour to let the flavors combine. Serve in lettuce cups, garnished with cilantro leaves.

MEDITERRANEAN SALAD WITH GRILLED TUNA

MAKES: 4 servings   **COOK:** 6 minutes

- ¼ cup olive oil
- 1 tablespoon lemon zest
- 1 tablespoon lemon juice
- ¼ cup Italian dressing
- 1 (12-ounce) tuna steak
- 1 (10-ounce) bag romaine lettuce
- 1 head radicchio, shredded
- 1 (8-ounce) package frozen green beans, thawed
- ½ cup pitted Kalamata olives
  Salt and pepper, to taste

1. In a large bowl, whisk together the olive oil with the lemon zest, juice, Italian dressing, and salt and pepper to taste. Place tuna steak in a shallow baking dish. Pour ½ of dressing over tuna, flipping to coat completely. Allow to marinate in dressing while preheating a grill pan over medium-high heat. Place tuna on grill pan and cook 3 minutes per side for medium rare. Remove from pan and let sit for 5 minutes.
2. In bowl with remaining dressing, toss the lettuce with uncooked green beans and olives to coat evenly. Slice tuna on the bias and serve atop tossed salad.

SEA BASS WITH ARTICHOKE PESTO

MAKES: 4 servings **BAKE:** 12 minutes

Nonstick cooking spray

4 (5 to 6-ounce) sea bass fillets, about ¾-inch thick

1 (12-ounce) jar marinated artichoke hearts

½ cup pesto

⅛ teaspoon red pepper flakes

2 tablespoons extra-virgin olive oil

Salt and pepper, to taste

1. Preheat oven to 400°F. Spray a baking dish with cooking spray and set aside.

2. Put the sea bass fillets in one layer, skin-side up, into the baking dish. Drain the artichoke hearts, pouring the liquid over the fish. Let marinate while you make the artichoke pesto.

3. To make the artichoke pesto, put artichoke hearts into the bowl of a food processor. Add pesto and red pepper flakes and process until chunky. Scrape down the sides of the bowl and start processing again. Drizzle in 1 to 2 tablespoons of olive oil, adding more as needed until you get a consistency that is thick but pourable. Taste and add salt and pepper if needed. Artichoke pesto can be refrigerated for up to 1 week.

4. Bake sea bass until cooked through, about 10 to 12 minutes. Spoon about 2 tablespoons of artichoke pesto onto each of 4 plates. Place the fish on top and add a generous spoonful of pesto.

SHANGHAI LOBSTER AND JASMINE RICE

MAKES: 4 servings   **COOK:** 37 minutes

2 tablespoons extra-virgin olive oil

4 tablespoons butter, divided use

4 lobster tails, thawed if frozen

¼ cup white wine

1 tablespoon peeled and chopped ginger

1 tablespoon chopped garlic

1 teaspoon curry powder

¼ teaspoon red pepper flakes

1 (8-ounce) bottle clam juice

1 cup heavy cream

1 tablespoon soy sauce

4 cups steamed jasmine rice

Salt and pepper, to taste

1. In a skillet over medium heat, add the oil and 2 tablespoons butter. When butter is melted, add the lobster tails, cover with a tight-fitting lid, and turn heat to low. Cook for 6 to 8 minutes. Remove lobster tails, cover, and keep warm. Add the wine to the skillet, turn heat to high, and cook until wine is reduced by half, about 3 to 4 minutes. Add the ginger, garlic, curry powder, and red pepper flakes and cook for 1 minute. Add the clam juice and cook until it is reduced by half, about 5 to 6 minutes. Put the lobster tails back into the skillet, pour in the cream, turn heat to low, cover, and cook for 6 to 8 minutes. Remove the lobster again and let cool a bit. Turn the heat to medium low and cook until the liquid is thickened and reduced by half, about 6 to 8 minutes. Stir in the soy sauce and remaining 2 tablespoons butter. Cook for 1 to 2 minutes, taste, and adjust the seasoning with salt and pepper.

2. To serve, crack the lobster tails and put them onto plates. Pour over some sauce. Serve with steamed jasmine rice.

SHRIMP, SCALLOP, AND LEMON SKEWERS

MAKES: 4 servings   **COOK:** 6 minutes

- ½   pound medium shrimp, peeled and deveined
- ½   pound sea scallops
- 4   lemons, cut into ½-inch wedges
- ¼   cup lemon juice
- 3   tablespoons citrus vodka
- ⅓   cup canola oil
- 2   teaspoons crushed garlic
- 2   teaspoons chopped fresh thyme leaves
- 3   tablespoons chopped flat-leaf parsley

1. Soak bamboo skewers in water for at least an hour. Rinse seafood under cold water and pat dry with paper towels. Thread shrimp and scallops onto skewers, alternating with lemon wedges. Place in a shallow baking pan and set aside. Stir lemon juice and vodka in a nonreactive bowl. Whisk in the oil a little at a time and stir in garlic, thyme, and parsley. Pour marinade over skewers and cover. Marinate in refrigerator for 30 minutes to 2 hours.

Outdoor Method: Set up a grill for direct cooking over medium heat. Remove skewers from marinade and discard marinade. Let stand at room temperature for 30 minutes. Brush and oil grate when ready to start cooking. Place skewers on hot, oiled grill and cook for 2 to 3 minutes per side or until shrimp is opaque. Serve hot or at room temperature.

Indoor Method: Preheat broiler. Remove skewers from marinade and discard marinade. Place skewers on a foil-lined baking sheet or broiler pan. Broil 6 to 8 inches from heat source for 2 to 3 minutes per side. Serve hot or at room temperature.

SPICY GRILLED LAMB CHOPS

MAKES: 4 servings   **COOK:** 12 minutes

8   loin lamb chops, 1 to 1½-inches thick

2   tablespoons fresh oregano leaves

1   tablespoon canned chopped jalapeños

1   tablespoon crushed garlic

2   teaspoons chopped ginger

1   cup lemon juice

2   tablespoons paprika

2   teaspoons spicy steak seasoning

¼   cup extra-virgin olive oil

1. Rinse lamb chops under cold water and pat dry. Place in a large zip-top bag and set aside. Place oregano, jalapeños, garlic, ginger, and ¼ cup lemon juice in a blender, and puree to make a paste. Add remaining lemon juice, paprika, and seasoning, and puree. With the blender running, drizzle in oil. Reserve ½ cup of the marinade for basting. Pour the remaining marinade into the bag with the lamb chops and seal. Gently massage bag to coat the lamb. Marinate in the refrigerator for at least 3 hours.

2. Preheat grill to medium-high heat. Let chops sit at room temperature for 30 minutes. Remove from marinade and discard marinade. Oil grate when ready to start cooking. Place chops on hot, oiled grill for 2 minutes, turn and baste with reserved marinade. Cook 10 to 12 minutes total for medium rare (135°–140°F), turning every few minutes and basting with marinade. Remove and brush with any remaining marinade.

SUMMER SOLSTICE STEAKS

MAKES: 4 servings   **COOK:** 10 minutes

4   New York strip steaks, 1-inch thick

1   cup ale-style beer

1   (6-ounce) can tomato juice

1   tablespoon steak sauce

1   (0.7-ounce) packet Italian salad dressing mix—Good Seasons

2   scallions, chopped

1   fresh jalapeño, chopped
    Nonstick cooking spray

1. Rinse steaks under cold water and pat dry with paper towels. Place in a large zip-top bag. Stir together remaining ingredients and pour into bag, coating the steaks. Squeeze air from bag and seal. Marinate in refrigerator for 4 hours to overnight.

2. Remove steaks from marinade and discard marinade. Let steaks stand at room temperature for about 30 minutes. Preheat broiler. Place steaks on a foil-lined baking sheet or broiler pan sprayed with cooking spray. Broil steak 6 to 8 inches from heat source for 4 to 5 minutes per side. Remove steaks and let rest for 5 minutes before serving.

SWEET AND STICKY BABY BACK RIBS

MAKES: 4 servings   **COOK:** 1 hour 45 minutes to 2 hours

3   racks pork baby back ribs

1   (12-ounce) bottle sesame oriental salad
    dressing

¼   cup orange juice concentrate

FOR THE SWEET AND STICKY GLAZE:

¾   cup hoisin sauce

½   cup orange marmalade

3   tablespoons orange juice concentrate

1   tablespoon chopped ginger—
    Gourmet Garden

1   tablespoon crushed garlic

1   tablespoon chili-garlic sauce

1. Rinse ribs with cold water and pat dry with paper towels. Remove thin membrane from the back of ribs and place ribs in a nonreactive roasting pan. In a bowl, stir together salad dressing and orange juice concentrate. Pour marinade over ribs and turn to make sure that marinade completely coats ribs. Cover and refrigerate for at least 2 hours, or as long as overnight, periodically turning ribs.

2. Set up a grill for indirect cooking over medium heat so that no heat source will be under the meat. Remove ribs from marinade and discard marinade. Place ribs in a rib rack over a drip pan on hot grill. Cover grill.

3. Cook 1½ to 2 hours. Rotate ribs around rack every 30 minutes. If using charcoal, add 10 briquettes to each pile of coals every hour.

4. While ribs are cooking, make glaze by combining ingredients in a small saucepan over medium heat. Simmer 10 minutes and remove from heat.

5. About 20 minutes before ribs are done, remove ribs from rib rack and lay meat-side down on grill. Generously brush with sauce and pile ribs in center of grill over a drip pan. Cover and cook 10 minutes. Turn ribs and brush on more sauce and re-pile. Cook an additional 10 minutes. Remove from grill and cut into servings. Serve hot with sauce on the side.

SWEET ONION PICNIC QUICHES

MAKES: 16 servings   **BAKE:** 22 minutes

Nonstick cooking spray

1½ cups egg substitute

1 teaspoon lemon and herb seasoning—McCormick

1 medium Vidalia or Maui onion, peeled and cut in half

½ cup crumbled bacon—Hormel

1 (2-ounce) jar diced pimientos, drained

¼ cup shredded Parmesan cheese

1 (16.3-ounce) roll flaky biscuits

Salt and pepper, to taste

1. Preheat oven to 350°F. Spray 12-cup muffin pans with cooking spray and set aside.

2. Whisk together egg substitute and seasoning in a medium mixing bowl with a spout. Grate both onion halves with a grater, and add to bowl. Add bacon, pimientos, and Parmesan cheese. Beat until well combined. Season with salt and pepper to taste.

3. Separate each biscuit from roll. Take one biscuit and pull apart by layers into two halves. Fit one half of biscuit into a muffin pan cup as a base. Repeat to make 16 biscuit cups. Pour egg mixture into each cup, filling three-quarters of the way.

4. Bake in preheated oven for 18 to 22 minutes or until egg filling is set and biscuit cup is golden brown. Remove from pan, carefully, and serve warm.

BERRIES WITH ITALIAN CUSTARD

MAKES: 4 servings   **COOK:** 10 minutes

½   pint raspberries

½   pint blueberries

¼   cup port wine, divided use

¼   cup plus 1 tablespoon sugar, divided use

4   large egg yolks

1. In a medium bowl, combine the berries with 1 tablespoon port and 1 tablespoon sugar. Allow to sit and macerate while you prepare the custard.
2. To make custard, bring a pot of water to a boil over medium heat. Mix egg yolks with remaining sugar in a bowl that will fit over top of pot. With an electric hand mixer, beat until pale. Place bowl over simmering water and, with beater running slowly, drizzle in remaining 3 tablespoons port. Continue to beat until mixture becomes very thick and has doubled in volume, about 5 to 10 minutes. Remove from heat.
3. Divide berries among 4 serving glasses. Top each with a generous dollop of custard, garnish with remaining berries, and serve immediately.

BLACKBERRIES WITH ORANGE-AMARETTO SHORTCAKE

MAKES: 6 servings   **BAKE:** 12 minutes

Zest and juice of 1 large orange

FOR THE BERRIES:

3   cups frozen blackberries

¼   cup sugar

FOR THE SHORTCAKE:

2⅓   cups baking mix—Bisquick®

¼   cup amaretto liqueur

3   tablespoons sugar

3   tablespoons butter, melted

FOR THE TOPPING:

1   teaspoon orange extract

8   ounces frozen whipped topping, thawed

¼   cup sliced almonds, toasted, for garnish

1. Preheat oven to 425° F.
2. Finely chop zest of orange. Juice zested orange.
3. For the berries, combine berries, sugar, 1 teaspoon orange zest, and ¼ cup orange juice in a small bowl. Set aside.
4. For the shortcake, stir together the baking mix, remaining zest, ¼ cup orange juice, amaretto, sugar, and butter until soft dough forms. Drop by 6 even spoonfuls onto ungreased cookie sheet. Bake for 10 to 12 minutes or until golden brown.
5. For the topping, stir orange extract into thawed whipped topping.
6. Split shortcakes and top with berries and whipped topping. Garnish with almonds.

CHOCOLATE BERRY CRISP

MAKES: 8 servings   **BAKE:** 30 minutes

1 (12-ounce) bag frozen mixed berries

1 (14-ounce) bag frozen unsweetened sliced strawberries

¾ cup packed brown sugar, divided use

1 tablespoon cornstarch

1 tablespoon lemon juice

¾ cup all-purpose flour

½ teaspoon pumpkin pie spice

4 tablespoons butter, cut into small pieces

½ cup crushed chocolate biscotti

½ cup nut toppings

Nonstick cooking spray

1. Set up a grill for direct cooking over medium heat.

2. In a large bowl, combine berries, ½ cup brown sugar, cornstarch, and lemon juice. Transfer to a 10-inch cast-iron skillet. In a bowl, combine flour, remaining ¼ cup brown sugar, and pumpkin pie spice. Cut butter into flour mixture until crumbly. Add crushed biscotti and nuts; sprinkle mixture evenly over fruit.

Outdoor Method: Place skillet in center of grate and cover grill. Cook 20 to 30 minutes or until lightly browned and bubbly. Serve hot.

Indoor Method: Preheat oven to 375°F. Lightly spray a 9 × 9-inch baking dish with cooking spray. Prepare berries and topping as directed and transfer to baking dish. Bake in preheated oven for 20 to 30 minutes or until lightly browned and bubbling. Serve hot.

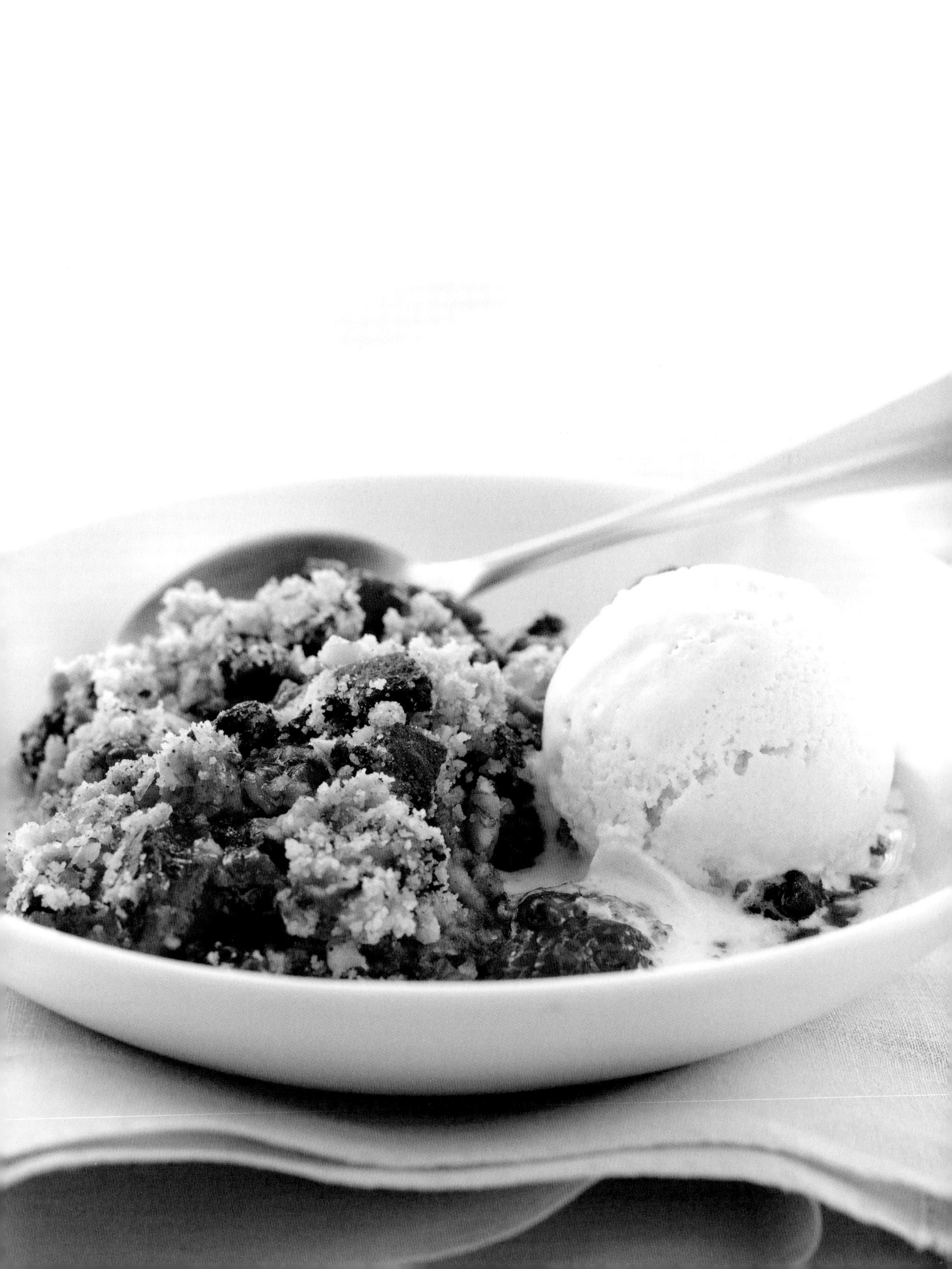

PEACHY PEAR

MAKES: 4 servings

1 (11.5-ounce) can peach nectar
1 (11.5-ounce) can pear nectar
2 cups sparkling water
¼ cup vodka, optional
¼ cup peach schnapps, optional
1 peach, sliced, for garnish

1. In a large pitcher, stir together all ingredients. Pour into ice-filled glasses and garnish with slices of peach, if desired.

REFRESHING MELON SMOOTHIE

MAKES: 2 servings

2 cups honeydew melon or cantaloupe, cubed
1 cup vanilla low-fat yogurt
2 tablespoons frozen apple juice concentrate
  Ice
  Cantaloupe, sliced, for garnish

1. Blend melon, yogurt, and apple juice concentrate in a blender until smooth. Add ice, with blender running, and continue until frothy. Pour into two 16-ounce glasses and garnish with sliced melon.

SHORTCAKES WITH WARM STRAWBERRY SAUCE

MAKES: 4 servings **BAKE:** 20 minutes

FOR THE BISCUITS:

2 ⅓ cups baking mix, Bisquick®

¾ cup cranberry juice

3 tablespoons butter, melted

2 tablespoons milk

1 tablespoon sugar

FOR THE SAUCE:

1 (16-ounce) bag frozen strawberries

¼ cup cranberry juice

¾ cup sugar

2 tablespoons cornstarch

1 cup heavy cream

3 tablespoons powdered sugar

1. Preheat oven to 425°F and line a baking sheet with parchment paper.
2. Stir together baking mix, cranberry juice, and butter in a large bowl until soft dough forms. Drop in 4 even mounds onto baking sheet. Brush the tops with milk and sprinkle with sugar. Bake for 15 to 20 minutes or until golden brown. Remove and cool completely.
3. In a saucepot, combine strawberries, cranberry juice, sugar, and cornstarch. Stir together and bring to a boil over medium heat, making sure to stir often. Turn down heat to low and simmer for 5 to 10 minutes until thick. Remove from heat and let cool slightly.
4. In a large chilled mixing bowl, whip the heavy cream until soft peaks form. Add the powdered sugar and continue to whip until stiff but not dry.
5. To serve, cut each cooled shortcake in half horizontally and place bottoms on serving plates. Spoon warm strawberry sauce over shortcake bottoms. Place shortcake tops on fruit. Top each with whipped cream.

JULY

Summer Star Cocktail, p. 231

CRAB SANDY

MAKES: 4 servings

2   English cucumbers, sliced into 1-inch-thick pieces
1   (12-ounce) container fresh crabmeat
1   avocado, diced
1   hard-boiled egg, diced
½   cup frozen asparagus tips, thawed
2   tablespoons chopped fresh parsley
3   tablespoons Thousand Island dressing
    Juice of ½ lemon
1   tablespoon hot sauce
    Salt and pepper, to taste

1. Using a melon baller, scoop out the center of each cucumber slice to form a small bowl. Finely chop cucumber centers and place in a large bowl.
2. Add all remaining ingredients to the bowl and gently toss to combine.
3. Spoon about a tablespoon of the crab mixture into each cucumber cup. Place on a platter and serve.

GRILLED FRUIT BRUSCHETTA

MAKES: 4 servings   **COOK:** 10 minutes

5   tablespoons butter, softened
1   baguette, cut into ¼-inch slices
2   tablespoons cinnamon sugar
8   large strawberries
2   plums, pitted and quartered
1   cup fresh pineapple chunks—Ready Pac, cut into 1-inch pieces
1   cup sliced mango—Ready Pac, cut into 1-inch cubes
    Canola oil cooking spray
2   tablespoons lime juice

1. Soak wooden skewers in water for at least an hour. Lightly butter both sides of baguette slices and sprinkle with cinnamon sugar. Set aside. Thread the fruit pieces alternately on presoaked skewers, with strawberries on both ends.
2. Set up a grill for direct cooking over medium heat. Oil grate when ready to start cooking. Lightly spray kebabs with cooking spray and place on hot, oiled grill. Cook 2 to 3 minutes per side or until fruit is warm and soft. Remove fruit from grill and toast baguette slices on the grill for 1 to 2 minutes per side.
3. Chop fruit, place in a medium bowl, and toss with lime juice. Serve fruit on toasted baguette slices.

HAWAIIAN POT STICKERS

MAKES: 4 servings **COOK:** 10 minutes

- 1 cup pulled pork, finely chopped, shredded
- 2 cloves garlic, minced
- 2 cloves garlic, chopped
- 1 pinch kosher salt
- 1 pinch freshly ground black pepper
- 1 scallion, thinly sliced
- 2 tablespoons chopped fresh cilantro leaves
- 12 small round wonton wrappers
- 2 tablespoons vegetable oil
- ½ cup soy sauce, for dipping

1. Combine the pork, garlic, salt, pepper, scallion, and half the cilantro in a small bowl. Mix ingredients together until well combined.

2. Working in batches of 4, lay the wonton wrappers on a clean surface. Spoon about 1 tablespoon of filling into the center of each wrapper. Brush the sides of each wrapper with a little water. Fold the opposite sides together to make a half circle and smooth out any air bubbles. Crimp the sides together to seal. Place on a plate and cover with a damp towel until ready to cook.

3. Heat vegetable oil in a large skillet over medium-high heat. Add pot stickers and cook for about 3 minutes per side, allowing each side to turn golden brown and crispy. Transfer to a serving platter. Garnish with remaining cilantro and serve with soy sauce, for dipping.

PORK EGG ROLLS

MAKES: 4 servings **COOK:** 10 minutes

- 3 cups vegetable oil
- 1 cup precooked pork roast, shredded
- 1 cup shredded cabbage
- 1 carrot, cut into 1-inch julienne strips
- 2 tablespoons Hawaiian marinade
- 8 large wonton wrappers

1. Preheat deep fryer or fill heavy-bottomed saucepan with vegetable oil and heat to 350°F.

2. In a medium bowl, combine pork, shredded cabbage, carrot, and Hawaiian marinade. Lay a wonton wrapper on a clean surface and place some filling in the center, about 2 tablespoons. Using a pastry brush, moisten all edges with water. Fold the top of the wrapper over the filling, then tuck the sides in and continue rolling until wrapped up, like a burrito. Set aside on a parchment-lined baking sheet. Repeat with remaining wrappers and filling.

3. Once all egg rolls are formed, add to hot oil in batches, frying egg rolls until they turn golden brown, about 2 to 3 minutes. Remove egg rolls to a paper towel–lined plate. Serve immediately.

POTATO AND CARAMELIZED ONION TART

MAKES: 4 servings   **COOK:** 50 minutes

½   box pie crust mix

2   tablespoons canola oil

2   large onions, thinly sliced

1   russet potato, thinly sliced

4   ounces cream cheese, softened

1   tablespoon spicy brown mustard

1   teaspoon Italian seasoning

Salt and pepper, to taste

1. Preheat oven to 375°F.

2. Prepare pie crust according to package directions. Flatten into a disk, wrap in plastic, and chill in the refrigerator while preparing the filling.

3. In a large sauté pan over medium heat, add oil, onions, and salt and pepper to taste. Cook, stirring occasionally, until onions are dark golden brown, 10 to 15 minutes. Remove from heat. In the meantime, using the slicing blade attachment of a food processor, slice potato into ⅛-inch-thick slices. Place in cold water to avoid browning.

4. In a small bowl, stir together the cream cheese with mustard, Italian seasoning, and salt and pepper to taste.

5. Remove pie crust from refrigerator and roll into a 12-inch round about ¼-inch thick. Place on a parchment-lined sheet pan. Spread cream cheese-and-mustard mixture in an even layer over pie crust. Dry potatoes thoroughly, and place an even layer on top of the cream cheese, overlapping slightly and keeping ½ inch from edge free. On top of potatoes, place an even layer of caramelized onions. Fold over edges of crust.

SALT AND PEPPER CALAMARI

MAKES: 4 servings   **COOK:** 15 minutes

2   cups canola oil

¾   cup cornstarch

1½   pounds calamari, cleaned, tubes cut into
     ¼-inch-thick rings

½   cup all-purpose flour

FOR THE DIPPING SAUCE:

¼   cup soy sauce

2   teaspoons minced garlic

½-inch piece ginger, grated

2   tablespoons sweet chili sauce

2   tablespoons lime juice

2   scallions, sliced, for garnish
    Salt and pepper, to taste

1. In a large heavy-bottomed skillet, heat canola oil over medium-high heat to 360 °F.

2. In a large bowl, stir together the cornstarch with a generous amount of salt and pepper. Toss the squid in the cornstarch, being sure to completely coat. Working in batches, lift the squid from the cornstarch, shake to remove excess, and place in oil. Fry until lightly golden and crisp, 3 to 4 minutes. Remove from oil and drain on a baking sheet lined with a brown paper bag. Repeat with remaining squid.

3. To make dipping sauce, stir together the soy sauce with garlic, ginger, chili sauce, and lime juice in a small bowl. Serve calamari garnished with scallions, with dipping sauce alongside.

BABY BACK RIBS WITH KEY LIME BARBEQUE SAUCE

MAKES: 4 servings   **COOK:** 1 hour 45 minutes to 2 hours

FOR THE RIBS:

3	racks pork baby back ribs
1	lemon, cut in half
⅓	cup pork rub—McCormick Grill Mates
2	teaspoons mustard powder

FOR THE BARBEQUE SAUCE:

1½	cups ketchup
½	cup key lime juice
2	tablespoons Worcestershire sauce
3	tablespoons chili-garlic sauce
3	tablespoons honey

1. Thirty minutes before cooking, soak hickory chips in water. Rinse ribs with cold water and pat dry. Remove thin membrane from back of ribs. Rub ribs with lemon and set aside. In a small bowl, combine pork rub with mustard powder. Sprinkle seasoning over ribs and pat in.

2. *Outdoor Method*: Set up a grill for indirect cooking over medium heat, so that no heat source will be under meat. Drain wood chips. Add some chips to the smoker box if using a gas grill, or place chips on hot coals if using charcoal. Place ribs in a rib rack over a drip pan on hot grill. Cover grill. Cook 1½ to 2 hours, rotating ribs around rack every 30 minutes. If using charcoal, add 10 briquettes to each pile of coals and another handful of soaked hickory chips every hour. For a gas grill, add wood chips to the smoker box every hour.

3. For the barbeque sauce, while ribs are cooking, combine ingredients in a saucepan over medium heat. Simmer for 10 minutes and remove from heat.

4. About 20 minutes before ribs are done, remove ribs from rib rack and lay meat-side down on grill. Generously brush with sauce and pile ribs in center of grill over drip pan. Cover and cook for 10 minutes. Turn ribs and brush on more sauce and re-pile. Cook for an additional 10 minutes. Remove from grill and cut into servings. Serve hot with sauce on the side.

Indoor Method: Prepare and rub ribs as directed above. Preheat oven to 350°F. Place ribs meat-side up on a rack in a shallow roasting pan. Tightly cover with foil. Bake for 1 hour. While ribs are baking, make sauce as directed above. Remove ribs from oven and carefully drain fat from roasting pan. Continue baking ribs, uncovered, for 30 to 45 minutes more or until tender, turning and brushing occasionally with sauce. Cut into servings and serve hot with sauce on the side.

BARBEQUE CHILI DOGS

MAKES: 8 servings   **COOK:** 45 minutes

1   pound lean ground beef

1½   cups brown sugar and hickory barbeque sauce

1   (1.25-ounce) packet chili seasoning mix

½   cup water

1   tablespoon molasses

1   tablespoon yellow mustard

8   all-beef franks

8   hot dog buns

Chopped white onion, for serving

1. In a large skillet over medium heat, brown ground beef, stirring frequently to break up clumps into a fine ground. Stir in barbeque sauce, chili seasoning, water, molasses, and mustard. Bring to a boil, reduce heat, and simmer for 30 minutes.

2. *Outdoor Method*: Set up a grill for direct cooking over medium heat. Oil grate when ready to start cooking. Place franks on hot, oiled grill. Cook for 12 to 15 minutes or until heated through, turning occasionally.

   Indoor Method: Prepare chili as directed. Preheat broiler. Place franks on a wire rack over a foil-lined baking sheet or broiler pan. Cook 6 to 8 inches from heat source for 12 to 15 minutes, turning occasionally.

3. Toast buns if desired. Place franks in buns and top with chili. Serve hot with chopped white onions.

BBQ CHICKEN WITH SWEET POTATO AND CORN SALAD

MAKES: 6 servings   **COOK:** 50 minutes

1 (16-ounce) bag frozen sweet potato patties—Bright Harvest

1 small red onion, cut into 1-inch squares

5 tablespoons vegetable oil, divided use

1½ cups frozen corn

⅓ cup frozen chopped green peppers—PictSweet

1 teaspoon water

2 teaspoons crushed garlic

4 teaspoons Dijon mustard

3 teaspoons key lime juice—Nellie & Joe's

1 (16-ounce) bag diced redskin potatoes

6 boneless chicken breasts

1 tablespoon mesquite chicken seasoning

1½ cups barbeque sauce

Salt and pepper, to taste

1. Preheat oven to 400°F. Line a baking sheet with foil.

2. Place sweet potatoes and onions on baking sheet. Drizzle 2 tablespoons oil over vegetables and toss to coat. Bake in preheated oven for 25 minutes.

3. Meanwhile, combine corn, green peppers, and water in a large microwave-safe bowl. Cover and microwave on 100 percent power for 3 minutes. Stir together garlic, mustard, 1 tablespoon oil, and lime juice in a small bowl and set aside.

4. Remove sweet potatoes and onions from oven and add redskin potatoes. Set aside to bake alongside the chicken.

5. Rinse chicken under cold water and pat dry with paper towels. Sprinkle chicken with mesquite seasoning. Heat remaining oil in a large nonstick skillet over medium-high heat. Add chicken to skillet and cook until golden, about 4 minutes per side. Transfer chicken to shallow baking dish and brush liberally with barbeque sauce. Bake pan of chicken and vegetables until chicken is cooked through, about 15 minutes.

6. Remove both pans from oven and set aside chicken. Pour vegetables into corn and green pepper mixture. Add mustard mixture and stir together gently. Season to taste with salt and pepper. Serve barbequed chicken and extra sauce with a helping of warm sweet potato and corn salad.

GRILLED CHILIES RELLENOS WITH SMOKED TOMATO SALSA

MAKES: 4 servings   **COOK:** 40 minutes

- 4 poblano chilies
- ½ cup part-skim ricotta cheese
- 2 cups Mexican-blend shredded cheese
- 1 cup Mexicorn—Green Giant
- 2 teaspoons Mexican seasoning—The Spice Hunter
- 2 cups chunky-style salsa, divided use
- ¼ teaspoon liquid smoke
- Salt and pepper, to taste

1. Cut chilies in half lengthwise to create a boat for filling. Scrape out seeds and membrane. In a medium bowl, stir together ricotta cheese, shredded cheese, corn, Mexican seasoning, and ½ cup salsa. Taste and adjust seasoning with salt and pepper. Spoon mixture into hollowed-out chilies.

2. Set up a grill for indirect grilling with medium heat so that no heat source will be under chilies. Place chilies in a foil baking pan. Place on grill away from direct heat and cook for 30 to 40 minutes or until chilies are tender and filling is bubbling.

3. While chilies cook, pour salsa and liquid smoke into a blender and puree until smooth. Serve chilies rellenos hot with salsa.

GRILLED GREEN PEPPERCORN RUBBED FILET MIGNON

MAKES: 4 servings   **COOK:** 16 minutes

4 (6-ounce) bacon-wrapped beef tenderloin steaks

3 tablespoons steak sauce

1 tablespoon brine-packed green peppercorns—Delicias, drained and chopped

1 teaspoon paprika

½ teaspoon dried thyme

1. Remove steaks from packaging, rinse under cold water, and pat dry with paper towels. Tie with butcher's twine to maintain shape. Stir to combine remaining ingredients in a small bowl. Coat steaks with rub and place in a zip-top bag. Squeeze air from bag and seal. Marinate in refrigerator for at least 4 hours, but preferably overnight.

2. Set up a grill for direct cooking over high heat. Oil grate when ready to start cooking. Let steaks stand at room temperature for 20 to 30 minutes before cooking.

3. Remove steaks from bag and place on hot, oiled grill. Cook for 6 to 8 minutes per side for medium (160°F). Transfer steaks to a platter and let rest for 5 minutes before serving. Serve hot.

GRILLED TURKEY COBB DOG

MAKES: 8 servings   **COOK:** 20 minutes

8 bun-length turkey franks

8 slices bacon

8 hot dog buns

1 cup creamy blue cheese dressing

1 cup diced tomatoes

1 cup diced avocado

½ cup crumbled blue cheese

1. Wrap each frank in a slice of bacon, securing the ends with wooden toothpicks.

   Outdoor Method: Set up grill for direct cooking over medium heat. Oil grate when ready to start cooking. Place bacon-wrapped franks on hot, oiled grill and cook for 16 to 20 minutes or until bacon is crispy, turning frequently and watching for flare-ups.

   Indoor Method: Preheat broiler. Place franks on a wire rack over a foil-lined baking sheet or broiler pan. Cook 6 to 8 inches from heat source for 16 to 20 minutes, turning frequently and watching for flare-ups.

2. Toast buns lightly while franks are cooking. Slather blue cheese dressing on buns and top with diced tomatoes, avocado, and crumbled blue cheese.

GRILLED SAUSAGE WITH TUSCAN BEANS

MAKES: 4 servings   **COOK:** 25 minutes

- 1 pound or 1 (6-count) package hot Italian sausage
- 2 tablespoons red wine vinegar
- ¼ cup olive oil
- 1 (14.5-ounce) can diced tomatoes, drained, juice reserved
- 1 teaspoon Italian seasoning
- 1 teaspoon chopped garlic
- 1 (15-ounce) can cannellini beans, drained and rinsed well
- 1 (15-ounce) can red beans, drained and rinsed well
- 2 tablespoons basil leaves, torn
  Salt and pepper, to taste

1. Preheat a grill pan over medium heat.
2. Place sausage on grill and cook for 20 to 25 minutes, turning every 4 to 5 minutes.
3. In a large bowl, whisk together the vinegar, olive oil, reserved juice from the can of tomatoes, Italian seasoning, and garlic. Season with salt and pepper to taste. Add beans to diced tomatoes and basil, and toss to coat. Serve with grilled sausage.

GYRO DOG

MAKES: 4 servings   **COOK:** 10 minutes

- 2 tablespoons finely chopped red onion
- ¼ cup finely chopped seeded cucumber
- 2 teaspoons finely chopped fresh mint
- ½ cup nonfat plain yogurt
- 4 chicken and apple sausages, butterflied
- 1 tablespoon Greek seasoning
- ½ teaspoon paprika
- 2 tablespoons lemon juice
- 4 pita breads
- 2 cups spring mix salad

1. Stir onion, cucumber, and mint into yogurt; cover and set aside in refrigerator until ready to use.

   Outdoor Method: Set up a grill for direct cooking over medium heat. Oil grate when ready to start cooking. Place butterflied sausages on hot, oiled grill and cook for 8 to 10 minutes or until heated through, turning once.

   Indoor Method: Prepare dressing and sausages as directed above. Preheat broiler. Place sausages on a foil-lined baking sheet or broiler pan. Cook 6 to 8 inches from heat source for 8 to 10 minutes or until heated through, turning once.

2. Slice sausages into 3 pieces horizontally. Place in a large bowl and toss together with Greek seasoning, paprika, and lemon juice. Cut pita breads in half and open pockets. Stuff with salad mix and sausages, and top with a dollop of yogurt dressing.

HAWAIIAN PIZZA

MAKES: 4 servings   **BAKE:** 20 minutes

FOR THE SAUCE:

2   tablespoons canola oil

2   teaspoons garlic, chopped

1   tablespoon ginger, chopped

½   can pineapple juice

1   (16-ounce) package frozen pizza dough, thawed

¼   pound baked ham, diced

½   (20-ounce) can pineapple chunks

1   small red onion, thinly sliced

1   cup shredded mozzarella cheese

Cilantro, for garnish

Salt and pepper, to taste

1. In a medium pot heat the oil over medium heat. Add garlic and ginger and saute until soft, about 2 minutes. Add the pineapple juice mixture, bring to a boil, then reduce heat and simmer for 10 minutes. Remove from heat and set aside.

2. Preheat oven to 450°F.

3. Lightly oil a medium-size baking pan. Roll or stretch dough to fit into pan. Evenly coat with the Hawaiian sauce, leaving a 1-inch border from the edge of the dough. Top with diced ham, pineapple chunks, and red onion. Sprinkle with cheese and season with salt and pepper to taste. Bake for about 20 minutes until the cheese has melted and the crust turns golden brown. Garnish with fresh cilantro. Slice and serve.

HAWAIIAN PULLED PORK SANDWICHES

MAKES: 4 servings **COOK:** 8 hours

3½ pounds pork shoulder

1 (1-ounce) packet teriyaki marinade

1 tablespoon paprika

1 teaspoon pepper

½ cup chicken broth

½ cup brown sugar

¼ cup soy sauce

1 cup chili sauce

1 (6-ounce) can pineapple juice

1 medium onion, chopped

2 carrots, chopped

FOR THE HAWAIIAN SAUCE:

2 tablespoons canola oil

2 teaspoons chopped garlic

1 tablespoon chopped ginger

8 hamburger rolls

1. Rinse pork roast with cold water and pat dry with paper towels. Set aside. In a small bowl, combine teriyaki mix, paprika, and pepper. Coat pork with rub mixture, patting until all rub is used. Place pork in a zip-top bag, squeeze out air, and seal. Let sit in refrigerator for 1 to 3 hours.

2. In a bowl, whisk together the chicken broth, brown sugar, soy sauce, chili sauce, and pineapple juice. Set aside.

3. Put the onion and carrots in a 5-quart slow cooker. Place the pork on top of the carrots and onion and pour half of the juice mixture over it. Reserve remainder for Hawaiian sauce. Cover and cook on low for 7 to 8 hours. The meat should fall apart easily. Remove the roast to a cutting board. Using two forks, carefully pull the meat into shreds.

4. To make the Hawaiian sauce, heat the oil over medium heat in a medium pot. Add garlic and ginger and sauté until soft, about 2 minutes. Add the remaining juice mixture, bring to a boil, then reduce heat and simmer for 10 minutes. Remove from heat and set aside. Serve drizzled over the pork on rolls or on the side.

LOBSTER SALAD WRAPS WITH MANGO SALSA

MAKES: 4 servings

8   ounces frozen mango chunks—
    Dole, finely diced

1   teaspoon canned diced jalapeños

3   tablespoons finely chopped cilantro,
    divided use

2   tablespoons lime juice, divided use

½   teaspoon salt, divided use

1½ cups cooked lobster meat, shredded

1   avocado, peeled and diced

2   scallions, finely chopped

⅛   teaspoon ground black pepper

⅓   cup mayonnaise

4   (10-inch) flour tortillas

1. In a small mixing bowl, toss together mango, jalapeños, 2 tablespoons cilantro, 1 tablespoon lime juice, and ¼ teaspoon salt. Set aside salsa in refrigerator to chill.

2. Place lobster and avocado in a bowl and sprinkle with remaining lime juice. Toss with scallions, remaining cilantro, remaining salt, and pepper. Gently stir in mayonnaise, cover, and chill thoroughly.

3. Lightly toast or warm tortillas to make pliable. Wrap lobster salad in tortillas and serve with mango salsa.

MARGARITA LOBSTER WITH CILANTRO-LIME BUTTER

MAKES: 4 servings **COOK:** 12 to 15 minutes

FOR THE LOBSTER:

    4   lobster tails, thawed if frozen
    1   cup ready-to-serve margarita
    2   teaspoons crushed garlic
    ¼   cup finely chopped fresh cilantro
    2   teaspoons Mexican seasoning

FOR THE CILANTRO-LIME BUTTER:

    2   sticks (1 cup) butter
    2   tablespoons lime juice
    ¼   cup finely chopped fresh cilantro
    1   teaspoon crushed garlic

1. Split lobster tails in half lengthwise using kitchen shears. Rinse under cold water and place meat-side up in a shallow baking dish. In a bowl, stir together margarita, garlic, cilantro, and Mexican seasoning. Pour over lobster. Cover and marinate in refrigerator for 30 minutes to 2 hours.

2. For the cilantro-lime butter, melt butter in small saucepan over medium-low heat. Skim foam from the top. Stir in lime juice, cilantro, and garlic. Set aside ⅓ cup for basting, while reserving the rest for dipping.

3. Remove lobster from marinade and discard marinade; pat lobster dry with paper towels. Brush meat of lobster tails lightly with butter mixture.

Outdoor Method: Set up a grill for direct cooking over medium heat. Remove lobster from refrigerator and let sit at room temperature for 30 minutes. Brush and oil grate before cooking. Grill lobster meat-side down for 2 to 3 minutes. Turn and grill shell-side down for 6 to 8 minutes more or until meat is opaque and firm but not dry. Do not overcook. Brush occasionally with butter mixture. Serve hot with remaining butter mixture for dipping.

Indoor Method: Prepare lobster and butter as directed. Preheat broiler. Place tails meat-side up on broiler pan and broil 6 to 8 inches from heat source for 4 to 5 minutes. Brush with butter and turn. Broil for another 6 to 8 minutes or until cooked through. Serve hot with remaining butter mixture for dipping.

PORK AND LIME NOODLE SALAD

MAKES: 4 servings **COOK:** 3 minutes

⅓ cup lite sesame, ginger, and soy dressing—Ken's Steak House

1 tablespoon lime juice

1 tablespoon smooth peanut butter

2 teaspoons chili-garlic sauce

2 (3-ounce) packages Oriental Flavor ramen noodle soup

1½ cups precooked pork roast, shredded

½ cup pre-shredded carrots

½ red bell pepper, thinly sliced

2 scallions, sliced diagonally

¼ cup mint leaves, loosely packed

½ cup cilantro leaves, loosely packed

¼ cup finely chopped peanuts

1. In a small bowl, whisk together dressing, lime juice, peanut butter, and chili-garlic sauce. Set aside.

2. In a large saucepan, bring 4 cups of water and noodle seasoning to a boil. Add noodles and cook for 3 minutes. Drain and rinse with cold water and set aside.

3. Combine pork, carrots, bell pepper, scallions, mint, and cilantro in a large bowl. Add noodles and dressing to bowl and gently toss to combine. Serve garnished with chopped peanuts.

ROASTED GARLIC AND SHRIMP SKEWERS

MAKES: 4 servings **COOK:** 45 minutes

1 head garlic
⅓ cup plus 1 tablespoon olive oil, divided use
1 tablespoon red wine vinegar
2 teaspoons dried oregano
2 pounds large shrimp, peeled and deveined with tails removed, thawed if frozen
   Salt and pepper, to taste

1. Preheat oven to 350°F.
2. Cut through the head of garlic near the top, removing stem end. Place on a 1-square-foot piece of aluminum foil, drizzle with 1 tablespoon olive oil, and season with salt and pepper. Wrap garlic in foil and roast for 30 to 40 minutes, until very soft and outside is browned. When cool enough to handle, squeeze cloves from skins into a large bowl. Whisk together with vinegar, remaining olive oil, and oregano, mashing cloves to break up slightly. Add shrimp, season with salt and pepper, and allow to sit in refrigerator to marinate for 30 minutes to 1 hour.
3. Soak 1 dozen bamboo skewers in water. Thread shrimp onto skewers at 2 points, making sure they lie flat.
4. Preheat a grill pan over medium-high heat. Place shrimp skewers on grill and cook until opaque and cooked through, about 3 minutes per side.

SAUSAGE STUFFED ZUCCHINI

MAKES: 4 servings **COOK:** 45 minutes

4 medium zucchini
2 tablespoons olive oil
½ pound pork sausage, casing removed
¾ cup frozen chopped onions, thawed
2 tablespoons chopped garlic
1 egg, lightly beaten
¾ cup stuffing mix, crushed
⅓ cup roasted red peppers, chopped
1 teaspoon Italian seasoning
½ cup marinara sauce
½ cup grated Parmesan cheese

1. Preheat oven to 400°F. Line a baking sheet with foil and set aside.
2. Cut zucchini in half lengthwise and scoop out insides with a small spoon. Reserve pulp. Place hollowed-out zucchini halves on prepared baking sheet and drizzle 2 tablespoons of oil over the top of them. Bake for 20 to 25 minutes.
3. Meanwhile, in a heavy skillet over medium heat, cook sausage with chopped onion and garlic. Drain off excess fat. Chop reserved zucchini pulp, add to the pan, and cook for 3 minutes more. Transfer to a mixing bowl and let cool for 5 minutes. Stir in remaining ingredients, except cheese.
4. Divide sausage mixture among zucchini shells. Sprinkle Parmesan cheese over the top of each. Return to oven and bake for 15 to 20 minutes. Remove and serve hot.

SOFT-SHELL CRABS WITH PINEAPPLE BARBEQUE SAUCE

MAKES: 4 servings   **COOK:** 10 minutes

12   jumbo soft-shell crabs, cleaned

1½   cups low-fat sesame ginger dressing—Newman's Own

2   scallions, chopped

½   cup hoisin sauce

½   cup pineapple juice

1. Place cleaned soft-shell crabs in a large zip-top bag. Pour dressing into bag and add chopped scallions. Squeeze air from bag and seal. Marinate in refrigerator for 30 minutes to 1 hour.

2. In a small saucepan, combine hoisin sauce and pineapple juice. Bring to a boil and reduce liquid until thickened and about 1 cup.

Outdoor Method: Set up a grill for direct cooking over medium-high heat. Remove crabs from refrigerator and let sit at room temperature 30 minutes. Remove crabs from marinade and discard marinade; pat dry with paper towels. Oil grate when ready to start cooking. Place crabs apart on hot, oiled grill. Cook for 2 to 3 minutes per side (claws will turn red). Brush each side with BBQ sauce. Serve immediately with extra sauce on the side.

Indoor Method: Prepare crabs as directed. Preheat broiler. Place crabs on a foil-lined baking sheet or broiler pan. Broil for 2 to 3 minutes per side (claws will turn red). Brush each side with BBQ sauce. Remove and serve immediately with extra sauce on the side.

SPICY SWEET STICKY WINGS

MAKES: 4 servings   **COOK:** 40 minutes

2   pounds chicken wings

½   cup orange marmalade

2   tablespoons chili sauce

1   tablespoon chicken seasoning

   Salt and pepper, to taste

1. Preheat oven to 375°F.
2. Rinse chicken wings under cold water and pat dry with paper towels. Season with salt and pepper and put in an ovenproof baking dish. Cover with foil and bake for 30 to 35 minutes or until chicken is cooked through.
3. While chicken is baking, combine marmalade, chili sauce, and chicken seasoning in a mixing bowl. When chicken is cooked through, turn oven to broil. Pour sauce over chicken and make sure wings are thoroughly coated. Broil 5 minutes, taking care not to burn the sauce.

SUMMER'S BOUNTY WITH HERB VINAIGRETTE AND PARMESAN

MAKES: 4 servings   **COOK:** 8 to 15 minutes

½   pound asparagus, trimmed

1   zucchini, thickly sliced

1   summer squash, thickly sliced

1   red bell pepper, seeded and cut into 1-inch pieces

1   orange bell pepper, seeded and cut into 1-inch pieces

1   large portobello mushroom, thickly sliced

¾   cup oil-and-vinegar salad dressing

¼   cup chopped fresh herbs (parsley, thyme, marjoram, oregano, basil)

½   teaspoon red pepper flakes

2   tablespoons shaved Parmesan cheese

1. Place vegetables in a zip-top bag. Whisk together salad dressing, herbs, and pepper flakes, then pour into bag over vegetables. Squeeze air from bag and seal. Marinate in refrigerator 30 minutes to 2 hours. Remove vegetables from bag, reserving marinade.
2. Set up a grill for direct cooking over medium heat. Brush and oil grate when ready to start cooking. Place vegetables on hot, oiled grill. Cook for 3 to 4 minutes per side or until grill-marked and cooked.
3. Transfer vegetables to a platter and drizzle with some of the reserved marinade. Sprinkle with shaved Parmesan and serve.

WHITE WINE STEAMED CLAMS WITH BLUEBERRY SALAD

MAKES: 4 servings   **COOK:** 10 minutes

FOR THE SALAD:

1½ tablespoons aged balsamic vinegar

2 teaspoons honey

1 (10-ounce) bag mixed salad greens

3 tablespoons extra-virgin olive oil

1 teaspoon salt

1 small yellow onion, peeled, cut into quarters, and thinly shaved lengthwise

4 ounces baby bella mushrooms, sliced

½ pint blueberries

½ pint grape tomatoes

4 ounces crumbled Gorgonzola cheese— Sargento

FOR THE CLAMS:

2 tablespoons butter, softened

4 tablespoons minced shallot

1 tablespoon chopped garlic

2 tablespoons ginger puree—Gourmet Garden

1 teaspoon Old Bay Seasoning

¼ cup minced fresh parsley

4 pounds live clams in the shell, scrubbed clean with brush

1 teaspoon salt

1½ cups white wine

2 green onions, finely sliced

1 crusty baguette

1. In a small box, mix together the vinegar and honey. Set aside.

2. Up to 30 minutes before serving, place the greens in a salad bowl and toss with the olive oil and salt. Arrange the onion, mushrooms, blueberries, tomatoes, and cheese on the greens. When ready to serve, toss with the vinegar and honey.

3. Examine clams and discard any that do not close when tapped on their shell.

4. Combine the butter with the shallot, garlic, ginger, Old Bay Seasoning, and parsley. Heat a medium saucepan over high heat and add the butter mixture. When the butter has melted and the pan is hot, add the clams and cover the pot immediately. Holding one hand on the lid and the other on the handle, give the pot a couple of really good shakes to coat the clams. Cook for 2 minutes and add the salt and wine, immediately replacing lid and shaking again. Lower the heat to medium high and cook 5 to 6 more minutes or until the clams open.

5. Spoon the clams into individual soup bowls and pour liquid over the top. Scatter with the green onions. Serve with lots of bread for sopping and the salad. Place an empty bowl on the table for discarded shells.

BALSAMIC STRAWBERRY SKEWERS

MAKES: 4 servings **COOK:** 10 minutes

½ cup balsamic vinegar

¾ cup semi-sweet chocolate chips

1 cup heavy cream

2 tablespoons strawberry syrup

16 large strawberries

  Nonstick cooking spray

1. Add vinegar to a small saucepan and bring to a boil. Reduce to ¼ cup and set aside in a bowl. Rinse and wipe pan dry, then add chocolate chips and cream. Cook and stir over medium heat until chocolate has melted and is incorporated into the cream. Remove from heat and stir in strawberry syrup. Set aside until ready to serve.

2. Thread 4 strawberries end-to-end on bamboo skewers that have been soaked in water for an hour. Lightly spray kebabs with cooking spray.

Outdoor Method: Set up a grill for direct cooking over medium heat. Oil grate when ready to start cooking. Place kebabs on hot, oiled grill. Cook 2 to 3 minutes per side or until fruit is warm and soft. Brush frequently with balsamic reduction. Serve immediately with chocolate sauce.

Indoor Method: Preheat broiler. Prepare balsamic reduction, chocolate sauce, and strawberries as directed. Place kebabs on a foil-lined baking sheet or broiler pan. Broil strawberries 2 to 3 minutes per side, 6 to 8 inches from heat source. Brush frequently with balsamic reduction. Serve immediately with chocolate sauce.

GRILLED BANANAS FOSTER

MAKES: 4 servings   **COOK:** 8 to 12 minutes

4   tablespoons butter

2   tablespoons dark rum

1   tablespoon banana liqueur

3   tablespoons brown sugar

1   teaspoon pumpkin pie spice

4   ripe medium bananas

     Vanilla ice cream

1. Melt butter in saucepan over medium heat. Add the rum, banana liqueur, brown sugar, and pumpkin pie spice. Bring to a boil over high heat, stirring frequently. Let the mixture boil until thickened, about 2 to 4 minutes. Remove from heat and set aside.

Outdoor Method: Set up a grill for direct grilling over medium heat. Brush and oil grate when ready to start cooking. Cut each banana in half lengthwise, leaving the skin on, and brush tops with butter sauce. Place the bananas on hot, oiled grill, cut-side down, and grill until caramelized, about 4 minutes. Turn bananas and grill about 4 minutes more or until skins are blackened and bananas are soft and warmed through. Baste frequently with butter sauce. Leaving skins on, transfer to serving bowls with a scoop of ice cream and drizzle with remaining butter sauce.

Indoor Method: In a large skillet, prepare butter rum sauce as directed. Peel and slice bananas lengthwise and add to sauce in a large skillet. Bring to a boil, reduce heat, and simmer 2 minutes. Transfer to serving bowls with a scoop of ice cream and drizzle with remaining butter sauce.

PINEAPPLE POUND CAKE

MAKES: 8 servings **BAKE:** 50 minutes

Nonstick cooking spray

1 (20-ounce) can pineapple slices, drained, juice reserved

1 (16-ounce) box pound cake mix

¾ cup pineapple juice

2 eggs

½ cup brown sugar

2 tablespoons butter

1. Preheat oven to 350°F. Spray a 9 × 5-inch loaf pan with cooking spray and set aside.

2. Reserve 3 pineapple rings and juice; set aside. Chop remaining pineapple rings into tiny pieces and set aside.

3. Combine cake mix, pineapple juice, and eggs in a large bowl and beat with an electric mixer on low speed for 30 seconds. Scrape down sides of bowl and beat for 3 minutes on medium speed. Stir in chopped pineapple until well combined. Pour into prepared loaf pan.

4. Bake in preheated oven for 45 to 50 minutes or until a tester inserted in cake comes out clean. Remove and cool completely.

5. Pour reserved pineapple juice and enough water to make ⅔ cup into a small skillet over medium-high heat. Add brown sugar and bring to a simmer. Add remaining pineapple rings and cook for 4 minutes or until sauce thickens slightly. Remove from heat and stir in butter until combined.

6. To serve, place pound cake on serving plate. Arrange pineapple rings on top and pour pineapple sauce over cake.

GRILLED PINEAPPLE TARTS

MAKES: 6 servings **COOK:** 6 minutes

1 (16-ounce) container fresh pineapple spears—Ready Pac

1 cup spiced rum, divided use

¾ teaspoon Jamaican jerk seasoning—divided use

1 (1-ounce) box fat-free cheesecake pudding mix

1½ cups low-fat milk, cold

1 package mini graham cracker pie crust
Nonstick cooking spray

2 tablespoons store-bought sweetened coconut, toasted

1. Place pineapple in a large zip-top bag. Add ¾ cup rum and ½ teaspoon jerk seasoning. Squeeze air from bag and seal. Marinate in refrigerator 30 minutes to overnight. In a medium mixing bowl, whisk together pudding mix, milk, remaining ¼ cup rum, and remaining ¼ teaspoon jerk seasoning for 2 minutes. Spoon ¼ cup of pudding mixture into each mini tart shell. Chill tarts in refrigerator.

2. Set up a grill for direct cooking over medium heat. Remove pineapple from marinade and pat dry with paper towels. Brush and oil grate when ready to start cooking. Spray each spear with cooking spray. Place pineapple on hot, oiled grill and cook for 2 to 3 minutes per side, or until warm and grill-marked on all sides. Transfer to a cutting board and roughly chop.

3. Remove filled tart shells from refrigerator and top with grilled pineapple. Sprinkle with toasted pineapple and serve.

PINEAPPLE FRESCA

MAKES: 4 drinks

1 (6-ounce) can pineapple juice

1 cup citrus soda—Fresca

4½ ounces (about ½ cup) vodka, optional

2 tablespoons frozen limeade concentrate

14 ice cubes

4 pineapple wedges, for garnish

1. **Combine all ingredients in a blender. Blend for 30 to 40 seconds until frothy. Pour into serving glasses. Garnish with a pineapple wedge.**

SUMMER STAR COCKTAIL

MAKES: 1 drink

2 ounces Smirnoff Raspberry Pomegranate vodka

1 teaspoon creme de cassis

1 splash lemon juice

Ginger ale

Sliced carambola (star fruit)

1. **In a rocks glass filled with ice, stir together vodka, creme de cassis, and lemon juice. Fill glass with ginger ale and garnish with a slice of star fruit.**

AUGUST

ASIAN SAUSAGE SALAD WRAPS

MAKES: 6 servings **COOK:** 8 minutes

1 (12-ounce) package smoked chicken and mango sausages—Aidells®

⅓ cup mayonnaise

2 tablespoons Chinese chicken salad dressing—Girard's®

⅓ cup finely chopped scallions

1 jalapeño pepper, stemmed, seeded, and finely chopped

1 (approx. 16-ounce) bag cole slaw mix

½ cup chopped red bell pepper

⅓ cup cashews, coarsely chopped

1 head butter lettuce, leaves separated, washed, and dried

Outdoor Method: Set up a grill for direct grilling over medium-high heat. Oil grate when ready to start cooking. Place sausages on hot, oiled grill and cook for 3 to 4 minutes per side.

Indoor Method: Preheat broiler. Place sausages on a wire rack over a foil-lined baking sheet or broiler pan. Cook 6 to 8 inches from heat source for 3 to 4 minutes per side.

1. Let sausages stand for 5 minutes. Dice sausages and set aside. In a large bowl, stir together mayonnaise, salad dressing, scallions, and jalapeño pepper. Add diced sausages, slaw mix, red pepper, and cashews. Toss until well combined. Cover and chill in the refrigerator for 1 to 2 hours. Serve spoonfuls of salad mix wrapped in lettuce leaves.

CHEDDAR-CHILI MASHED POTATOES

MAKES: 4 servings **COOK:** 10 minutes

1 (24-ounce) bag Steam n' Mash frozen cut russet potatoes—Ore-Ida®

2 tablespoons butter, cut into pieces

⅔ cup milk

1 (4.5-ounce) can chopped green chilies, drained

1 teaspoon chopped garlic
Salt and pepper, to taste

1. Microwave potatoes according to package directions. Stir in green chilies and garlic. Add salt and pepper to taste. Transfer potatoes to a serving dish and loosely cover with foil until ready to serve.

CORN AND BLACK-EYED PEA SALAD

MAKES: 4 servings

1 (15-ounce) can black-eyed peas, rinsed and drained

1 (16-ounce) bag frozen pepper stir-fry, thawed and chopped—Birds Eye

2 cups frozen corn kernels, thawed

1 tablespoon minced garlic

1 tablespoon hot sauce

1 tablespoon Cajun seasoning

⅓ cup honey mustard dressing

1. In a large bowl, combine all ingredients. Stir to make sure everything is evenly coated. Cover and keep in refrigerator until ready to serve.

ISLAND POTATO SALAD WITH PASTA

MAKES: 4 servings   **COOK:** 20 minutes

1 (24-ounce) package frozen Steam n' Mash potatoes—Ore-Ida®

4 ounces elbow macaroni or pasta shells

1 red onion, finely chopped

2 celery stalks, finely chopped

2 medium carrots, grated

1 red bell pepper, finely chopped

2   scallions, finely sliced

2 tablespoons fresh parsley, finely chopped

¼ cup sour cream

¼ cup mayonnaise

½ cup Hawaiian marinade

2 eggs, hard-boiled and quartered

   Salt and pepper, to taste

1. Cook potatoes in a microwave oven according to package directions, but do not mash. Carefully open the package and let the potatoes cool.

2. Bring a large pot of water to a boil over high heat. Add a big pinch of salt and the pasta. Cook according to package directions until the pasta is tender. Drain pasta, rinse with cold water, and set aside.

3. In a large bowl, add the potatoes, pasta, onion, celery, carrots, red pepper, scallions, and parsley. In a small bowl, mix together the sour cream, mayonnaise, and marinade. Add half the dressing to the large bowl and mix everything together. Add more dressing if you desire. Taste and adjust seasoning with salt and pepper. Refrigerate for 1 hour to let the flavors combine. When ready to serve, transfer to a serving bowl, and garnish with hard-boiled eggs.

SESAME GRILLED ASPARAGUS SPEARS

MAKES: 6 servings   **COOK:** 10 minutes

1   pound asparagus, trimmed

1   teaspoon canola oil

2   teaspoons toasted sesame oil, divided use

½   cup mayonnaise

2   tablespoons rice vinegar

1   teaspoon soy sauce

1   teaspoon crushed garlic

1   tablespoon toasted sesame seeds,
    for garnish

Outdoor Method: Set up a grill for direct cooking over medium heat. Place asparagus on a baking sheet and drizzle with canola oil and 1 teaspoon sesame oil.

1. In a bowl, stir together mayonnaise, vinegar, soy sauce, garlic, and remaining 1 teaspoon sesame oil. Set aside.

2. Brush and oil grate before cooking. Place asparagus on hot, oiled grill. Cook for 8 to 10 minutes or until fork-tender, turning frequently. Remove and garnish with sesame seeds. Serve warm with sesame dipping sauce.

Indoor Method: Preheat oven to 400°F. Prepare asparagus and dipping sauce as directed above. Roast asparagus for 8 to 10 minutes or until fork-tender. Serve warm with sesame dipping sauce.

NEW ENGLAND CLAM & CORN CHOWDER

MAKES: 4 servings   **COOK:** 20 minutes

2 tablespoons butter

1 tablespoon canola oil

1 medium onion, diced

1 tablespoon garlic, chopped

2 tablespoons all-purpose flour

3 russet potatoes, peeled, quartered, and cut into ¼-inch-thick slices

1 teaspoon chopped fresh thyme leaves

4 cups milk

2 (6.5-ounce) cans minced clams, drained, juice reserved

1 cup frozen corn

Salt and freshly ground black pepper

1. In a large pot, over medium heat, add the butter and the oil. Once the butter is melted add the onion and garlic and cook for 3 to 4 minutes until slightly tender. Mix in the flour and cook until the flour is a very pale golden color, about 2 to 3 minutes. Add the potatoes and thyme. Stir in the milk and the juice from the canned clams. Reduce the heat and simmer until the potatoes are cooked through, about 10 minutes.

2. Remove 2 cups of the chowder and puree in a blender until smooth. Add pureed chowder, clams, and corn to the pot. Season with salt and pepper, to taste, and let simmer for another 5 minutes. Transfer to individual soup bowls or a large soup bowl and serve.

BRATS ON A STICK WITH SWEET MUSTARD GLAZE

MAKES: 4 servings   **COOK:** 10 minutes

¼ cup spicy brown mustard

¼ cup apple jelly

1 teaspoon honey BBQ seasoning mix

5 tablespoons olive oil, divided use

2 tablespoons apple cider vinegar

4 cooked bratwurst links, each sliced into 4 pieces

1 red bell pepper, cut into 1-inch pieces

8 medium white mushrooms, cut in half

1½ cups (about 16) frozen pearl onions, thawed and dried

Salt and pepper, to taste

1. Soak 8 bamboo skewers in water for at least an hour. Preheat barbeque grill or indoor grill pan to medium heat.

2. In a small bowl, stir together mustard, jelly, BBQ seasoning, 2 tablespoons olive oil, and apple cider vinegar. Set aside.

3. Alternating between bratwurst, red peppers, mushrooms, and pearl onions, thread 2 pieces of each onto each skewer. Brush with remaining olive oil and season with salt and pepper. Place on a hot, oiled grill and cook for 3 minutes. Turn and liberally brush with glaze. Grill an additional 3 minutes then turn and brush with glaze. Grill for an additional 2 minutes per side, brushing again with glaze.

4. Remove from grill heat and serve. Any remaining glaze can be brushed onto the skewers or served alongside as a dipping sauce.

CHILI RUBBED RIBS

MAKES: 4 servings **COOK:** 2 hours 30 minutes

- 2   racks pork spareribs
- 2   (1.25-ounce) packets chili seasoning
- 3   tablespoons granulated garlic
- 1   tablespoon paprika
- 2   tablespoons steak seasoning
- 2   tablespoons packed brown sugar

FOR BARBEQUE SAUCE:

- (18-ounce) bottle barbeque sauce
- ⅓   cup dark brown sugar
- 1   tablespoon molasses
- 1   tablespoon steak sauce

1. Preheat oven to 350°F.
2. Rinse ribs with cold water and pat dry with paper towels. Remove thin membrane from the back of ribs. Mix together chili seasoning, garlic, paprika, steak seasoning, and 2 tablespoons sugar. Reserve 2 tablespoons rub mix and sprinkle remaining mix over ribs and pat in. Set aside to cure for 15 to 30 minutes. For the sauce, stir together BBQ sauce, dark brown sugar, molasses, steak sauce, and remaining rub mix. Set aside.
3. Place ribs meat-side up on a rack in a shallow roasting pan. Tightly cover with foil. Bake in preheated oven for 1 hour. Remove ribs from oven and carefully drain fat from roasting pan. Continue baking ribs, uncovered, for 1 to 1½ hours more or until tender, turning and brushing occasionally with sauce.
4. Remove from oven and let rest 10 minutes before cutting into servings. Serve hot with sauce on the side.

CLAMS CASINO

MAKES: 6 servings **COOK:** 8 minutes

1 stick (½ cup) unsalted butter

1 tablespoon citrus herb seasoning

1 tablespoon crushed garlic

1 tablespoon lemon juice

1 small shallot, minced

1 cup dried Italian seasoned bread crumbs

2 tablespoons grated Parmesan cheese

24 large clams, shucked

8 slices precooked bacon, cut in 2-inch-long pieces

2 to 3 cups sea salt or kosher salt, for serving

1. Preheat oven to 450°F.

2. In a small pot, combine butter, citrus herb seasoning, garlic, lemon juice, and shallot. Heat over a low flame until butter is melted. Set aside.

3. In a large bowl, combine bread crumbs, cheese, and melted butter mixture. Mix well to combine.

4. Place open clams on a baking sheet. Place a piece of bacon on top of each clam. Top with 1 tablespoon of bread crumb mixture. Bake for 7 minutes.

5. To serve, place about 2 to 3 cups of coarse sea salt or kosher salt onto a large platter. Arrange the clams on the platter, lightly pressing them into the salt so they are nestled in.

CUBANO DOG

MAKES: 4 servings   **COOK:** 10 minutes

FOR THE DRESSING:

½ cup olive-oil-and-vinegar salad dressing

1 tablespoon orange juice concentrate

1 tablespoon finely chopped fresh parsley

2 teaspoons finely chopped fresh oregano

1 teaspoon crushed garlic—Gourmet Garden

FOR THE SANDWICHES:

8 bun-length franks, butterflied

8 French rolls, split horizontally

¼ pound deli-shaved honey-roasted ham

16 slices deli Swiss cheese, thinly sliced

Sandwich pickle slices

2 medium tomatoes, thinly sliced

1. Whisk together all ingredients for the dressing and set aside.

Outdoor Method: Set up a grill for direct cooking over medium heat. Oil grate when ready to start cooking. Place butterflied franks on hot, oiled grill and cook for 8 to 10 minutes or until heated through, turning once.

Indoor Method: Prepare dressing as directed. Preheat broiler. Place butterflied franks on a foil-lined baking sheet or broiler pan. Cook 6 to 8 inches from heat source for 8 to 10 minutes or until heated through, turning once.

2. Toast rolls lightly while franks are cooking.

3. Re-whisk dressing and drizzle a little on the toasted rolls. Divide ham, franks, cheese, pickles, and tomatoes to build sandwiches. Drizzle with a bit more dressing and serve.

GRILLED PORK CHOPS AND CAJUN POTATO SALAD

MAKES: 4 servings   **COOK:** 22 minutes

FOR THE POTATO SALAD:

1 (16-ounce) bag precooked and diced red potatoes

2 tablespoons mayonnaise

1 tablespoon stone-ground mustard

2 tablespoons sour cream

1 teaspoon Cajun seasoning

½ teaspoon salt

1 teaspoon crushed garlic

½ cup diced tomatoes, drained

1 scallion, thinly sliced

FOR THE CHOPS:

4 pork loin chops

1 tablespoon pork rub—McCormick Grill Mates

1 tablespoon Cajun seasoning

1. Place potatoes in a microwave-safe bowl, cover, and cook on high for 8 to 10 minutes.

2. While potatoes are cooking, mix mayonnaise, mustard, sour cream, Cajun seasoning, salt, and garlic in a large bowl until well blended. Add warm potatoes and toss to coat well. Lightly toss in the tomatoes and scallion. Refrigerate for at least 1 hour, tossing occasionally to evenly chill.

3. While salad chills, rinse pork chops with cold water and pat dry with paper towels. Stir together pork rub and Cajun seasoning; rub and pat into pork chops, using all the rub mixture. Set aside to cure for at least 15 minutes.

4. Set up a grill for direct cooking over medium heat. Place chops on a hot, oiled grill. Cook for 5 to 6 minutes per side, or until slightly pink in the center and the juices run clear (160°F).

GRILLED RIB EYE WITH TANGERINE-CHILI MIGNONETTE

MAKES: 4 servings **COOK:** 14 minutes

- 4   beef rib eye steaks
- 4   tablespoons steak rub
-     Zest and juice of 2 tangerines
- ¼   cup white wine vinegar
- 2   tablespoons minced shallot
- 1   jalapeño, seeded and minced

1. Rinse steaks under cold water, pat dry with paper towels, and set aside. In a small bowl, combine steak rub with grated zest of 1 tangerine. Rub mixture into both sides of steaks. Set aside to cure for 15 to 30 minutes. Meanwhile, grate zest from remaining tangerine and squeeze juice from both into a small bowl. Stir in zest, vinegar, shallots, and jalapeño. Set aside.

Outdoor Method: Set up a grill for direct cooking over high heat. Let steaks stand at room temperature for 20 to 30 minutes before grilling. Oil grate when ready to start cooking. Place steaks on hot, oiled grill and cook for 5 to 7 minutes per side for medium (160°F). Transfer steaks to a platter and let rest for 5 minutes before serving. Serve hot with a spoonful of tangerine-chili mignonette.

Indoor Method: Prepare steaks and tangerine-chili mignonette as directed. Preheat broiler. Place steaks on a foil-lined baking sheet or broiler pan. Broil 6 to 8 inches from heat source for 5 to 7 minutes per side for medium (160°F). Serve hot with a spoonful of tangerine-chili mignonette.

ITALIAN SAUSAGE STUFFED TROUT

MAKES: 4 servings   **COOK:** 25 minutes

4   hot Italian sausages, casings removed

2   teaspoons crushed garlic

2   scallions, chopped

1   tablespoon Italian seasoning

4   trout, scales removed, cleaned and boned
    Kosher salt

¾   cup marinara sauce

2   tablespoons finely chopped flat-leaf parsley,
    for garnish
    Salt and pepper, to taste

1. Brown sausages in a large skillet, stirring often to break up clumps. Stir in garlic, scallions, and Italian seasoning, and season to taste with salt and pepper. Remove from heat and let cool to room temperature.

Outdoor Method: Set up a grill for indirect cooking over medium heat, so that no heat source will be under fish. Make sure you have a very clean grill, or the fish will stick. Brush and oil grate before cooking.

2. Rinse fish under cold water and pat dry with paper towels, inside and out. Fill the cavity of each fish with a quarter of the sausage mixture and secure closed with toothpicks. Spray both sides of fish with cooking spray and season well with kosher salt. Place fish onto a very clean grill over a drip pan. Close grill and cook 12 to 15 minutes per side. To test for doneness, use a sharp knife to cut a slit down the back to check if fish is opaque. Brush both sides of the fish with marinara and remove fish from grill carefully so it doesn't stick. Transfer fish to a platter. Brush once more with marinara and garnish with chopped parsley.

Indoor Method: Prepare fish as directed. Preheat oven to 450°F. Put the fish on a wire rack in a roasting pan and roast for 18 to 20 minutes. Transfer fish to a platter. Brush with marinara and garnish with chopped parsley.

LEMONGRASS RUBBED CHICKEN BREASTS

MAKES: 4 servings   **COOK:** 40 to 50 minutes

4   bone-in chicken breasts

¼   cup lemongrass paste—Gourmet Garden

1   tablespoon ginger paste—Gourmet Garden

1   tablespoon mild chili-pepper paste—
Gourmet Garden

2   teaspoons crushed garlic

2   teaspoons lime zest

1   teaspoon salt

1. Rinse chicken under cold water and pat dry with paper towels. Cut away any excess skin. Stir together remaining ingredients and rub and pat all over chicken. Place in a zip-top bag, squeeze out air, and seal. Marinate in refrigerator for at least 2 hours, and up to overnight.

Outdoor Method: Set up a grill for direct cooking over medium heat. Let chicken stand at room temperature for 20 to 30 minutes before grilling. Oil grate when ready to start cooking. Remove chicken from bag and place skin-side down on hot, oiled grill. Cook for 18 to 22 minutes per side or until no longer pink at the bone and the juices run clear (170°F). Transfer chicken to a platter and let rest for 5 minutes before serving. Serve hot.

Indoor Method: Prepare chicken breasts as directed above. Preheat oven to 375°F. Place chicken on foil-lined baking sheet and roast for 40 to 50 minutes or until no longer pink at the bone and the juices run clear (170°F). Transfer chicken to a platter and let rest for 5 minutes before serving. Serve hot.

MEDITERRANEAN SALAD WITH GRILLED CHICKEN

MAKES: 4 servings   **COOK:** 10 minutes

1   pound (about 2) boneless, skinless chicken breasts
¼   cup olive oil
     Juice and zest of 1 lemon
1   teaspoon Italian seasoning
1   teaspoon sugar
1   large head romaine lettuce, cleaned and torn into bite-size piece
8   ounces frozen green beans, thawed
½   medium red onion, sliced
¼   cup pitted Kalamata olives, roughly chopped
½   cup crumbled feta cheese
     Salt and pepper, to taste

1. Preheat grill over medium heat.
2. Rinse chicken under cold water and pat dry with paper towels. Slice each chicken breast across horizontally to get 4 large, thin pieces. When the grill is hot, brush the grill grates with cooking oil to prevent the chicken from sticking. Season the chicken with salt and pepper and grill for 4 minutes per side. Let rest for a few minutes, then slice into strips.
3. In a large bowl, whisk together olive oil, lemon juice, half the zest, Italian seasoning, and sugar, and season with a pinch of salt and pepper. Reserve 2 tablespoons of the dressing to pour over the salad.
4. In bowl with remaining dressing, add the lettuce, green beans, onion, olives, and cheese, and toss to coat evenly. Divide the salad among 4 plates or one large serving platter. Top with the sliced chicken and drizzle with reserved dressing.

NECTARINE SALSA ON QUESADILLA ROUNDS

MAKES: 30 quesadilla rounds **COOK:** 1 hour

FOR THE SALSA:

- 3 nectarines, peeled and finely chopped
- 1 cup frozen corn kernels, thawed
- 1 cup black beans
- 1 cup salsa fresca (pico de gallo)
- 1 tablespoon diced canned jalapeños
- 2 tablespoons finely chopped cilantro

FOR THE QUESADILLAS:

- 2 (13-ounce) bags fajita-size flour tortillas
- 2 cups shredded Mexican blend cheese, divided use
- 1 (1-ounce) packet Mexican taco seasoning
- 1 (8-ounce) container sour cream, for serving

1. For the salsa, stir together all ingredients in a medium bowl until well combined. Chill in refrigerator for at least 1 hour, or as long as overnight.

2. For the quesadillas, cut out 3 circles from each tortilla with a 3-inch round cutter. Repeat to use all tortillas.

3. Spray a large skillet with cooking spray and heat on medium high. Place as many tortilla rounds as will fit comfortably in skillet. Top each round with a heaping tablespoon of shredded cheese, being careful not to burn your fingers. Sprinkle a little bit of Mexican seasoning on top of cheese. Top each with another tortilla round. Heat for 2 minutes then flip quesadillas with a spatula. Heat for 2 more minutes. Repeat to make 30 quesadilla rounds.

4. To serve, top each quesadilla round with a tablespoon of salsa and a dollop of sour cream.

ORIGINAL TOMMY'S BURGER

MAKES: 4 servings **COOK:** 38 minutes

FOR THE CHILI SAUCE:

- 1 pound ground beef
- 2 tablespoons less-sodium chili mix—McCormick
- 2 tablespoons beefy onion soup mix—Lipton®
- 2 tablespoons finely grated and chopped carrot
- 1¾ cups lower-sodium beef broth

FOR THE BURGERS:

- 1½ pounds ground beef
- 2 tablespoons beefy onion soup mix—Lipton®
- 2 teaspoons steak seasoning
- ¼ cup lower-sodium beef broth
- 8 slices cheddar cheese
- 4 plain burger buns
  Yellow mustard
- 1 onion, chopped
- 1 cup pickle-flavor chips
- 1 beefsteak tomato, sliced

1. For the chili sauce, place all ingredients in a large skillet over medium heat, stirring frequently to break up meat into fine grind. Reduce heat and simmer gently for 15 to 30 minutes or until liquid is absorbed. Set aside.

2. For the burgers, combine ground beef, soup mix, steak seasoning, and beef broth in a large bowl. Mix thoroughly. Form into 8 patties slightly larger than buns. Cover and chill if not cooking immediately.

Outdoor Method: Set up a grill for direct cooking over high heat. Oil grate when ready to start cooking. Place patties on hot, oiled grill. Cook for 3 to 4 minutes per side for medium (160°F). Sandwich 2 slices of cheese between 2 burgers and place on bottom of bun, spread with mustard. Top with chili sauce, onions, pickle chips, tomato, and top of bun.

Indoor Method: Prepare patties as directed. Preheat broiler. Place patties on a wire rack over foil-lined baking sheet or broiler pan. Broil 6 to 8 inches from heat source for 3 to 4 minutes per side for medium (160°F). Serve as directed.

PEACH TEA CHICKEN

MAKES: 4 servings   **COOK:** 40 minutes

4   boneless, skinless chicken breasts

2   tablespoons extra-virgin olive oil

½   cup peach-flavored iced tea

½   cup peach preserves

¼   cup chili sauce

2   tablespoons molasses

Salt and pepper, to taste

1. Rinse chicken under cold water and pat dry with paper towels. Season chicken with salt and pepper. Heat oil in a large skillet over medium-high heat. Brown chicken on both sides, about 3 minutes per side, and transfer to a plate.

2. Remove skillet from heat and carefully add peach tea. Return pan to heat and deglaze pan by scraping up browned bits. Stir in remaining ingredients and bring to a boil. Reduce to a simmer and return chicken plus any accumulated juices to the pan.

3. Cover and cook until chicken is cooked through, about 20 to 30 minutes.

SESAME TERIYAKI LONDON BROIL

MAKES: 6 servings   **COOK:** 18 minutes

- 1 (1½-pound) top round London broil, about 1 ¼-inches thick
- 1¼ cup teriyaki sauce
- 2 teaspoons toasted sesame oil
- 2 teaspoons crushed garlic
- 2 scallions, thinly sliced
- 1 tablespoon sesame seeds

1. Rinse steak under cold water and pat dry with paper towels. Place steak in a large zip-top bag and set aside. Stir to combine remaining ingredients in a small bowl. Pour marinade into bag with steak. Squeeze air from bag and seal. Marinate in refrigerator for at least 4 hours, but preferably overnight.

2. Set up a grill for direct cooking over medium-high heat. Let steak stand at room temperature for 20 to 30 minutes before grilling. Remove steak from bag and discard marinade. Oil grate when ready to start cooking. Place steak on hot, oiled grill and cook for 7 to 9 minutes per side for medium rare (145°F). Transfer steak to a cutting board and let stand 10 minutes. Holding a knife at a 45-degree angle, cut steak across grain into thin slices and serve.

SUMMER GRILLED SAUSAGE AND APRICOT CREPES

MAKES: 4 servings   **COOK:** 15 minutes

- ¼ cup sweet chili sauce
- ¼ cup chili sauce
- 1 (12-ounce) package smoked chicken and mango sausages—Aidells®
- 6 apricots, pitted and quartered
- 2 tablespoons canola oil
- 4 premade crepes—Frieda's
- 2 tablespoons honey
- 2 teaspoons Thai seasoning
- 1 tablespoon cilantro, finely chopped

1. In a bowl, stir together sweet chili sauce and chili sauce. Set aside.

2. Set up a grill for direct grilling over medium-high heat. Place sausages on hot, oiled grate and cook for 3 to 4 minutes per side. Brush apricots with oil and grill for 2 to 3 minutes per side, until warm and grill-marked. Transfer sausages and apricots to a cutting board. Slice sausages and roughly chop apricots.

3. Place crepes on hot grill for 30 seconds per side. Remove, brush one side with honey, and sprinkle with Thai seasoning and cilantro. Divide sausage and apricots among the crepes and roll up tightly. Serve immediately, drizzled with chili sauce mix.

SWEET-AND-SOUR CHICKEN SKEWERS

MAKES: 4 servings   **COOK:** 25 minutes

½ cup apple cider vinegar

¼ cup brown sugar

1 tablespoon corn starch, mixed with 1
   tablespoon water

1 pound chicken thighs, boneless

½ (20-ounce) can pineapple chunks, juice
   reserved

1 red bell pepper, cut into 1-inch pieces

   Salt and pepper, to taste

1. Place vinegar, sugar, reserved pineapple juice, and corn starch slurry into a small saucepan. Bring to a boil, then reduce to a simmer and cook until the sauce thickens, about 8 minutes. Remove from heat and set aside.

2. Preheat grill pan on your stovetop.

3. Rinse chicken under cold water and pat dry with paper towels. On each of 8 skewers that have been soaked in water for at least an hour, place 1 piece of red pepper, then a chunk of pineapple, followed by a chicken thigh half and another red pepper. Repeat with remaining chicken and peppers. Season with salt and pepper. Place skewers on hot grill, cooking for 6 minutes on each side or until the chicken is cooked all the way through. Remove skewers from grill and immediately brush with sweet-and-sour sauce. Serve hot alongside remaining sauce for dipping.

TERIYAKI SHRIMP AND PINEAPPLE SKEWERS

MAKES: 4 servings   **COOK:** 6 to 8 minutes

12 large shrimp, peeled and deveined

¾ cup teriyaki sauce

¾ cup pineapple juice

2 tablespoons soy sauce

1 tablespoon Thai seasoning

12 pineapple chunks

1 tablespoon sesame seeds

1. Soak 4 bamboo skewers in water for at least an hour. Rinse shrimp with cold water and place in a zip-top bag. In a bowl, stir together teriyaki sauce, pineapple juice, soy sauce, and Thai seasoning. Reserve half of the sauce and pour the other half into the bag with the shrimp. Squeeze air from bag and seal. Marinate in refrigerator for 2 to 4 hours.

Outdoor method: Set up a grill for direct cooking over medium heat. Remove shrimp from marinade and discard marinade. Thread 3 shrimp on each skewer, alternating with 3 chunks of pineapple. Oil grate when ready to start cooking. Place skewers on hot, oiled grill. Cook for 3 to 4 minutes per side or until shrimp are opaque and cooked through. Brush liberally with reserved marinade after shrimp have been turned. Turn and brush once more with marinade before transferring to a platter. Serve hot.

Indoor Method: Prepare shrimp skewers and marinade as directed. Preheat broiler and thread 3 shrimp onto each skewer, alternating with 3 chunks of pineapple. Place skewers on a foil-lined baking sheet or broiler pan. Broil 6 to 8 inches from heat source for 2 to 3 minutes per side, or until shrimp are opaque and cooked through, basting liberally with reserved marinade. Serve hot.

TEXAS COWBOY STEAK

MAKES: 4 servings   **COOK:** 24 minutes

2   (about 20-ounce) bone-in rib eye steaks

2   tablespoons olive oil

2   tablespoons steak seasoning

1   (6-ounce) can French Fried Onions—
    French's

2   scallions, thinly sliced for garnish
    Salt and pepper

1. Rub the steaks with olive oil, and then rub with steak seasoning, salt, and pepper. Cover and set aside to allow to come to room temperature, about 30 minutes. Set up a grill for direct cooking over medium-high heat. Oil grate when ready to start cooking. Place steaks on hot oiled grill and cook for 10 to 12 minutes per side for medium (155°F). Transfer steaks to a cutting board, cover, and let rest 10 minutes before serving.

2. Slice 4 to 5 slices out of the eye on the large side of the steak for one portion, leaving some meat on the bone for another portion. Serve garnished with fried onions and scallions.

ZESTY LEMONADE GRILLED CHICKEN

MAKES: 6 servings   **COOK:** 50 minutes

FOR THE CHICKEN:

- 4 pounds chicken breast, thighs, and drumsticks
- 2 tablespoons chicken rub—McCormick Grill Mates
- ¼ teaspoon cayenne pepper

FOR THE LEMONADE BASTING SAUCE:

- 1 stick (½ cup) butter
- ⅓ cup frozen lemonade concentrate, thawed
- ¼ cup soy sauce
- 1 tablespoon hot sauce

1. Rinse chicken under cold water and pat dry with paper towels. Cut away any excess skin. Stir together rub and cayenne pepper, then sprinkle chicken pieces with mixture and pat in.

   Set up a grill for direct cooking over medium heat. Let chicken stand at room temperature for 20 to 30 minutes before grilling.

2. For the basting sauce, melt butter in a small saucepan, stir in all ingredients, and remove from heat.

3. Oil grate when ready to start cooking chicken. Dip chicken pieces in basting sauce and place skin-side down on hot, oiled grill. Cook for 35 to 45 minutes total, turning and basting every few minutes up to the last 2 minutes of cooking. Discard any remaining basting sauce. Chicken is done when it is no longer pink at the bone and the juices run clear (170°F for breast halves; 180°F for thighs and drumsticks). Transfer chicken to a platter and let rest for 5 minutes before serving. Serve hot.

CHERRY PIE POCKETS

MAKES: 6 servings **BAKE:** 40 minutes

FOR THE PIES:

- 1 package double pie crust mix
- 1 (20-ounce) can cherry pie filling
- ½ teaspoon pumpkin pie spice
- 2 tablespoons milk
- 2 teaspoons sugar

FOR THE BLUEBERRY SAUCE:

- 1 pint fresh blueberries; reserve ¼ cup for garnish
- 2 tablespoons sugar
- 2 tablespoons water
- 2 cups vanilla ice cream

1. Preheat oven to 400°F.
2. Prepare pie crust according to package directions. Divide into 6 equal portions, roll into balls, and refrigerate covered for at least 1 hour. On a lightly floured surface, roll each into a circle about ¼-inch thick.
3. *For Pies*: Place each of the rolled-out circles onto the baking sheet. Divide cherry pie filling into the center of each of the 6 pie crusts and sprinkle each with the pumpkin pie spice. Fold the edges of the pie dough over the cherry pie filling, making sure to leave the center of the pie exposed. Place a few of the reserved blueberries on top of each pie. Brush the sides of the pies with milk and sprinkle with 2 teaspoons of the sugar. Place pies in the oven and bake for 30 minutes, or until crust is golden brown and filling is bubbling. Remove from oven and allow to cool slightly.
4. *For Blueberry Sauce*: In a medium sauce pan over medium heat, stir together blueberries, sugar, and two tablespoons water. Bring to a boil, reduce heat, and simmer for 10 minutes. Turn off the heat and allow to cool to room temperature.
5. To serve, place 1 warm pie on 6 plates, and top each pie with a scoop of vanilla ice cream and a generous drizzle of the blueberry sauce.

GRILLED S'MORES CAKES

MAKES: 4 servings **COOK:** 5 minutes

4 pre-made dessert shortcake shells

½ stick (¼ cup) unsalted butter, melted

¼ cup chocolate hazelnut spread

¼ cup crushed graham crackers (about 2 crackers)

½ cup mini marshmallows

¼ cup chocolate sauce

1. Preheat the grill to medium heat.

2. Brush all sides of the shortcakes and a 12-inch square of aluminum foil with the melted butter. Spoon a heaping tablespoon of the chocolate hazelnut spread into the well of each shortcake shell. Sprinkle with about 1 tablespoon crushed graham crackers. Top each with mini marshmallows. Place the prepared foil on top of the grill grate. Place the cakes onto the foil. Close the cover and cook until the marshmallows are browned and toasted, about 5 minutes.

3. Remove from the grill, place on a plate and drizzle with the chocolate sauce.

PEACH FRANGIPANE CROSTATA

MAKES: 8 servings **BAKE:** 28 minutes

1   (15-ounce) can sliced peaches, drained

2   tablespoons sugar, divided use

¼   teaspoon ground ginger

½   teaspoon cinnamon

½   teaspoon cornstarch

½   cup almond cake-and-pastry filling—Solo®

¼   cup, plus more if needed, peach chardonnay—Arbor Mist®, chilled, divided use

1   egg, lightly beaten

1   teaspoon water

1⅓ cups pie crust mix

1   cup whipped topping

1. Preheat oven to 425°F. Line a baking sheet with parchment paper.

2. Toss together peaches, 1 tablespoon sugar, ginger, cinnamon, and cornstarch in a small bowl. Set aside.

3. Stir together almond filling and 2 tablespoons peach chardonnay in a small bowl until well combined. Set aside.

4. Stir pie crust mix and remaining 2 tablespoons peach chardonnay in a medium bowl with a wooden spoon until mixture comes together. (Add more peach chardonnay 1 teaspoon at a time, if needed.) Roll into a ball and turn out onto a lightly floured surface. Roll pie dough into a 10-inch-diameter circle and transfer to prepared baking sheet. Spread half of almond mixture in a thin layer on pie dough, leaving a two-inch border. Starting at the center, arrange peach slices on top of almond layer. Pour any accumulated juices over peaches. Fold border over peaches.

5. Stir together egg and water, then brush mixture on outside crust and sprinkle with remaining 1 tablespoon sugar. Bake in preheated oven for 25 to 28 minutes or until crust is golden brown.

6. Gently stir whipped topping into remaining half of almond mixture. Slice and serve crostata with a dollop of almond cream.

PEACHES 'N CREAM CUPS

MAKES: 4 servings

1   cup heavy cream
1   tablespoon sugar
1   (8-ounce) package cream cheese, at room temperature
1   cup peach preserves
1   teaspoon vanilla extract
1   small peach, sliced, for garnish
4   ladyfinger cookies, for garnish

1. In a large bowl, combine heavy cream and sugar, and whip with a hand mixer until medium peaks form. Cover and set aside in refrigerator.
2. In another large bowl, combine the cream cheese, peach preserves, and vanilla extract, and beat with a hand mixer until light and fluffy. Fold whipped cream into cream cheese mixture.
3. Divide the mixture among 4 dessert glasses and refrigerate. When ready to serve, garnish each with a few slices of peach and a ladyfinger cookie.

TROPICAL FRUIT SPLITS

MAKES: 8 servings   **COOK:** 8 to 10 minutes

¼   cup spiced rum
¾   cup semi-sweet chocolate chips
1   cup heavy cream
½   teaspoon cinnamon extract
½   (20-ounce jar) mango slices
½   (24-ounce) jar papaya slices
½   (10.5-ounce) container fresh pineapple chunks—Ready Pac
      Canola oil cooking spray
1   tablespoon Jamaican jerk seasoning
3   pints macadamia nut ice cream—Häagen-Dazs®
      Sweetened flaked coconut, toasted

1. Add rum to a small saucepan and bring to a boil. Reduce to 2 tablespoons and set aside in a bowl. Wipe pan dry and add chocolate chips and cream. Cook and stir over medium heat until chocolate has melted and is incorporated into the cream.
2. Remove from heat and stir in rum-and-cinnamon extract. Set aside.
3. Set up a grill for direct cooking over medium heat. Brush and oil grate. Drain fruit on paper towels and pat dry. Spray fruit with cooking spray and sprinkle with jerk seasoning. Place on hot, oiled grill and cook for 1 to 2 minutes per side.
4. Divide fruit among serving bowls and top with ice cream and chocolate rum sauce. Serve garnished with toasted coconut.

COCONUTTY GRAPE

MAKES: 4 servings

2   cups grape juice, chilled

1   (12-ounce) can coconut water, chilled

1   lime, juiced

2   cups seltzer water, chilled

6   ounces white rum, optional

1. In a large pitcher, combine grape juice, coconut water, lime juice, and seltzer water. Pour into ice-filled glasses. For a cocktail, add 1½ ounces rum to each glass.

PINEAPPLE-STRAWBERRY SMOOTHIE

MAKES: 2 servings

2   scoops vanilla frozen yogurt

2   cups frozen strawberries

1   (11.5-ounce) can pineapple coconut nectar—Kern's

½   cup coconut rum

1. Puree all ingredients in a blender until smooth. Pour into two 16-ounce glasses. Serve immediately.

SEPTEMBER

To cook al dente pasta, boil 4 to 6 quarts of water per pound of dry pasta. Salt water generously. Stir in the pasta and bring water back to a boil. Cook pasta until it begins to soften and is tender but still firm when you bite into it. Drain pasta in colander.

APRICOT-PEACH BREAKFAST POCKETS

MAKES: 8 servings **BAKE:** 18 minutes

1 egg
1 teaspoon water
1 (16.3-ounce) can butter-flavored
   refrigerated biscuits
8 teaspoons apricot preserves
½ cup raisins
1 cup canned sliced peaches

1. Preheat oven to 350°F. Line a baking sheet with parchment paper and set aside.
2. Lightly whisk egg with water to make an egg wash. Set aside.

3. On a lightly floured surface, use a rolling pin to roll out each biscuit to a 5-inch circle. Take a rolled biscuit and top with 1 teaspoon apricot preserves, 1 tablespoon raisins, and 1 peach slice. Use a pastry brush to brush perimeter of biscuit with egg wash. Fold one side of biscuit over filling to close, and press edges together to seal. Repeat to make 8 pockets.
4. Place pockets on prepared baking sheet and brush tops with remaining egg wash. Bake for 15 to 18 minutes. Remove and let cool to touch.

GRILLED NECTARINES WITH PROSCIUTTO

MAKES: 6 servings   **COOK:** 6 to 15 minutes

1   cup balsamic vinegar
3   ripe nectarines, pitted and quartered
1   (3-ounce) package prosciutto
1   (5-ounce) bag baby arugula
1   package crumbled goat cheese
     Nonstick cooking spray

1. Place vinegar in a small saucepan over medium heat. Bring to a boil and reduce to ⅓ to ½ cup, about 20 to 25 minutes. Set aside to cool.

   Outdoor Method: Set up a grill for direct cooking over medium heat. Oil grate when ready to start cooking. Wrap each quarter nectarine with a piece of prosciutto. Place on hot, oiled grill and cook for 2 to 3 minutes per side.

   Indoor Method: Preheat oven to 400°F. Reduce balsamic vinegar and prepare nectarines as directed. Place nectarines on a foil-lined baking sheet that has been lightly sprayed with cooking spray. Roast nectarines for 12 to 15 minutes or until prosciutto starts to crisp at the edges.

2. To serve, divide arugula among 4 salad plates. Top with grilled nectarines, sprinkle with goat cheese, and drizzle with balsamic reduction.

BLUE CORN CHIP NACHOS WITH PEPPER JACK CHEESE

MAKES: 4 servings   **COOK:** 10 minutes

1   (9-ounce) bag blue corn chips
1   (15-ounce) can red beans, drained and rinsed
1   (15-ounce) can black beans, drained and rinsed
1   (15-ounce) can no-bean chili
2   cups grated pepper jack cheese
1   cup sour cream
1   tablespoon chili powder
4   scallions, finely sliced
½   cup pickled jalapeño slices, for garnish
2   plum tomatoes, diced

1. Preheat grill over medium-high heat.
2. Place a single layer of corn chips on the bottom of four 8 × 5 ¼-inch foil au gratin pans. Sprinkle each with 2 tablespoons of beans, 3 tablespoons chili, and ¼ cup cheese. Repeat to make another layer.
3. Turn heat down to medium-low. Place pans on grill, cover, and cook for about 10 minutes or until cheese is melted, bubbling, and lightly browned.
4. In a small bowl, combine the sour cream and chili powder, and mix until well blended. Top with sour cream mixture, sliced scallions, jalapeño slices, and diced tomatoes.

HEARTY SKILLET RICE

MAKES: 4 servings   **COOK:** 25 minutes

2   tablespoons canola oil, divided use
2   large eggs
1   medium onion, chopped
1   medium zucchini, chopped
¼   pound slice deli ham, diced
¼   teaspoon red pepper flakes
3   cups white or brown rice, cooked
1   tablespoon chopped fresh parsley
    Salt and pepper

1. In a large skillet over medium heat, add 1 tablespoon of oil. Crack the eggs into a bowl and beat them, adding a little salt and pepper to taste. Add the eggs to the skillet and cook until just set. Transfer eggs to a clean bowl and set aside.
2. Put the skillet back onto medium heat and add the remaining 1 tablespoon oil. When the oil is hot, add the onion, zucchini, ham, and red pepper flakes. Cook until the vegetables begin to lightly brown, about 6 to 8 minutes. Add the rice and cook, stirring frequently, until the rice is hot. Stir in the eggs and cook for another minute or two until the eggs are heated through. Serve garnished with parsley.

HERBED FOCACCIA

MAKES: 6 servings   **BAKE:** 28 minutes

3   tablespoons olive oil, divided use
1   (15-ounce) package refrigerated pizza dough, at room temperature
2   teaspoons Italian seasoning
2   plum tomatoes, thinly sliced
½   onion, chopped
1   teaspoon salt
¼   teaspoon freshly ground black pepper

1. Preheat oven to 425°F.
2. Coat a 13 × 9-inch sheet pan with 1 tablespoon of olive oil. Spread out the pizza dough to fit the sheet pan.
3. In a small bowl, mix together the Italian seasoning and remaining olive oil. Brush the seasoned oil all over the top of the dough, making sure to reserve about 2 teaspoons. Using your fingers, punch dimples about halfway down into the dough. Bake for about 8 minutes.
4. Remove the focaccia from the oven, top with tomatoes and diced onion, and sprinkle with salt and pepper. Brush with remaining oil mixture, return to the oven, and bake until the focaccia is gold brown, about 15 to 20 minutes. Cut into squares and serve warm with Tuscan Peasant Soup with Tortellini.

PUMPED-UP POTATO SALAD

MAKES: 4 servings   **COOK:** 20 minutes

- 1 (24-ounce) package prepared mashed potatoes
- 1 cup elbow macaroni (uncooked about 4 ounces)
- ¼ cup honey mustard dressing
- ¼ cup mayonnaise
- ¼ cup sour cream
- 1 tablespoon apple cider vinegar
- 1 cup pre-shredded carrots
- 2 celery stalks, finely chopped
- 2 hard-boiled eggs, chopped
- 1 red bell pepper, finely chopped
- 2 scallions, sliced
- Salt and pepper, to taste

1. Bring a large pot of water to a boil over high heat. Add a big pinch of salt and the pasta, and cook according to the package directions until the pasta is tender. Drain the pasta, rinse with cold water, and set aside.
2. In a large bowl, mix together the honey mustard dressing, mayonnaise, sour cream, and apple cider vinegar. Add the pasta, potatoes, carrots, celery, eggs, and bell peppers. Mix until all the ingredients are well coated.
3. Taste and adjust the seasoning with salt and pepper. Refrigerate until ready to serve. When ready, put into a serving bowl and garnish with the scallions.

SHOESTRING FRIES WITH CREAMY KETCHUP

MAKES: 4 servings   **COOK:** 20 minutes

FOR THE FRIES:
- 2 russet potatoes
- 1½ cups canola oil
- Salt, to taste

FOR THE KETCHUP:
- ¼ cup ketchup
- 2 tablespoons sour cream

1. Wash and peel potatoes and cut into sticks ¼-inch thick. Rinse under hot tap water and drain well. Dry potatoes between several sheets of paper towels. In a 12-inch skillet, over medium heat, add the oil and heat to 360°F. Add the potatoes and fry until golden brown and crisp. Drain fries on a paper towel–lined plate and sprinkle with salt to taste.
2. For the creamy ketchup, mix together the ketchup and sour cream and serve with the fries.

SWEET POTATO FRIES

MAKES: 4 servings   **BAKE:** 20 minutes

2   sweet potatoes, washed

3   tablespoons canola oil

1   tablespoon low-sodium chili seasoning mix
Salt and pepper, to taste

1. Preheat oven to 400°F. Place a baking sheet in the oven.

2. Slice the sweet potatoes in half lengthwise. Slice each half into 6 wedges. Place wedges in a large bowl and add oil. Season with chili seasoning mix, salt, and pepper and toss to coat all the fries.

3. Place the fries on the hot baking sheet and bake for 15 to 20 minutes, turning fries halfway to crisp on both sides.

TRICOLOR POTATO SALAD

MAKES: 4 servings   **COOK:** 15 minutes

- ½ pound Yukon gold potatoes, washed and cut into 1-inch cubes
- ½ pound sweet potatoes, washed and cut into 1-inch cubes
- ½ pound purple potatoes, washed and cut into 1-inch cubes
- 1 tablespoon salt, divided use
- ½ cup mayonnaise
- ½ cup sour cream
- 2 tablespoons brown mustard
- 1 tablespoon cider vinegar
- ½ teaspoon grill seasoning
- 3 scallions, sliced

1. Place the Yukon gold and sweet potatoes in a large pot, cover with water, and add 2 teaspoons of salt. Bring to a light boil over medium heat and boil for 12 to 15 minutes or until potatoes are tender but still hold their shape. Drain and let cool until just slightly warm.

2. Place the purple potatoes in a medium pot, cover with water, and add 1 teaspoon of salt. Bring to a light boil over medium heat and boil for 10 to 12 minutes or until potatoes are tender but still hold their shape. Drain and let cool until just slightly warm.

3. In a large bowl, combine remaining ingredients and mix until blended. Add potatoes and gently mix until all potatoes are completely coated.

TURKEY SAUSAGE PASTRY WRAPS

MAKES: 4 servings **COOK:** 45 minutes

1 sheet frozen puff pastry, thawed
Flour, for dusting board

1 teaspoon vegetable oil

1 tablespoon butter

1 cup frozen seasoning blend—PictSweet, thawed

10 (1-ounce) smoked turkey sausage links—Jennie-O, casings removed

1 teaspoon poultry seasoning—McCormick

½ teaspoon salt

¼ teaspoon pepper

⅓ cup bread crumbs

1 egg, lightly beaten with 1 teaspoon water
Maple syrup, for serving

1. Preheat oven to 400°F.

2. Unroll puff pastry sheet on a lightly floured surface and fold in half. Roll sheet into a 18 × 6-inch rectangle with a rolling pin. Refrigerate until ready to use.

3. Heat oil and butter in a small skillet over medium-high heat. Add seasoning blend and sauté until tender, about 5 minutes. Remove from heat and cool completely.

4. Mix turkey sausage, poultry seasoning, salt, pepper, bread crumbs, and cooled seasoning blend in a large bowl. Shape into a long roll and place off-center on puff pastry rectangle. Brush egg wash on the perimeter of puff pastry with a pastry brush. Tightly fold one side of pastry over sausage roll and press edges securely together.

5. Slice roll gently with a floured, sharp knife to make 8 rolls. Make 3 small slashes on the top of each roll and place on an ungreased baking sheet. Refrigerate for 15 minutes.

6. Brush the top of each roll with egg wash. Bake in preheated oven for 35 to 40 minutes or until puffed and golden brown. Remove and cool for 10 minutes. Serve warm with maple syrup.

5-SPICE BRINED PORK CHOPS WITH SPICY HOISIN SAUCE

MAKES: 4 servings   **COOK:** 20 minutes

FOR THE CHOPS:

- 4   center-cut bone-in pork chops, 1-inch thick
- 2   cups water, divided use
- 2   tablespoons salt
- 2   tablespoons brown sugar
- 1   tablespoon five-spice powder
- 1   tablespoon soy sauce
- 1   tablespoon crushed garlic
- 1   tablespoon chopped ginger
- 2   scallions, finely chopped

FOR THE SAUCE:

- ½   cup hoisin sauce
- 2   tablespoons rice vinegar
- 1   tablespoon soy sauce
- ½   teaspoon red pepper flakes
- 1   teaspoon crushed garlic
- 1   teaspoon chopped ginger
   Nonstick cooking spray

1. Rinse chops with cold water and pat dry with paper towels, then place in a large zip-top bag and set aside.

2. In a small pan, combine ½ cup water, salt, and sugar. Bring to a boil, reduce heat, and simmer until sugar and salt have dissolved. Remove from heat. Stir in 1½ cups cold water, five-spice powder, soy sauce, garlic, ginger, and scallions. Pour mixture over chops in bag. Squeeze air from bag and seal. Marinate in refrigerator 2 to 4 hours.

3. For the spicy hoisin sauce, add all sauce ingredients to a small saucepan. Bring to a boil, reduce heat, and simmer for 5 minutes. Set aside until ready to grill.

Outdoor Method: Set up a grill for direct cooking over medium heat. Oil grate when ready to start cooking. Let pork chops sit at room temperature for 30 minutes. Remove from brine and pat dry with paper towels. Discard brine. Lightly spray both sides of the chops with cooking spray, and place chops on hot, oiled grill. Cook for 5 to 6 minutes per side or until slightly pink in the centers and juices run clear (160°F). Remove from grill and brush with hoisin sauce. Serve hot with extra hoisin sauce on the side.

Indoor Method: Prepare chops and sauce as directed. Preheat broiler. Place pork chops on a foil-lined baking sheet or broiler pan. Broil 6 to 8 inches from heat source for 5 to 6 minutes per side, or until slightly pink in the centers and juices run clear (160°F). Remove and brush with hoisin sauce. Serve hot with extra hoisin sauce on the side.

AUSSIE LAMB ON THE BARBIE

MAKES: 4 servings   **COOK:** 12 minutes

8   lamb loin chops, 1 to 1½ inches thick
1   (11.5-ounce) can mango nectar
1   (1-ounce) packet onion soup mix
1   teaspoon yellow curry powder
2   teaspoons chopped ginger
2   teaspoons steak seasoning

1. Rinse lamb chops under cold water and pat dry with paper towels. Place in a large zip-top bag and set aside. In a bowl, stir together remaining ingredients, except steak seasoning. Pour marinade into the bag with the lamb chops. Squeeze air from bag and seal. Gently massage bag to coat the lamb. Marinate in the refrigerator for 3 hours or as long as overnight.

Outdoor Method: Preheat grill to medium-high heat. Let chops sit at room temperature for 30 minutes. Brush and oil grate when ready to start cooking. Remove chops from marinade and discard marinade. Season chops with steak seasoning and place on hot, oiled grill. Cook 10 to 12 minutes total for medium (135°–140°F), turning every few minutes. Watch for flare-ups. Remove and let lamb chops rest for 5 minutes before serving. Serve hot.

ASIAN INSPIRED SLOPPY JOES

MAKES: 4 servings   **COOK:** 35 minutes

FOR THE SAUCE:
1   (15-ounce) can tomato sauce
¼   cup soy sauce
2   tablespoons tomato paste
1   teaspoon chopped ginger
1   teaspoon chopped garlic
1   teaspoon hot sauce
¼   cup light brown sugar
2   tablespoons cider vinegar

FOR THE PORK:
2   teaspoons canola oil
1   green bell pepper, chopped
1   medium onion, chopped
1   pound ground pork
2   green cabbage leaves
4   hamburger buns, toasted
    Salt and pepper, to taste

1. For the tomato hoisin sauce, whisk together all ingredients in a bowl until blended. Set aside.
2. In a large skillet over medium heat, add the oil. When it is hot, add the pepper and onion and cook until soft, about 6 to 8 minutes. Push the vegetables to one side of the pan and add the

ground pork. Break up any lumps and season with salt and pepper. Cook until the pork is lightly browned, about 6 to 8 minutes. Spoon some of the fat out and discard it. Add the sauce to the pan, bring to a simmer, and cook until pork mixture has thickened but is still a bit loose, about 15 to 20 minutes.

3. Remove 2 outer leaves from a cabbage, roll them up like a cigar, and slice them into very thin strips. Divide the sloppy joe mixture among the hamburger buns. Garnish with the sliced cabbage and serve.

BAKED CHICKEN NUGGETS WITH SWEET MUSTARD

MAKES: 6 servings   **COOK:** 20 minutes

FOR THE CHICKEN NUGGETS:

2   pieces (about 3 lbs) chicken breast with ribs

¼   cup all-purpose flour

1   egg

1   cup panko bread crumbs

1   teaspoon poultry seasoning

Salt and pepper, to taste

FOR THE SWEET MUSTARD:

¼   cup brown mustard

1   tablespoon packed brown sugar

1. Preheat oven broiler to 350°F. Line a baking sheet with parchment paper and set aside.

2. Rinse the chicken and pat dry with paper towels. Remove chicken breasts from the bone and cut into 2-inch "nuggets."

3. Put the chicken in a zip-top plastic bag with the flour, shake to coat, and set aside. Whisk the egg in a bowl and set aside. Season the bread crumbs with poultry seasoning, salt, and pepper, and put in a shallow dish or pie plate. Remove chicken from bag and shake off excess flour. Coat in the egg, than dredge the chicken in the panko bread crumbs. Place in a single layer on baking sheet, allowing space in between.

4. Bake for 15 to 20 minutes or until golden brown and chicken is cooked through.

5. For the sweet mustard, combine the mustard and brown sugar in a small saucepan over medium heat. Heat just until the sugar dissolves completely. Cool to room temperature and serve with the chicken nuggets.

BLACK BEAN BURGERS

MAKES: 4 servings   **COOK:** 20 minutes

½   medium yellow onion, roughly chopped

1   tablespoon chopped garlic

2   (15-ounce) cans black beans, rinsed and drained

2   tablespoons chopped fresh cilantro

2   tablespoons chopped fresh parsley

1   egg

½   teaspoon red pepper flakes

½   cup bread crumbs

2   tablespoons canola oil

4   hamburger buns

     Salt and pepper, to taste

OPTIONAL TOPPINGS:

4   small Romaine lettuce leaves, or any other type you have on hand

1   tomato, sliced

¼   cup ketchup

1. Heat a grill pan over medium-high heat.

2. In a food processor, pulse onion and garlic until finely chopped. Add 1 can black beans, cilantro, parsley, egg, and red pepper flakes, and pulse to combine. Transfer mixture to a large mixing bowl, add the remaining can of black beans and the bread crumbs. Season with salt and pepper, to taste, and mix until well combined.

3. Divide remaining mixture into 4 portions and form into patties. Place on hot, oiled grill over medium-low heat and cook about 6 minutes a side or until heated through. Toast hamburger buns on a grill. Place a burger on the bottom of each bun. Top with lettuce, tomato, and ketchup. Cover the burgers with the tops of the buns and serve.

CHATEAUBRIAND WITH GRILLED ARTICHOKES AND BÉARNAISE SAUCE

MAKES: 4 servings   **COOK:** 30 minutes

1   (2-pound) center-cut beef tenderloin

1   tablespoon garlic salt

2   teaspoons black pepper

1   tablespoon plus 1 teaspoon herbes de Provence, divided use

1   (8-ounce) box frozen artichokes, thawed

½   cup balsamic vinaigrette

1   teaspoon crushed garlic

1   (6-ounce) can hollandaise sauce—Aunt Penny's

1   teaspoon white wine vinegar

1   teaspoon dried tarragon, crushed

2   cups canola oil, as needed for grilling

1. Trim away any excess fat from meat, rinse under cold water, then pat dry with paper towels. Season with garlic salt, pepper, and 1 tablespoon herbes de Provence, and set aside. Thread artichokes onto 4 wooden skewers that have been soaked in water for at least an hour and place in a shallow pan. Stir together vinaigrette, garlic, and remaining herbes de Provence. Pour over artichokes and set aside.

Outdoor Method: Set up a gas grill for direct cooking over high heat. Oil grate when ready to start cooking. Place beef on hot, oiled grill and sear for 3 to 4 minutes per side. Reduce heat to medium and continue cooking another 15 minutes, turning occasionally, about 25 to 30 minutes total or until internal temperature reaches 150°F for medium. During the last 10 minutes, place artichokes on grill for 3 to 4 minutes per side. Remove beef and artichokes to a platter and tent with foil for 10 minutes before serving.

2. Meanwhile, stir together hollandaise, vinegar, and tarragon in a microwave-safe bowl. Microwave for 30-second intervals until heated through, stirring each time.

3. Slice beef into 4 thick servings. Serve immediately with artichokes and béarnaise sauce.

Indoor Method: Preheat oven to 425°F. Prepare beef and artichokes (omit skewers) as directed above. Heat ⅛-inch canola oil in a heavy-bottomed skillet over high heat. When oil is very hot, add beef and brown for 2 to 4 minutes per side. Transfer to a roasting pan with a wire rack. Roast in preheated oven for 25 to 35 minutes per pound or until internal temperature reaches 150°F for medium. Add artichokes to pan for the last 15 minutes of roasting. While meat is roasting, prepare sauce as directed above. Remove beef and artichokes to a platter and tent with foil for 10 minutes before serving. Slice beef into 4 thick servings. Serve immediately with artichokes and béarnaise sauce.

CHERRY SPICED
PORK CHOPS

MAKES: 4 servings   **COOK:** 50 minutes

- 4   center-cut pork chops, 1-inch thick
- 1   teaspoon ground allspice—McCormick
- 1   teaspoon garlic salt
      Freshly ground black pepper, to taste
- ½   cup olive oil
- 1   cup frozen pitted cherries—Dole, thawed
- ½   cup frozen chopped onions
- ½   cup cherry preserves
- ½   cup balsamic vinegar

1. Rinse pork chops under cold water and pat dry with paper towels. Season pork chops with allspice, garlic salt, and black pepper.
2. In a large skillet, thoroughly brown pork chops on both sides in olive oil. Remove pork and set aside.
3. Drain excess fat from pan and add remaining ingredients to make cherry sauce. Bring to a boil and reduce to a simmer, stirring constantly until preserves have melted.
4. Return pork chops to pan with any accumulated juices. Cover and simmer 30 to 40 minutes or until pork is cooked through. Serve hot with cherry sauce.

HAWAIIAN
PULLED PORK

MAKES: 6 servings   **COOK:** 4 to 6 hours

FOR THE PORK:
- 3½   pounds pork shoulder roast
- 1   (1.06-ounce) packet teriyaki marinade mix—McCormick Grill Mates
- ¼   cup paprika
      Hawaiian sweet rolls—King's, for serving

FOR THE MOP SAUCE:
- ½   cup pineapple juice
- ½   cup teriyaki sauce
- ½   cup Hawaiian marinade
- 1   cup chili sauce

1. Rinse pork roast with cold water, pat dry, and set aside. In a bowl, combine teriyaki mix and paprika. Coat roast with rub mixture, patting until all rub is used. Place in a zip-top bag. Squeeze out air and seal. Let cure in refrigerator 1 to 3 hours. Prepare sauce by combining all sauce ingredients in saucepan. Bring to a boil, reduce heat, and simmer for 10 minutes. Remove from heat and set aside.
2. Turn grill to medium heat. Oil grate when ready to start cooking. Let pork sit at room temperature for 30 to 40 minutes before grilling.
3. Oil grate. Place roast over a drip pan on heated grill. Cook covered 4 to 6 hours or until internal temperature reaches 180°–190°F. If using charcoal, add 10 briquettes to each pile of coals every hour. Brush roast with sauce at hourly intervals and every 15 minutes during last hour of cooking. Remove from grill and chop meat. Serve on sweet rolls with sauce on the side.

OVEN BAKED FRIED CHICKEN

MAKES: 4 servings   **BAKE:** 40 minutes

2   pieces each chicken legs, thighs, and wings
1   cup buttermilk
1   teaspoon hot sauce
2   cups panko bread crumbs
1   teaspoon garlic powder
1   teaspoon onion powder
    Salt and pepper, to taste

1. Rinse the chicken pieces under cold water, pat dry with paper towels, and put into a large bowl or baking dish. Set aside. In a small bowl, mix together buttermilk with the hot sauce. Pour over chicken pieces and turn to completely coat. Cover and let sit in the refrigerator for 30 minutes.

2. Preheat oven to 350°F. Line a baking sheet with parchment paper.

3. In a large zip-top bag, combine the bread crumbs, garlic powder, and onion powder. Remove chicken pieces from buttermilk and drain excess liquid. Place chicken in bag with bread crumb mixture and shake to coat completely. Place chicken on baking sheet and bake for 30 to 40 minutes until bread crumbs are golden brown and chicken reaches an internal temperature of 175°F.

PEPPER AND ONION PERSONAL PIZZAS

MAKES: 6 pieces   **BAKE:** 18 minutes

1 (13.8-ounce) can refrigerated pizza crust dough

   Nonstick cooking spray

¾ cup Alfredo sauce

¼ cup pesto sauce

1 (12-ounce) jar roasted red peppers, drained and sliced

1 (14-ounce) can artichoke hearts, drained and quartered

½ cup frozen chopped onions, thawed

1½ cups shredded mozzarella cheese

1. Preheat oven to 400°F. Spray a baking sheet with cooking spray.
2. Roll out and stretch dough onto the baking sheet. Using a pizza cutter, slice the dough into 6 squares.
3. In a small bowl, mix together the Alfredo sauce and pesto. Evenly spread the sauce on each of the 6 dough squares, making sure not to go all the way to the edge, so as to leave a crust. Top each with some red peppers, artichoke hearts, onions, and ¼ cup of cheese.
4. Bake for 15 to 18 minutes or until crust is golden brown and cheese is bubbling.

PLUM, BLUE CHEESE, AND WALNUT STUFFED PORK CHOPS

MAKES: 6 servings   **COOK:** 35 minutes

FOR THE CHOPS:

Nonstick cooking spray

6 (10-ounce) double-cut pork chops

1 teaspoon salt

1 teaspoon freshly ground black pepper

1 tablespoon olive oil

FOR THE STUFFING:

½ cup chopped walnuts

½ cup crumbled blue cheese

1 (15-ounce) can plums in heavy syrup, pitted, chopped, juice reserved

1 tablespoon minced fresh thyme

2 tablespoons bread crumbs

FOR THE SAUCE:

3 cups Merlot wine

Reserved juice from canned plums, strained

6 cloves garlic, peeled

¼ teaspoon salt

½ teaspoon black pepper

2 tablespoons red currant jelly

1 tablespoon honey

3 tablespoons butter, cold and cubed

1. Preheat oven to 400°F. Spray a rimmed baking sheet with cooking spray.

2. For the chops, rinse under cold water and pat dry with paper towels. Rub salt and pepper on chops. Cut a pocket into each pork chop by carefully inserting a sharp paring knife into the long side of the chop. Make the opening small but the pocket large enough to insert stuffing. If the opening is too large, stuffing will ooze out during cooking.

3. For the stuffing, combine stuffing ingredients in a medium bowl, adding just enough bread crumbs to absorb the juice. Stuff pork chops with a thin, even layer of stuffing, about ⅓ cup per chop.

4. Heat oil in a large skillet over high heat. When hot, add the stuffed chops and cook until browned, about 3 minutes per side. Transfer to baking sheet and bake for 10 to 12 minutes or until golden brown. Meat should register 150°F on a thermometer inserted into the meat, not into the stuffing.

5. For the sauce, heat the skillet in which you cooked the chops over high heat. When hot, remove pan from heat and whisk in the wine. Return to heat. Add reserved plum juice and garlic. Bring to a boil and reduce to 2 cups, about 12 to 15 minutes. Whisk in salt, pepper, currant jelly, and honey, and heat through. Discard garlic, remove pan from heat, and whisk in the butter gradually. To serve, lay chops on serving plates and cover with sauce.

SWORDFISH WITH THAI DRESSING

MAKES: 4 servings   **COOK:** 8 minutes

⅓ cup sesame ginger dressing

¼ cup sweet chili sauce—Lee Kum Kee

2 tablespoons lime juice

¼ cup finely chopped mint

2 tablespoons finely chopped cilantro

4 (6-ounce) swordfish steaks

   Nonstick cooking spray

   Salt and pepper, to taste

1. Preheat broiler. Whisk together dressing, chili sauce, lime juice, mint, and cilantro in a small mixing bowl. Set aside.

2. Season swordfish with salt and pepper and place on a foil-lined baking sheet or broiler pan that has been sprayed with cooking spray. Lightly spray the swordfish. Broil 4 to 6 inches from heat source for 3 to 4 minutes per side. Serve steaks immediately with a spoonful of dressing.

THIN CRUST PIZZA WITH FIGS, SWEET ONION, AND BLUE CHEESE

MAKES: 6 servings   **BAKE:** 17 minutes

   Nonstick cooking spray

1 (13.8-ounce) can refrigerated pizza crust dough

¼ cup balsamic salad dressing

2 cups shredded Monterey Jack cheese

½ sweet onion, thinly sliced

4 fresh figs, sliced

½ cup crumbled blue cheese—Sargento

1. Preheat oven to 425°F. Lightly spray a cookie sheet with cooking spray.

2. Unroll pizza dough and place on cookie sheet. Stretch dough to about 9 by 13 inches and bake in preheated oven for 7 minutes. Remove from oven and brush balsamic dressing over crust, leaving a 1-inch border. Top with shredded cheese, onion, sliced figs, and blue cheese. Return to oven for 8 to 10 minutes or until crust is golden and cheese is melted and beginning to bubble. Serve hot.

BROWN SUGAR BANANA SPICE CAKE

MAKES: 8 servings   **COOK:** 8 hours

Nonstick cooking spray

2 cups baking mix—Bisquick®

¾ cup sugar

2 ½ teaspoons pumpkin pie spice, divided use

2 ripe bananas, mashed

1 egg

¼ cup canola oil

¼ cup light brown sugar

FOR THE CHOCOLATE WHIPPED CREAM:

½ pint whipping cream

3 tablespoons powdered sugar

1 tablespoon cocoa powder

1. Lightly spray a 6-cup loaf pan with cooking spray. In a large mixing bowl, combine baking mix, 2 teaspoons pumpkin pie spice, bananas, egg, and oil. Using a hand mixer, beat batter for 2 minutes. Remove ½ cup batter and place in a small bowl with brown sugar and remaining ½ teaspoon pumpkin pie spice. Mix well and reserve. Make a foil ring and place on bottom of slow cooker. Place loaf pan on top of foil ring.

2. Cover slow cooker with 5 paper towels before securing with lid. Cook on low setting until tester comes out clean, about 4 hours Cool cake on wire rack.

3. For the chocolate whipped cream, beat cream with a hand mixer until it starts to thicken. Add powdered sugar and cocoa and continue beating until whipped. Serve with banana spice cake.

GAME DAY CAKE

MAKES: 24 servings   **BAKE:** 45 minutes

Nonstick baking spray

2 (18.25-ounce) boxes chocolate fudge cake mix, divided use

6 eggs, divided use

1 cup vegetable oil, divided use

2⅔ cups low-fat chocolate milk, divided use

2 teaspoons mint extract, divided use

2 (16-ounce) cans buttercream frosting

3 cups sweetened coconut flakes

Green food coloring

FOR THE COOKIES:

1 (17.25-ounce) package sugar cookie mix

½ cup all-purpose flour

4 tablespoons butter, softened

¼ cup cream cheese, softened

1 egg

1 teaspoon lemon extract—McCormick

Flour, for dusting board

FOR THE ICING:

1 pound powdered sugar

¼ cup pasteurized egg whites

1 teaspoon lemon extract

Food coloring

1. Preheat oven to 350°F. Lightly spray one 10-inch, one 8-inch, and two 6-inch round cake pans with baking spray.

2. For cake mix, prepare each box of cake mix separately, combining 1 cake mix, 3 eggs, ½ cup vegetable oil, 1⅓ cups chocolate milk, and 1 teaspoon mint extract in a large mixing bowl. Beat on medium speed for 2 minutes. Transfer to the 4 prepared pans so that the batter is the same height in each pan. Bake in preheated oven for 30 to 35 minutes. The 6-inch cakes will finish baking about 5 minutes before the others. Let cakes cool.

3. For the cookies, preheat oven to 375°F. Line baking sheet(s) with kitchen parchment.

4. Whisk together cookie mix and flour in a large mixing bowl to combine. Stir in butter, cream cheese, egg, and lemon extract until a soft dough forms.

5. Split dough in half and shape each half into a disk. Roll out on a lightly floured surface to ¼-inch thick. Using 2 to 3-inch sports-themed cookie-cutters, cut out cookies. Scraps can be gathered up and rerolled once with good results. Chill cookies in refrigerator for 15 minutes before baking. Bake in preheated oven for 9 to 11 minutes or until edges are just golden. Cool on baking sheet for 2 minutes, then cool completely and decorate with colored icing.

6. For the icing, combine ingredients in a medium mixing bowl. Beat on low speed until incorporated, then beat on medium speed until medium peaks form. If icing is too thin, add more powdered sugar. Thin with a few drops of water if too stiff. Color if desired. Use immediately to frost cookies.

7. To decorate, if cakes have crowned, level the tops with a serrated knife. Trim one of the 6-inch cakes to 4 inches in diameter. Tint the frosting and the coconut with green food coloring. Frost between the layers, and then stack the cakes largest to smallest. Now frost the sides of the cake and press coconut into each layer. Finish decorating with cookies around the perimeter of the cake layers.

CHERRY LATTICE PIE

MAKES: 8 servings **BAKE:** 40 minutes

- 1 (21-ounce) can cherry pie filling
- 12 ounces frozen mixed berries, thawed and drained
- 1 tablespoon cherry liqueur
- 1 (15-ounce) package refrigerated pie crust
  Flour for dusting
- 1 egg, lightly beaten
- 1 tablespoon sugar for sprinkling

1. Preheat oven to 375°F.
2. In a large bowl, combine cherry pie filling, mixed berries, and cherry liqueur. Set aside.
3. Gently press 1 sheet of pie crust into a flour-dusted 9-inch pie plate. Pour berry filling into unbaked crust. Using a pie plate as a guide, cut a circle for the top crust from second sheet of pie crust. Use a generously floured lattice pie-top cutter to cut a pattern from the circle. Top pie with lattice top. Press along rim to seal, and trim edges. Press fork into edges or crimp to make decorative edge. Brush top crust with beaten egg and sprinkle lightly with sugar.
4. Bake in preheated oven about 40 minutes or until filling bubbles. Cover pie with foil halfway through baking to prevent overbrowning. Let stand for 20 minutes before serving.

CHOCOLATE RICE PUDDING

MAKES: 4 servings **COOK:** 15 minutes

- 3 cups whole milk
- 2 cups cooked rice
- ½ cup sugar
- 1 pinch salt
- 1 teaspoon vanilla extract
- ½ cup chocolate chips

1. In a medium pot over medium heat, stir together the milk, rice, sugar, and pinch of salt. Bring to a boil, turn the heat to low, cover, and cook until the mixture is thickened, about 10 minutes. Remove from the heat, stir in the vanilla and chocolate chips, and let rest for 5 minutes. Serve warm or cover and cool in refrigerator for at least 1 hour.

SLOW COOKER CHEESECAKE WITH PEACH TOPPING

MAKES: 8 servings   **COOK:** 1 hour 30 minutes

FOR THE CHEESECAKE:

- 1 (15-ounce) container ricotta cheese
- ¾ cup sugar
- 3 eggs
- 1 teaspoon vanilla extract
- 1 orange, zested
- 1 pinch salt
- 1 (9-inch) prepared graham cracker crust

FOR THE TOPPING:

- 1 (15-ounce) can peaches, chopped, juice reserved
- 1 orange, juiced
- 2 teaspoons cornstarch
- 1 tablespoon sugar
- 1 pinch salt

1. Puree ricotta cheese in a food processor until smooth. Scrape down the sides, add sugar, and puree for approximately 1 minute so that it is not grainy. Add the eggs, vanilla, orange zest, and salt. Puree until smooth.

2. Place a small bowl in the bottom of a 5-quart slow cooker and place a small plate on top of the bowl. Place pie crust on top of the plate and pour the filling into the crust. Place 4 paper towels over the top of slow cooker bowl, making sure not to let the towels touch the top of the cheesecake. Secure with lid and cook on high setting for 1½ hours or until set. Remove from slow cooker and let sit for 30 minutes, then refrigerate for 30 minutes or until chilled.

3. For the topping, whisk together the reserved peach juice, orange juice, cornstarch, sugar, and salt in a saucepan. Stir in the chopped peaches and heat over medium heat. Cook until liquid thickens, about 5 minutes. Remove from heat and serve warm over a slice of cheesecake.

PEACH AND WHITE CHOCOLATE MELBA PIZZA

MAKES: 6 servings   **COOK:** 15 minutes

¼ cup heavy cream

1 cup white chocolate chips

1 (13.8-ounce) can refrigerated pizza crust dough

1 (16-ounce) bag frozen peaches, thawed and chopped

½ cup raspberry pie filling

2 tablespoons slivered almonds, toasted
  Nonstick cooking spray

1. Pour cream into a small microwave-safe bowl, and microwave until very hot, about 45 to 60 seconds. Add chips and stir until they begin to melt. Place bowl in microwave, stirring at 30-second intervals, until the chips have melted and are incorporated into the cream. Set aside until cooled and spreadable.

Outdoor Method: Set up a grill for direct cooking over medium heat. Brush and oil grate when ready to start cooking. Carefully remove pizza dough from can. Unroll dough and gently place on hot, well-oiled grill. Let cook 3 minutes, and turn over using a cookie sheet. Cover grill and cook for an additional 5 to 7 minutes and remove. Spread with white chocolate spread and top with chopped peaches. Drop teaspoonfuls of raspberry pie filling all over pizza and sprinkle with slivered almonds.

Indoor Method: Prepare white chocolate spread as directed. Preheat oven to 425°F. Lightly spray a baking sheet with cooking spray and set aside. Carefully unroll dough and place on prepared baking sheet. Press out dough with fingers to form a 13 × 9-inch rectangle. Bake in preheated oven for 7 to 10 minutes or until crust begins to brown. Remove crust from oven and top as directed above.

SPICED CAKE WITH ALMONDS AND CARAMELIZED ORANGES

MAKES: 12 servings   **BAKE:** 35 minutes

Nonstick cooking spray

1 (18.25-ounce) box spice cake mix—Betty Crocker

1½ cups vanilla low-fat yogurt

3 eggs

1 cup water

1 cup sugar

2 tablespoons garam masala, divided use

1 orange, thinly sliced

1 (16-ounce) can cream cheese frosting

2 cups sliced almonds, toasted

1. Preheat oven to 350°F. Lightly coat two 8-inch cake pans with cooking spray. Set aside.

2. For the cake, combine cake mix, yogurt, and eggs in a large mixing bowl. Beat with an electric mixer on low speed for 30 seconds. Scrape down sides of bowl and beat on medium speed for 2 more minutes. Pour batter into prepared cake pans and bake in preheated oven for 30 to 35 minutes or until a tester inserted into center comes out clean. Cool cakes in pans for 10 minutes and then turn out onto wire racks to cool completely.

3. For the caramelized oranges, combine water, sugar, and 1 tablespoon garam masala in a large skillet. Bring mixture to a boil and boil for 5 minutes. Add orange slices and continue boiling for an additional 5 minutes. With tongs, carefully remove orange slices and place on waxed paper to cool.

4. To assemble, combine frosting and remaining 1 tablespoon of garam masala in a small bowl. Spread cake with a thin layer of frosting between layers and on top and sides. (The frosting is just the "glue" for the almonds and oranges.) Gently press toasted sliced almonds onto side of cake. Arrange caramelized orange slices on top of cake.

OCTOBER

Favorite Baked Macaroni
and Cheese, p. 308

Pot Roast with Roasted
Vegetables, p. 320

Hot Spiced Cider, p. 333

BEER BISCUITS

MAKES: 4 servings **BAKE:** 10 minutes

1 cup beer
2¼ cups baking mix—Bisquick®
2 tablespoons sugar

1. Preheat oven to 375°F.
2. In a large mixing bowl, mix all ingredients with a whisk until just combined. Using 2 spoons, divide dough into 4 even mounds and put on a baking sheet. Bake for 8 to 10 minutes until golden brown.

CRISPY FINGERLING POTATOES

MAKES: 6 servings **COOK:** 40 minutes

1½ pounds fingerling potatoes
¼ cup olive oil
1 tablespoon grill seasoning
2 teaspoons paprika
Pepper, to taste

1. Put the potatoes into a large pot and cover with water. Add a big pinch of salt, cover, and bring to a boil over high heat. Uncover and cook for 10 minutes, just until potatoes start to soften but are not cooked all the way through. Drain potatoes and return them to the warm pot. Shake potatoes around to roughen up the sides. Let them dry out and sit in the warm pot.
2. Preheat oven to 425°F. Place a baking sheet in the oven to preheat.
3. Add the olive oil, grill seasoning, paprika, and pepper to the potatoes and toss to coat. Spread potatoes out on the hot baking sheet and roast them until cooked through and crispy, about 20 to 25 minutes, flipping once halfway through. Remove the potatoes from the oven to a serving bowl and serve.

CHICKEN SAUSAGE PO'BOY WITH APPLE SLAW

MAKES: 4 servings   **COOK:** 8 minutes

⅓   cup mayonnaise

⅓   cup ranch dressing

1   cup apple, finely diced

1   (approx. 16-ounce) bag cole slaw mix

¼   cup finely chopped fresh parsley

1   (12-ounce) package chicken and apple sausages

4   hoagie sandwich rolls

Dijon mustard, for serving

1. In a large bowl, stir together mayonnaise, ranch dressing, apple, slaw mix, and parsley. Toss until well combined. Cover and chill in the refrigerator until ready to serve.

2. Preheat broiler. Place sausages on a wire rack over a foil-lined baking sheet or broiler pan. Cook 6 to 8 inches from heat source for 3 to 4 minutes per side. To serve, spread rolls liberally with mustard, add the sausages, and top with plenty of apple slaw.

FAST FOOD CHEESE BURGERS

MAKES: 4 servings   **COOK:** 8 minutes

½   pound ground beef, 80 percent lean

Salt and freshly ground black pepper

4   slices American cheese

¼   cup ketchup

¼   cup sour cream

1   tablespoon mayonnaise

4   hamburger buns

¼   head iceberg lettuce, shredded

2   dill pickles, sliced

1. Divide the ground beef. Shape into 4 patties and season with salt and pepper. Place in a skillet that has been sprayed with nonstick cooking spray over medium-high heat and cook patties 3 minutes on each side. In the last minute of cooking, top the meat patties with cheese so it will melt.

2. In a small bowl, mix together the ketchup, sour cream, and mayonnaise, spread half onto the hamburger buns, and reserve the leftover for a dipping sauce for french fries. Place the burgers on the buns and top with lettuce and pickles.

SPICED PUMPKIN SOUP

MAKES: 6 servings **COOK:** 30 minutes

1 cup frozen chopped onions—Ore-Ida®

2 ribs celery, diced

1 cup frozen sliced carrots

1 teaspoon crushed garlic—Gourmet Garden

3½ cups vegetable broth, divided use

1 (15-ounce) can solid-pack pumpkin—Libby's

2 cups applesauce

1½ teaspoons pumpkin pie spice

1½ teaspoons ground ginger

Sour cream, for serving

Salt and pepper, to taste

1. In a medium microwave-safe bowl, combine onions, celery, carrots, garlic, and 1 cup broth. Cover and cook on high for 8 minutes. Transfer to a large pot and add remaining broth and remaining ingredients. Stir to combine and bring to a boil. Reduce heat and simmer for 20 minutes.

2. Working in batches, puree soup in blender. To prevent spilling, only fill blender half-full and cover lid with kitchen towel. Return to pot and adjust seasoning with salt and pepper to taste. Serve hot with a dollop of sour cream.

FAVORITE BAKED MACARONI AND CHEESE

MAKES: 12 servings **COOK:** 1 hour

Nonstick cooking spray

1 pound elbow macaroni

5 tablespoons melted butter, divided use

½ pound sharp cheddar cheese, grated

½ pound Italian shredded four-cheese blend

2 (12-ounce) cans evaporated milk

2 cups water

4 eggs, lightly beaten

2½ teaspoons mustard powder

1 teaspoon salt

2 teaspoons Worcestershire sauce

¼ teaspoon hot sauce

1 cup panko bread crumbs

1 teaspoon paprika

1. Preheat oven to 350°F. Lightly coat a 9 × 13-inch baking dish with cooking spray.

2. In a large bowl, toss uncooked macaroni with 3 tablespoons melted butter to coat. Add cheese and combine thoroughly. Transfer to prepared baking dish.

3. In a medium bowl, whisk together evaporated milk, water, eggs, mustard powder, salt, Worcestershire sauce, and hot sauce. Pour over macaroni mixture. Bake in preheated oven for 55 to 60 minutes.

4. Combine bread crumbs, paprika, and remaining 2 tablespoons butter. Sprinkle over baked macaroni and cheese. Return to oven and place on top rack position under broiler for 1 to 2 minutes or until golden brown.

GREEN GOBLIN MAC AND CHEESE

MAKES: 6 servings **COOK:** 55 minutes

5 quarts water

1 tablespoon salt

1½ teaspoons green food coloring—McCormick

16 ounces fusilli pasta

2 cups 2 percent milk

1 (1.8-ounce) packet four-cheese sauce mix—Knorr

1 teaspoon red food coloring

½ teaspoon yellow food coloring

1½ cups shredded cheddar cheese

1. Preheat oven to 350°F. Lightly coat a 9 × 13-inch glass baking dish with cooking spray.

2. In a large pot over high heat, bring water, salt, and green food coloring to a boil. Add pasta and cook according to package directions. Drain cooked pasta and rinse with cold water until water runs clear. Set aside.

3. In a small saucepan over medium-high heat, whisk together milk, sauce mix, and red and yellow food coloring. Bring mixture to a boil while stirring constantly. Reduce heat to medium and simmer 1 minute.

4. Add cheese and stir until melted.

5. Fold together pasta and cheese and pour into baking dish. Bake in preheated oven for 35 to 40 minutes or until heated through and bubbling.

GRILLED HENS WITH SOUTHERN-STYLE CORNBREAD STUFFING

MAKES: 4 servings   **COOK:** 1 hour 20 minutes

FOR THE STUFFING:

1½ cups less-sodium chicken broth

4 tablespoons butter

2 cups frozen seasoning blend—PictSweet

1 teaspoon red pepper flakes

1 (6-ounce) box cornbread stuffing mix—
Stove Top

FOR THE HENS:

4 (1 to 1½-pound) game hens

1½ tablespoons Montreal chicken seasoning—
McCormick Grill Mates

1½ cups cranberry juice cocktail

2 tablespoons frozen apple juice concentrate,
thawed

2 teaspoons Dijon mustard

1. For the stuffing, combine broth, butter, seasoning blend, and red pepper flakes in a medium saucepan. Bring to a boil. Stir in stuffing mix, cover, and remove from heat. Let stand 5 minutes, then fluff with a fork. Spread out on a baking sheet to cool.

2. For the hens, remove neck and giblets from cavity and discard. Trim excess fat and skin. Rinse skin and cavity under cold water and pat dry with paper towels. Season hens inside and out with chicken seasoning. Spoon ¼ of cooled stuffing into cavity of each bird. Do not pack stuffing in. Close openings with toothpicks.

3. In a small saucepan, reduce cranberry juice by half (about ¾ cup) over medium-high heat. Stir in apple juice concentrate and mustard. Bring to a boil, then remove from heat.

4. Set up a grill for indirect grilling over medium heat (no direct heat source under hens). Oil grate before cooking.

5. Place hens breast-side up, with wings tucked under, on hot, oiled grill over a drip pan. Cover grill. Roast for 1 to 1 ¼ hours or until no longer pink at the bone and the juices run clear (180°F at the thigh). During the last 15 minutes of cooking, brush hens liberally with cranberry glaze every 5 minutes, covering grill after each time. Transfer hens to a platter and let rest for 5 minutes before serving. Serve hot.

GUINNESS SAUSAGES

MAKES: 5 servings **COOK:** 45 minutes

2 onions, thinly sliced

1 (19.76-ounce) package uncooked bratwurst
sausages

3 (12-ounce) bottles beer—Guinness

2 tablespoons canola oil

5 hot dog buns
Stone-ground mustard, for serving

1. Arrange the onion slices on the bottom of a large straight-sided skillet. Place sausages on top and add beer (and water, if necessary) to cover. Bring to a simmer over medium heat and poach sausages for about 10 minutes or until almost cooked through. Remove sausages and set aside. Retaining onions in skillet, drain beer from skillet, reserving 2 cups for basting. Add oil and caramelize onions over medium-low heat, about 20 minutes.

Outdoor Method: Set up a grill for direct grilling over medium-high heat. Oil grate when ready to start cooking. Place sausages on hot, oiled grill and cook for 4 to 6 minutes per side or until the casings are brown and crisp. Internal temperature should be 160°F. Baste sausages frequently with reserved beer. Serve on buns piled with caramelized onions and plenty of mustard.

Indoor Method: Prepare onions and bratwurst as directed. Preheat broiler. Place poached sausages on a wire rack over a foil-lined baking sheet or broiler pan. Cook 6 to 8 inches from heat source for 4 to 6 minutes per side or until the casings are brown and crisp. Internal temperature should be 160°F. Baste sausages frequently with reserved beer. Serve on buns piled with caramelized onions and plenty of mustard.

HALIBUT WITH APPLE VERDE SALSA

MAKES: 4 servings **COOK:** 8 minutes

FOR THE HALIBUT:

- 4 (6-ounce) halibut fillets
- ½ cup salsa verde
- 2 teaspoons crushed garlic
- 1 tablespoon lime juice
- ¼ cup finely chopped cilantro

FOR THE SALSA:

- 1 cup diced Granny Smith apples
- 1 tablespoon lime juice
- 1 cup salsa verde
- 2 tablespoons coarsely chopped fresh cilantro
- 2 scallions, finely chopped
- ¼ cup chopped walnuts, lightly toasted

1. Rinse halibut under cold water and pat dry with paper towels. Place in a large zip-top bag and set aside. Stir to combine salsa, garlic, lime juice, and cilantro. Pour into bag with halibut. Squeeze air out and seal bag. Gently massage bag to coat fish with marinade. Marinate in refrigerator for 30 minutes to 2 hours.

2. For the salsa, stir to combine all ingredients in a medium bowl. Cover with plastic wrap and refrigerate until ready to use.

3. Preheat broiler. Place fish on foil-lined baking sheet or broiler pan. Broil 6 to 8 inches from heat source for 3 to 4 minutes per side, or until fish flakes easily with a fork. Serve fish hot with apple verde salsa.

HEARTY BEEF STEW

MAKES: 4 servings **COOK:** 4 to 6 hours

- 2 tablespoons all-purpose flour
- 1 (14-ounce) can less-sodium beef broth
- 1 cup water
- 1 tablespoon red wine vinegar
- 1 pound chuck roast, cut into bite-size chunks
- ½ medium onion, chopped
- 4 celery ribs, chopped
- 3 carrots, sliced into thick rounds
- 1 medium potato, peeled and chopped into large dice
- 1 (14.5-ounce) can diced tomatoes
- 2 teaspoons minced garlic
- 1 teaspoon hot sauce
- 1 teaspoon chopped fresh thyme
- 1 bay leaf
- 2 tablespoons chopped fresh parsley
   Salt and pepper, to taste

1. Stir together all ingredients except parsley in a 4-quart slow cooker. Cover and cook on high for 4 to 6 hours. Remove bay leaf. Season with salt and pepper to taste. Garnish with fresh parsley.

HERBED PORTERHOUSE WITH HORSERADISH BUTTER

MAKES: 4 servings   **COOK:** 30 minutes

FOR THE STEAK:

- 2 (1 pound each) porterhouse steaks, 1-inch thick
- ¼ cup oil-and-vinegar salad dressing
- 1 tablespoon crushed garlic
- 2 tablespoons Dijon mustard
- ¼ cup finely chopped fresh parsley
- 2 tablespoons finely chopped rosemary
- 2 tablespoons finely chopped thyme

FOR THE HORSERADISH BUTTER:

- 4 tablespoons butter, softened
- 4 tablespoons prepared horseradish (not creamy)—Morehouse, moisture squeezed out
- ½ teaspoon Worcestershire sauce
  Salt and pepper, to taste

1. Rinse steaks under cold water, pat dry with paper towels, and place in a large zip-top bag. In a small bowl, stir to combine salad dressing, garlic, mustard, and herbs. Pour into bag with steaks. Squeeze air from bag and seal. Marinate in refrigerator for at least 4 hours, but preferably overnight, turning occasionally.

2. For the horseradish butter, place all ingredients in a small bowl and mash together with a fork. Set aside until ready to serve.

3. *Outdoor Method*: Set up a grill for direct cooking over medium heat. Oil grate when ready to start cooking. Let steaks stand at room temperature for 20 to 30 minutes before grilling.

4. Remove steaks from marinade and discard marinade. Place steaks on hot, oiled grill and cook for about 5 minutes per side for medium (160°F). Move steaks to cooler parts of the grill if starting to burn. Transfer to cutting board and let rest, tented with foil, for 5 minutes. Cut meat away from bones and thinly slice across the grain of the meat. Spread slices with horseradish butter and serve guests a few slices from each side of the bone.

Indoor Method: Prepare steaks and horseradish butter as directed. Preheat broiler. Place steaks on a foil-lined baking sheet or broiler pan. Broil 6 to 8 inches from heat source for 5 minutes per side for medium (160°F). Serve as directed.

MEATBALL SUB

MAKES: 4 servings   **COOK:** 40 minutes

FOR THE MEATBALLS:

½ pound ground beef

1 tablespoon garlic, chopped

½ cup Italian seasoned dried bread crumbs

2 tablespoons finely chopped fresh parsley
   leaves

2 tablespoons grated Parmesan

1 egg
   Salt and freshly ground black pepper

2 tablespoons canola oil

1 cup tomato sauce, jarred or homemade,
   recipe follows

½ cup shredded mozzarella

FOR THE SUB:

2 sub rolls

FOR THE CHUNKY TOMATO SAUCE:

2 tablespoons olive oil

½ medium onion, diced

1 tablespoon chopped garlic

1 (28-ounce) can diced tomatoes

2 tablespoons freshly chopped basil leaves

2 tablespoons freshly chopped parsley leaves
   Salt and freshly ground black pepper

1. Preheat oven to 400°F.

2. For meatballs, in a large bowl mix together all ingredients except the canola oil, tomato sauce, and mozzarella, until well combined. Using wet hands, form walnut-size pieces into balls. Heat the oil in a medium skillet over medium-high heat and fry the meatballs until browned on all sides.

3. Slice the rolls in half lengthwise and put on a baking sheet. Top each half with ¼ cup of the tomato sauce, 4 meatballs, and some mozzarella cheese. Put in the oven and bake for 10 minutes or until the cheese is melted. Transfer to a serving platter and serve.

4. For the sauce, in a medium pot, add the oil and heat over medium heat. Add the onion and garlic and sauté for 3 minutes. Add the remaining ingredients and simmer for another 15 minutes.

PESTO AND MOZZARELLA SAUSAGE SANDWICH

MAKES: 4 servings **COOK:** 25 minutes

⅓ cup mayonnaise

3   tablespoons pesto

4   sweet Italian sausages

1   loaf ciabatta bread, cut lengthwise

2   cups mixed baby greens

4   canned artichoke hearts, drained, thinly sliced

2   Roma tomatoes, thinly sliced

8   thin slices fresh mozzarella cheese

1. Stir together mayonnaise and pesto. Cover and store in the refrigerator until ready to use.

2. Place sausages in a large skillet and cover with water. Bring to a simmer over medium heat for 10 minutes or until almost cooked through. Remove sausages with a slotted spoon. Preheat broiler. Place poached sausages on a wire rack over a foil-lined baking sheet or broiler pan. Cook 6 to 8 inches from heat source for 4 to 6 minutes per side. Remove and halve sausages lengthwise. Broil for 1 minute, cut-sides up.

3. Spread pesto mayonnaise over both sides of bread. To the bottom half add mixed greens, artichokes, and tomatoes. Top with sausages and mozzarella. Add top half of bread and cut into serving-size sandwiches.

PHILLY CHEESESTEAK BURGER

MAKES: 4 servings **COOK:** 25 minutes

FOR THE TOPPING:

1   tablespoon extra-virgin olive oil

1   (8-ounce) package presliced mushrooms

1   green bell pepper, cut into strips

1   medium onion, thinly sliced

½   teaspoon steak seasoning

FOR THE BURGERS:

1½ pounds ground sirloin

¼   cup less-sodium beef broth

1   (1-ounce) package onion soup & dip mix

4   slices provolone cheese

4   sandwich rolls

1   cup store-bought pizza sauce, heated

1. For the topping, heat oil in a large skillet over medium-high heat. Add mushrooms, green pepper, and onion. Sauté until vegetables are soft, about 10 to 12 minutes. Set aside.

2. For the burgers, combine ground sirloin, broth, and soup mix in a large bowl. Mix thoroughly. Form into 4 patties to fit rolls. Cover and chill in refrigerator until ready to use.

3. Preheat broiler. Place patties on a wire rack over a foil-lined baking sheet or broiler pan. Broil 6 to 8 inches from heat source for 4 to 5 minutes per side for medium (160°F). Place cheese slices on patties and broil for 1 to 2 minutes more or until cheese is melted. Serve hot on rolls topped with sautéed vegetables and pizza sauce.

PIMIENTO CHEESE-STUFFED BURGERS

MAKES: 4 servings   **COOK:** 10 minutes

1½   pounds ground beef

3   tablespoons chili seasoning mix

3   tablespoons beer

½   cup pimiento cheese—Price's

8   hamburger buns, toasted

½   head lettuce, for serving, optional

1   large tomato, sliced, for serving, optional

1   red onion, sliced, for serving, optional
    Condiments (mustard, ketchup,
    mayonnaise), optional

1. In a large bowl, combine ground beef, chili seasoning, and beer. Shape into 8 patties slightly larger than the buns. Spoon 2 tablespoons of pimiento cheese onto 4 patties. Top with remaining patties and press around edges to seal. Refrigerate if not cooking immediately.

2. Preheat broiler. Place patties on a wire rack over a foil-lined baking sheet or broiler pan. Broil 6 to 8 inches from heat source for 4 to 5 minutes per side for medium (160°F). Serve on hot toasted buns with your favorite condiments.

POMEGRANATE PORK TENDERLOIN WITH ONIONS

MAKES: 6 servings   **COOK:** 60 minutes

3 cups pomegranate juice

2 pork tenderloins, about 1 to 1½ pounds each

¼ cup coarse mustard

1½ tablespoons chopped garlic

2 tablespoons minced fresh thyme

1½ pounds red onion, cut into ½-inch-thick slices

2 tablespoons lemon juice

¼ cup extra-virgin olive oil

¼ cup water

Thyme sprigs, for garnish

Salt and pepper, to taste

1. Boil the pomegranate juice over high heat until reduced by half, about 15 minutes. Let cool to room temperature.

2. Rinse pork under cold water and pat dry with paper towels. Season pork with salt and pepper and place in a large zip-top bag. Combine juice, mustard, garlic, and 1 tablespoon thyme in a bowl. Pour into bag with pork. Squeeze air from bag and seal. Gently massage bag to coat pork. Marinate overnight in refrigerator, turning bag occasionally.

3. Preheat oven to 425°F.

4. Separate the onions into rings and toss with lemon juice, remaining thyme, and 2 tablespoons olive oil on a large nonstick baking pan. Season with salt and pepper. Roast onions, stirring occasionally, until tender and beginning to brown, about 10 minutes. Remove pan from oven and push onions to one side, leaving just enough room for pork on the other side. Remove pork from bag and transfer to pan. Reserve marinade. Drizzle remaining olive oil over pork and return pan to oven. Add ¼ cup water after 15 minutes and continue to cook until onions are golden brown and an instant-read thermometer inserted in pork registers 155°F, about 30 minutes total.

5. In a medium saucepan, bring reserved marinade to a boil. Boil until reduced by half, about 5 minutes, and set aside.

6. Transfer onions to one side of a serving platter, cover, and keep warm. Transfer pork to cutting board and let stand 10 minutes before carving into ¼-inch-thick slices.

7. Arrange pork slices next to onions on platter, drizzle oil over all, and spoon sauce over top of meat. Garnish with sprigs of fresh thyme.

POT ROAST WITH ROASTED VEGETABLES

MAKES: 4 servings **COOK:** 8 hours

FOR THE POT ROAST:

1½	pounds bottom round roast beef
2	teaspoons salt, plus more for seasoning
½	teaspoon pepper, plus more for seasoning
2	tablespoons all-purpose flour
2	tablespoons canola oil
1	medium yellow onion
2	carrots, cut into 2-inch pieces
2	stalks celery
1	(15-ounce) can beef broth
1	cup water
1	tablespoon minced fresh garlic
2	tablespoons Worcestershire sauce
4	sprigs fresh thyme

FOR THE ROASTED ROOT VEGETABLES:

2	carrots, cut into 3-inch pieces
2	russet potatoes, cut into 1-inch cubes
½	pound turnips, cut into wedges
1	red onion, sliced
2	tablespoons canola oil
1	teaspoon fresh rosemary
1	teaspoon fresh thyme
	Salt and pepper, to taste

1. For the pot roast, season beef with salt and pepper and lightly coat with flour. Heat oil in a large skillet on medium-high heat and brown meat on all sides, several minutes per side. Set aside. Place onion, carrots, and celery in bottom of a slow cooker and top with seared beef. Add broth, water, garlic, Worcestershire sauce, and thyme, and set cooker on low for 8 hours. When finished, remove meat, blend remaining vegetables and broth in a blender, and serve as gravy with pot roast and roasted root vegetables.

2. For the roasted root vegetables, preheat oven to 400°F one hour before the pot roast is done cooking. In a bowl, toss vegetables with oil, rosemary, and thyme, season with salt and pepper, and spread out on a sheet tray. Roast for 30 minutes, then toss and roast another 30 minutes.

PRETZEL CRUSTED CHICKEN LEGS

MAKES: 6 servings   **BAKE:** 45 minutes

FOR THE CHICKEN:

12   whole chicken legs

¾   cup Dijon mustard

2   cups crushed pretzels

Nonstick cooking spray

FOR THE DIPPING SAUCE:

¼   cup honey

½   cup Dijon mustard

2   tablespoons sour cream, optional

1. Preheat oven to 425°F. Spray a baking pan with cooking oil.
2. For the chicken, rinse under cold water and pat dry with paper towels. Rub chicken with the mustard, dredge in the crushed pretzels, and set on the baking pan about 1-inch apart. Let stand for 15 minutes at room temperature. Spray thoroughly with cooking spray and bake chicken for 30 to 45 minutes or until browned.
3. For the dipping sauce, combine the honey, mustard, and sour cream in a small bowl until smooth. Serve dipping sauce with warm chicken.

SESAME-SOY RUBBED FLANK STEAK

MAKES: 4 servings   **COOK:** 10 minutes

1½   pounds beef flank steak

2   tablespoons sesame seeds, toasted

1½   tablespoons soy sauce

1   tablespoon mirin sweet cooking wine

1   tablespoon canola oil

2   teaspoons sesame oil

2   teaspoons crushed garlic

1   teaspoon minced ginger

1. Rinse steak under cold water and pat dry with paper towels. Lightly score both sides of steak with a sharp knife in a diamond pattern. Set aside. Stir to combine remaining ingredients in a small bowl. Coat steak with sesame-soy mixture and place in a large zip-top bag. Squeeze air from bag and seal. Marinate in refrigerator for at least 4 hours, but preferably overnight.
2. Preheat broiler. Place steak on a foil-lined baking sheet or broiler pan. Broil 6 to 8 inches from heat source for 4 to 5 minutes per side for medium (160°F).
3. Transfer steak to cutting board and let rest for 5 minutes before thinly slicing across the grain. Serve hot or at room temperature.

SPICED TENDERLOIN WITH BUTTERNUT SQUASH PILAF

MAKES: 4 servings   **COOK:** 30 minutes

1 tablespoon olive oil

1 large garlic clove, mashed

2 tablespoons pork rub—McCormick Grill Mates

1 teaspoon ground cinnamon

¼ teaspoon ground cloves

1½ pounds pork tenderloin

FOR THE BUTTERNUT SQUASH:

1 (12-ounce) bag butternut squash—Mann's

½ teaspoon ground cinnamon

2 cups chicken broth

1 tablespoon butter

¼ teaspoon turmeric

1 box rice pilaf—Near East®, with spice packet

1 cup canned chickpeas

Salt and pepper, to taste

1. Preheat oven to 450°F.

2. Mix together oil, garlic, pork rub, cinnamon, and cloves in a small bowl. Rinse pork under cold water and pat dry with paper towels. Rub pork with spice mixture and salt and pepper. Place on a foil-lined baking sheet. Roast until thermometer inserted into center of pork registers 150°F, about 20 minutes. Transfer pork to cutting board and let rest 5 minutes before slicing.

3. Meanwhile, cut each butternut squash piece in half. Toss together with cinnamon in a small bowl and set aside. Heat chicken broth, butter, and turmeric in a medium saucepan over medium-high heat. Bring to a boil. Stir in rice and spice packet, cover, and reduce heat. Simmer for 10 minutes. Stir in squash and garbanzo beans, cover, and simmer for another 10 to 12 minutes. Remove from heat and season with salt and pepper to taste.

SPANISH CHICKEN WITH SPICY LEMON RICE

MAKES: 4 Servings   **COOK:** 4 hours 15 minutes

1 tablespoon garlic powder

2 tablespoons paprika

3 tablespoons all-purpose flour

Salt and pepper

4 chicken thighs (about 1 pound)

¼ cup canola oil

1 (14.5-ounce) can diced tomatoes

2 green bell peppers, diced into 2-inch pieces

1 onion, sliced into thick pieces

2 tablespoons tomato paste

2 cups chicken broth

2 cups water

Zest and juice of 1 lemon, divided use

½ teaspoon crushed red pepper flakes

1 cup rice

½ cup pitted green olives with pimientos

lemon

1. In a large zip-top bag, mix together garlic, paprika, flour, salt, and pepper. Add chicken pieces and toss to coat completely. In a large saucepan over medium heat, heat canola oil. Add chicken and brown all sides, cooking 3 to 4 minutes per side. While the chicken is cooking, to a slow cooker add the tomatoes, peppers, and onions. Top with the chicken thighs.

2. In the same skillet used to brown the chicken, add the tomato paste and cook for 1 minute, stirring constantly. Add the chicken broth and bring to a simmer, stirring to scrape any browned bits off the bottom of the pan. Pour over top of the chicken in the slow cooker. Cook on low for 4 hours, or until the chicken is extremely tender.

3. In a medium pot, combine 2 cups water, the rice, red pepper flakes, lemon zest, juice of half the lemon and a pinch of salt. Bring to a boil, reduce to a simmer and cook, covered, until the rice is tender and has absorbed all the liquid.

4. To serve, spoon the rice onto a deep-sided platter and ladle the Spanish chicken and vegetables over top. Garnish with the olives and squeeze over the remaining lemon juice.

SPARERIBS WITH BROWN SUGAR BARBEQUE SAUCE

MAKES: 4 servings   **COOK:** 2 hours 30 minutes

2   racks pork spareribs
⅓   cup pork rub (suggested: McCormick Grill Mates)

FOR THE SAUCE:

1   (12-ounce) bottle chili sauce
⅔   cup dark brown sugar
1   tablespoon molasses
1   tablespoon steak sauce
¼   teaspoon liquid smoke
1   (1.31-ounce) packet sloppy joe seasoning mix—suggested: McCormick
    Wood chips

1. Rinse spareribs with cold water and pat dry with paper towels. Remove the thin membrane from the back of ribs. Sprinkle pork rub over ribs and pat in.

Outdoor Method: Soak wood chips before preparing grill. Set up a grill for indirect cooking over medium heat so that no heat source will be under meat. Drain wood chips. Add some chips to the smoker box if using a gas grill, or place chips on hot coals if using charcoal. Place ribs in a rib rack over a drip pan on hot grill. Cover grill. Cook 2 to 2½ hours, rotating ribs around rack every 30 minutes. If using charcoal, add 10 briquettes to each pile of coals and another handful of soaked hickory chips every hour. For a gas grill, add wood chips to the smoker box every hour.

2. For the sauce, while ribs are cooking, combine sauce ingredients in a small saucepan over medium heat. Simmer for 10 minutes and remove from heat.

3. About 20 minutes before ribs are done, remove ribs from rib rack and lay meat-side down on grill. Generously brush with sauce and pile ribs in center of grill over a drip pan. Cover and cook for 10 minutes. Turn ribs and brush on more sauce and re-pile. Cook an additional 10 minutes. Remove from grill and cut into servings. Serve hot with sauce on the side.

Indoor Method: Prepare and rub ribs as directed above. Preheat oven to 350°F. Place ribs meat-side up on a rack in a shallow roasting pan. Tightly cover with foil. Bake for 1 hour. While ribs are baking, make sauce as directed above. Remove ribs from oven and carefully drain fat from roasting pan. Continue baking ribs, uncovered, for 1 to 1½ hours more or until tender, turning and brushing occasionally with sauce. Cut into servings and serve hot with sauce on the side.

STETSON STEAK

MAKES: 4 servings   **COOK:** 10 minutes

1 tablespoon grill seasoning

1 teaspoon finely ground coffee

1 teaspoon ancho chili powder

2 tablespoons adobo sauce

1 (2-pound) London broil

1. Preheat a grill or grill pan over high heat.
2. In a small bowl, mix together all ingredients except meat. Rub mixture into steak on all sides. Let sit at room temperature while grill is heating.
3. Rinse steak under cold water and pat dry with paper towels. Place steak on grill and cook for 1 to 2 minutes per side to sear. Lower heat and cook for an additional 3 minutes per side for medium. Remove from heat and allow to rest 5 minutes before slicing. Holding a knife at a 45-degree angle, cut steak across grain into thick slices and serve.

SYRAH MARINATED FILET

MAKES: 4 servings **COOK:** 16 minutes

FOR THE STEAK:

4   (6-ounce) bacon-wrapped beef tenderloin
    steaks (bacon is cooked)

1½ cups Syrah wine

2   teaspoons crushed garlic

2   tablespoons finely chopped tarragon leaves

1   tablespoon steak seasoning

1   tablespoon Worcestershire sauce

FOR THE TARRAGON BUTTER:

2   tablespoons finely chopped tarragon leaves

1   teaspoon crushed garlic

½   teaspoon salt

½   teaspoon black pepper

½   cup butter, softened

1. Rinse steaks under cold water and pat dry with paper towels. Tie with butcher's twine to maintain shape. Place in a zip-top bag. Whisk to combine wine, garlic, tarragon, steak seasoning, and Worcestershire sauce in a medium bowl, then pour into bag with steaks. Squeeze air from bag and seal. Marinate in refrigerator for at least 4 hours, but preferably overnight.

2. For the tarragon butter, work tarragon, garlic, salt, and pepper into butter with a fork. Form into a log and wrap with plastic wrap. Set aside in refrigerator until ready to serve.

3. Preheat broiler. Place steaks on a foil-lined baking sheet or broiler pan. Broil 6 to 8 inches from heat source for 6 to 8 minutes per side for medium (160°F).

4. Transfer steaks to a platter and let rest for 5 minutes before serving. Serve hot with slices of tarragon butter.

TURKEY SALAD WITH CRANBERRY VINAIGRETTE AND CORNBREAD CROUTONS

MAKES: 4 servings   **COOK:** 26 minutes

1 (12-ounce) package butternut squash—Mann's

1 tablespoon extra-virgin olive oil

1 teaspoon pumpkin pie spice

1 big slice store-bought cornbread, cut into bite-size cubes

Nonstick cooking spray

1 teaspoon garlic salt

½ cup whole cranberry sauce

2 tablespoons orange juice

1 teaspoon sugar

2 tablespoons balsamic vinaigrette

10 cups spring mix salad

1 cooked turkey breast half from deli, sliced

2 tomatoes, cut into eighths

1 cucumber, sliced

½ cup glazed pecans—Emerald

1. Preheat oven to 400°F. Line 2 baking sheets with foil and set aside.

2. Toss squash with oil and pumpkin pie spice. Roast in preheated oven for 15 to 20 minutes or until fork-tender. Remove and set aside.

3. Spread cornbread cubes in an even layer on prepared baking sheets. Spray with cooking spray and sprinkle with garlic salt. Bake in preheated oven until golden brown, about 6 minutes. Remove croutons and set aside to cool.

4. Heat the cranberry sauce and orange juice in a small saucepan over medium heat until boiling. Remove from heat and let cool. Strain cranberry mixture into a large bowl with a fine mesh strainer. Whisk in sugar and vinaigrette until well combined.

5. Add salad mix to bowl and toss with tongs until lettuce is coated. Divide salad on serving plates. Top with sliced turkey, squash, tomatoes, cucumber, and croutons. Garnish with glazed pecans and serve.

BAT BARK

MAKES: Approx. 8 servings   **COOK:** 5 minutes

Nonstick cooking spray

12 Halloween sandwich cookies—Oreo, chopped

1½ cups white fudge–covered pretzels, chopped

⅓ cup peanut butter chips

1½ pounds white chocolate, broken into squares

2 cups candy corn

Black bat sprinkles

1. Spray a 9 × 13-inch baking pan with cooking spray. Sprinkle with chopped sandwich cookies, broken pretzels, and peanut butter chips. Set aside.

2. Melt chocolate in a large microwave-safe bowl on 50 percent power for 5 minutes, stirring every 30 seconds. Pour melted chocolate over mixture in baking pan and spread with a spatula. Top with candy corn and bat sprinkles. Let cool until firm. Break into pieces and store in an airtight container.

HONEY GLAZED FIG AND APPLE KEBABS

MAKES: 4 servings   **COOK:** 7 to 11 minutes

¼   cup honey

1   tablespoon frozen lemonade concentrate

½   teaspoon dried culinary lavender, finely chopped

1   (14-ounce) package green apple slices— Chiquita

8   Mission figs, halved

4   ounces soft goat cheese
    Baguette-style French bread slices, toasted
    Nonstick cooking spray

1. *Outdoor Method*: Set up a grill for direct cooking over medium heat. In a small saucepan, combine honey, lemonade concentrate, and lavender. Simmer over medium-low heat for 2 minutes and set aside.

2. Beginning and ending with apples, alternately thread fig halves and apples onto skewers that have been soaked in water at least an hour. Spray fruit on both sides with cooking spray. Brush and oil grate when ready to start cooking. Place skewers on hot, oiled grill for 2 to 4 minutes per side or until fruit is tender and grill-marked. Brush with honey glaze and cook each side 1 minute more. Serve warm with goat cheese and toasted baguette slices drizzled with extra honey glaze.

Indoor Method: Prepare lavender honey glaze and fruit kebabs as directed. Preheat broiler. Place kebabs on a foil-lined baking sheet or broiler pan that has been sprayed with cooking spray. Broil 6 to 8 inches from heat source for 1 to 3 minutes. Brush with honey glaze and cook each side 1 minute more. Serve as directed above.

JELLY SLUG CUPCAKES

MAKES: 24 servings **BAKE:** 30 minutes

FOR THE CUPCAKES:

- 1 (18.25-ounce) box moist devil's food cake
- 1⅓ cups soda—Dr Pepper®
- 3 eggs
- ½ cup canola oil
- 12 Gummy worms, cut in half
- ½ package cream-filled chocolate cookies, filling removed and cookies crushed

FOR THE FROSTING:

- 2 cans (16 ounces) white frosting
- 20 drops yellow food coloring
- 10 drops red food coloring
- 1½ teaspoons orange extract
- 1 cup powdered sugar, sifted

1. Preheat oven to 350°F. Place cupcake papers in muffin pans. Set aside.

2. In a large mixing bowl, combine cake mix, soda, eggs, and oil. Beat on medium speed for 2 minutes, scraping sides of bowl often. Fill cupcake papers ⅔ full with cake batter. Bake in preheated oven for 25 to 30 minutes. Cool in pan for 10 minutes before removing from pan. Cool completely on wire racks before frosting.

3. For the frosting, combine frosting, food coloring, orange extract, and sifted powdered sugar in a medium mixing bowl. Spoon frosting into a zip-top bag or a pastry bag fitted with a ¼-inch round decorating tip. Pipe frosting onto top of cupcake by starting at the outside edge, circling twice, and then working toward the center.

4. Finish cupcakes by sticking gummy worms into frosting and sprinkling tops with crushed cookie "dirt."

MONSTER CANDY BAR CAKE

MAKES: 12 servings   **BAKE:** 30 minutes

Nonstick cooking spray

1   (18.25-ounce) box chocolate cake mix

1⅓   cups cola

3   large eggs

½   cup vegetable oil

2½   cups various candy bars, coarsely chopped, divided use

1 (16-ounce) can chocolate frosting

1. Preheat oven to 350°F. Prepare two 9-inch-round pans with cooking spray. Cut parchment-paper circles to fit in bottom of pans. Place circles in pans and give them a light spray of oil.

2. In a large mixing bowl, combine cake mix, cola, eggs, and oil. Beat with mixer on low speed until combined, then continue beating on medium speed for 2 minutes, occasionally scraping bowl with spatula. Fold in 1½ cups chopped candy.

3. Divide batter between the 2 cake pans. Place in preheated oven and bake for 25 to 30 minutes or until a toothpick inserted into center comes out clean. Cool in pans for 10 minutes. Invert cakes onto cooling racks to cool completely.

4. To finish cake, remove parchment circles and place one layer on a cake plate or stand. Spread a layer of frosting and sprinkle with ½ cup candy. Place second layer on top and finish frosting cake. Decorate cake by sprinkling remaining candy on top and sides of cake.

HOT SPICED CIDER

MAKES: 20 servings   **COOK:** 3 hours

4   (11.5-ounce) cans peach nectar

3   cups water

1   cup packed brown sugar

1   cup Canadian whisky, Crown Royal®

½   cup lemon juice

1   teaspoon ground allspice

3   cinnamon sticks

1½   cups peaches, sliced (about 3 peaches)

1. In a 4-quart slow cooker, combine all ingredients except peach slices. Cover and cook on low heat setting for 2 to 3 hours. Remove cinnamon sticks. Serve in mugs. Garnish with peach slices.

NOVEMBER

Herb and
Pear Glazed Turkey, p. 347

Melted Leek
Mashed Potatoes, p. 337

ARTICHOKE RATATOUILLE

MAKES: 4 servings   **COOK:** 25 minutes

3   tablespoons olive oil
1   small eggplant, diced into 1-inch cubes
1   (16-ounce) bag frozen pepper stir-fry
    vegetables—Birds Eye, thawed
1   (9-ounce) package frozen artichoke hearts,
    thawed
½   teaspoon red pepper flakes
1   tablespoon minced garlic
1   (14.5-ounce) can diced tomatoes
¼   cup chopped fresh basil
    Salt and pepper, to taste

1. In a high-sided skillet, heat oil over medium heat. Add eggplant, stir-fry vegetables, artichoke hearts, red pepper flakes, and garlic and season with salt and pepper. Sauté for about 5 minutes or until vegetables are almost completely cooked through. Add diced tomatoes, cover, and simmer on low for 15 to 20 minutes until eggplant is soft and ratatouille is thickened slightly. Just before serving, stir in the basil. Taste and adjust seasoning if necessary.

HORSERADISH MASHED POTATOES

MAKES: 4 servings   **COOK:** 3 minutes

1   (24-ounce) container homestyle mashed
    potatoes
2   tablespoons sour cream
1   tablespoon prepared horseradish
1   teaspoon Worcestershire sauce
    Black pepper, to taste

1. In a large microwave-safe bowl, stir together the mashed potatoes, sour cream, horseradish, Worcestershire sauce, and pepper. Cover with a damp paper towel and return to microwave. Cook on high setting for 3 minutes.

MELTED LEEK MASHED POTATOES

MAKES: 8 servings   **COOK:** 25 minutes

- 4 pounds russet potatoes
- 1 pound leeks, white parts cleaned and finely chopped
- 6 tablespoons butter, divided use
- 1 cup milk
- 2 cloves garlic, peeled
- 2 sprigs fresh thyme
  Salt and pepper

1. Peel the potatoes, cut them into 1-inch pieces, and put them into a large pot of cold water. Add a big pinch of salt and put the pot over high heat. When it comes to a boil, cook until potatoes are just cooked through, about 20 minutes. Drain in a colander, put the colander over the pot, and let the potatoes dry out a bit while you finish the leeks.

2. While the potatoes are cooking, put a medium skillet over medium-low heat and add 2 tablespoons butter. When the butter is melted, add leeks and season with salt and pepper. Cover the pan and cook leeks for about 20 minutes until they are very soft, being careful not to let them color or burn.

3. In a small pot over low heat, add the milk, remaining 4 tablespoons butter, garlic, and thyme and warm through. Dry the large pot and add the potatoes. Mash with a potato masher, breaking up the big lumps. Strain the garlic and thyme from the warm milk and stir the milk into the potatoes, using a wooden spoon. Stir in the leeks, taste, and season with salt and pepper. Cover and keep warm.

MUSHROOM AND WATER CHESTNUT STUFFING

MAKES: 8 servings   **COOK:** 60 minutes

 1 loaf of your favorite bread
 3 tablespoons butter, divided use
 1 (8-ounce) package sliced fresh mushrooms
 1 small onion, chopped
 2 stalks celery, chopped
 1¼ cups low-sodium chicken broth
 1 (8-ounce) can sliced water chestnuts,
    drained and rinsed
 1 tablespoon soy sauce
 1 tablespoon chopped fresh parsley
 2 large eggs, beaten
    Salt and pepper, to taste

1. The night before, cut the bread into large cubes and spread out on a baking sheet. Leave uncovered overnight to go stale.

2. Preheat oven to 350°F. Grease a 9 × 13-inch baking dish with 1 tablespoon of butter.

3. Put a large skillet over medium heat and add the remaining 2 tablespoons of butter. When it is melted, add the mushrooms and cook until they release their liquid, about 4 to 5 minutes. Add the onion and celery and season with salt and pepper. Cook until all the vegetables have softened, about 6 to 8 minutes. Let cool for a few minutes, then stir in the broth, water chestnuts, soy sauce, and parsley, and cook for another minute. Fold in the stale bread. Fold in the beaten eggs. If the mixture seems too dry, add more broth or a little water. Spread the mixture in the prepared baking dish, which can be covered and refrigerated overnight until you are ready to bake. Let dish come to room temperature before baking.

4. Cover the dish with foil and put it in the oven for about 20 to 25 minutes. Uncover and cook until the top is browned, about another 20 minutes. Let rest for 5 minutes before serving.

THREE BREAD STUFFING

MAKES: 8 servings **COOK:** 70 minutes

½ loaf sourdough bread

½ loaf rye bread

4 tablespoons butter, plus more for greasing

1 cup frozen chopped onions, thawed

3 stalks celery, chopped

2 medium carrots, chopped

1 (14-ounce) bag cornbread stuffing

2 cups chicken broth

1 cup turkey gravy

2 large eggs, beaten

1 tablespoon poultry seasoning

½ cup grated Parmesan cheese

Salt and pepper

1. **Preheat oven to 300°F.**
2. **Cut the breads into 1-inch cubes and spread them out on baking sheets. Bake for 30 minutes to dry them out.**
3. In a large skillet over medium heat, add butter. When it is melted add the onions, celery, and carrots and season with salt and pepper. Cook until vegetables are soft, about 10 minutes. Turn off the heat and let cool a bit.
4. Preheat oven to 350°F. Butter a 9 × 13-inch baking dish.
5. Put the bread cubes into a large bowl with the cornbread stuffing and add the cooled vegetables. In a medium bowl, whisk together broth, gravy, eggs, and poultry seasoning. Pour over bread and mix. The mixture should be fairly moist, but not wet. If it seems too dry, add some more broth. Fill the baking dish with the stuffing and top with the Parmesan. Bake until the top is browned and the stuffing is cooked through, about 35 to 40 minutes.

PECAN CHEESE TURKEY WITH PITA TAIL FEATHERS

MAKES: 12 servings   **BAKE:** 22 minutes

FOR THE TURKEY:

8   ounces goat cheese, softened

16   ounces cream cheese, softened

2   tablespoons tarragon, stems removed

1   (10-ounce) bag whole pecans

FOR TURKEY NECK AND FEATHERS:

3   sundried tomato basil tortilla wraps—
Mission

4   teaspoons paprika

1   teaspoon black pepper

2   teaspoons garam masala

3   teaspoons dried tarragon

2   eggs, lightly beaten
Crackers, to serve

1. For the turkey, combine goat cheese, cream cheese, and tarragon in a food processor. Process until smooth. Transfer to an airtight container and chill in refrigerator for at least 4 hours. Once chilled, shape into turkey body. Working from the back end of the turkey body, insert a row of pecans into cheese at an angle to resemble feathers. Continue until cheese is covered and looks as if the pecans are rows of feathers. Cover with plastic wrap and place in the refrigerator until ready to serve.

2. For turkey neck and feathers, preheat oven to 375°F. Line a baking sheet with aluminum foil and set aside.

3. Take one tortilla and fold in half. Use a paring knife, carefully cut out a turkey head from the folded tortilla (use a stencil from a craft store or make your own by drawing a turkey head with neck and wattle). Once cut, place both turkey heads on prepared baking sheet. Make sure one turkey head is facing left and the other is facing right. Use a pastry brush to lightly brush each head with egg wash. Sprinkle 1 teaspoon of paprika on wattle part of each turkey head. Sprinkle a small dot of black pepper on each head to give the turkey eyes. Bake in oven on top rack for 8 to 10 minutes, until crisp. Remove and let cool completely.

4. Take remaining 2 tortillas and cut straight across the bottom one-third of each tortilla. Discard the smaller portion. Cut the larger portion into 5 wedges or triangles. Arrange triangles on prepared baking sheet, evenly spaced. Brush each with egg wash and sprinkle with the various herbs and spices to simulate feathers of different colors. Bake in oven on top rack for 10 to 12 minutes, until crisp. Remove and let cool completely.

5. To serve, remove cheese turkey body from refrigerator and let soften for 15 minutes. Place tortilla turkey heads back to back and insert into cheese. Insert tortilla feathers into the back end of cheese body in an alternating color pattern. Serve as edible centerpiece with crackers.

BACON ROASTED TURKEY WITH CRANBERRY AND WILD RICE DRESSING

MAKES: 15 servings **COOK:** 5 hours

FOR THE TURKEY:

- 1 (15-pound) turkey, thawed if frozen
- 1 packet onion soup mix
- 1 tablespoon lemon and herb seasoning—McCormick
- 2 teaspoons garlic salt—Lawry's
- ½ teaspoon black pepper
- ¼ cup olive oil
- 1 small onion, thickly sliced
- 1 small orange, thickly sliced
- 8 leaves fresh sage
- 10 sprigs fresh thyme
- 1 pound bacon
- 1 (14-ounce) can chicken broth

FOR THE DRESSING:

- 4 (6.2-ounce) boxes fast-cooking long grain and wild rice
- 3 cups low-sodium chicken broth
- 4 cups frozen seasoning blend (mixed diced vegetables including onion, celery, red and green peppers, and parsley)
- 3 (11-ounce) cans mandarin orange segments, drained
- 1⅓ cups chopped pecans
- 2 cups whole cranberry sauce

1. Preheat oven to 400°F. Move rack to lowest position in oven.
2. For the turkey, remove the bird from refrigerator and let sit 30 to 40 minutes at room temperature. Stir together soup mix, lemon and herb seasoning, garlic salt, and pepper in a small bowl. Rinse turkey inside and out and pat dry with paper towels. Pour and rub oil all over outside of turkey. Sprinkle seasoning mixture all over and rub into skin. Fill cavity with onion slices, orange slices, sage, and thyme. Truss bird and wrap bacon slices around it, tucking into place and securing with toothpicks when necessary. Place on rack in roasting pan, breast-side down. Pour chicken broth into pan.
3. Roast for 30 minutes, then reduce oven temperature to 350°F and roast for 2 hours, basting with pan juices every 30 minutes. Reduce temperature to 275°F and roast another 1½ to 2½ hours, basting every 30 minutes or until thermometer inserted into thigh reads 180°F. Remove and tent with foil. Let sit for 20 minutes before slicing.
4. For the dressing, stir together rice, chicken broth, and seasoning blend in a large saucepan. Bring to a boil. Cover and reduce heat. Simmer for 5 minutes. Remove from heat and let sit for 5 minutes or until broth is absorbed. Stir in remaining ingredients.
5. Carve bird and place on platter. Serve cranberry and wild rice dressing alongside turkey on platter.

BLACK PEPPER BEEF RIBS

MAKES: 4 servings **COOK:** 2 hours 30 minutes

12 long meaty beef ribs

¾ cup hickory smoke barbeque sauce—Bull's Eye, divided use

3 cups beef broth

1 cup bourbon

1 cup steak sauce

½ cup brown sugar

2 tablespoons ground black pepper

1 tablespoon mustard powder

4 scallions, finely chopped

1. Rinse ribs with cold water, pat dry with paper towels, and place in a roasting pan. In a large saucepan, combine ¼ cup of the barbeque sauce and remaining ingredients. Bring to a boil and reduce heat to a simmer for 10 minutes. Cool completely, then pour over the ribs. Ribs should be completely submerged in the marinade. Cover and refrigerate overnight.

2. Remove ribs from marinade and let sit at room temperature for 30 minutes. Reserve 1 cup of marinade and discard the rest.

3. Preheat oven to 350°F. Place ribs meat-side up on a rack in a shallow roasting pan. Tightly cover with foil. Bake for 1 hour. While ribs are baking, make sauce. In a small saucepan, bring reserved marinade to a boil and reduce by half. Stir in remaining ½ cup barbeque sauce and remove from heat.

4. Remove ribs from oven and carefully drain fat from roasting pan. Continue baking ribs, uncovered, for 1 to 1½ hours more or until tender, turning and brushing occasionally with sauce.

COUNTRY MUSTARD RUBBED PORK CHOPS

MAKES: 4 servings **COOK:** 14 minutes

½   cup country Dijon mustard
2   teaspoons herb blend seasoning
1   teaspoon crushed garlic
1   teaspoon honey
2   tablespoons chopped fresh parsley
1½ pounds boneless pork loin chops, thick-cut

1. In a small bowl, combine mustard, seasoning, garlic, honey, and parsley. Reserve ¼ cup of the mixture.

2. Transfer mustard mixture to a large zip-top bag. Rinse pork chops under cold water and pat dry with paper towels. Add pork chops to bag and thoroughly rub chops with the mustard mixture. Let the pork chops sit for at least 5 minutes and as long as overnight in the refrigerator before grilling.

3. Heat a grill pan over medium heat. Place pork chops on hot, oiled grill for 6 to 7 minutes per side. Serve pork chops with reserved rub.

DUCK BREAST WITH APPLE SAUCE, POTATOES, AND FENNEL

MAKES: 4 servings   **COOK:** 1 hour 10 minutes

FOR THE DUCK:

 4 (5-ounce) boneless, skinless duck breast halves
 ½ teaspoon salt
 1½ teaspoons black pepper, divided use
 5 tablespoons extra-virgin olive oil, divided use

FOR THE VEGETABLES:

 2 teaspoons garlic salt
 1 (20-ounce) bag frozen roasted potatoes—Ore-Ida®
 2 heads fennel, trimmed of greens and stems, quartered

FOR THE SAUCE:

 1 tablespoon chopped garlic
 3 tablespoons brandy
 ½ cup low-sodium chicken broth
 1 (20-ounce) can apple pie filling
 2 tablespoons apple cider vinegar

1. Preheat oven to 375°F.

2. Rinse duck breasts, pat dry with paper towels, and trim any excess fat. Score the surface diagonally and season with salt, 1 teaspoon pepper, and 1 tablespoon olive oil. Cover with plastic wrap and set aside.

3. For the vegetables, mix garlic salt and remaining black pepper with 1 tablespoon olive oil in a large bowl and toss with the potatoes and fennel. Spread out on a rimmed baking sheet lined with foil. Bake for 35 to 40 minutes or until golden brown.

4. For the duck, heat 1 tablespoon olive oil in a medium ovenproof sauté pan over medium-high heat. Cook breasts, turning once, until lightly browned on both sides, about 4 minutes. Pour off any fat from the pan and transfer pan to the oven. Roast the duck until an instant-read thermometer reads 150°F, about 12 to 15 minutes. Transfer the duck breasts to a cutting board, wrap with foil to keep warm, and allow to rest for 10 minutes.

5. For the sauce, heat the same sauté pan over medium-high heat, add 2 tablespoons olive oil and garlic, stirring often to scrape up the browned bits and toast the garlic without burning. When the garlic is golden brown, add brandy. Stir in the chicken broth and apple pie filling. Bring to a boil, reduce the heat to low, and cook until thickened, about 6 to 8 minutes. Stir in cider vinegar.

6. To serve, slice the duck breasts diagonally across the grain. Pour some sauce on individual serving plates and arrange the duck, fanning out slices alongside the potatoes and fennel.

HAM STEAKS AND WHIPPED SPICY SWEET POTATOES

MAKES: 4 servings **COOK:** 15 minutes

1 (24-ounce) bag Steam n' Mash sweet potatoes—Ore-Ida®

2 tablespoons butter

2 tablespoons maple syrup

2 teaspoons Mexican seasoning—The Spice Hunter

¼ cup sour cream

1 tablespoon canned diced jalapeños

¼ cup crumbled bacon—Hormel

2 (16-ounce) center-cut ready-to-eat ham steaks

Salt and pepper, to taste

1. Heat potatoes in microwave according to package directions. Empty into a large mixing bowl, add butter, syrup, and Mexican seasoning, and whip with electric mixer on low speed until smooth. Stir in sour cream, jalapeños, and bacon. Season to taste with salt and pepper.

2. Preheat broiler. Broil ham (do not turn) until brown at edges, about 3 minutes.

3. Serve broiled ham steaks hot, topped with whipped potatoes.

HERB AND PEAR GLAZED TURKEY

MAKES: 8 servings   **COOK:** 3 hours

1   (14-pound) fresh turkey

1   stick (½ cup) butter, softened

1   (1.5-ounce) packet Honey BBQ Chicken
     Glaze seasoning mix—McCormick

1   pear

1   bunch mixed fresh herbs such as parsley,
     sage, thyme, and rosemary

1   (12-ounce) can pear nectar

1. Preheat oven to 350°F.

2. Rinse turkey under cold water and pat dry with paper towels. Mix the butter with the seasoning mix. Reserve 2 tablespoons seasoned butter for the glaze, and rub the remaining 6 tablespoons all over the turkey, inside and out, as well as under the skin. Cut the pear into quarters and put them into the cavity along with the herbs. Tie up the legs and put the turkey, breast-side up, onto the rack in a roasting pan. Pour ½ cup water into the pan and roast for 2 hours, basting with the pan juices every 15 minutes, while you prepare the glaze.

3. In a small pot over medium-high heat, add pear nectar. Cook, stirring frequently, until nectar is reduced by a third, about 10 minutes. Remove from heat and stir in the reserved seasoned butter to make a glaze. When the turkey has cooked for 2 hours, start basting the turkey with the glaze every 15 minutes until the internal temperature is 165°F in the breast and 180°F in the thigh. Remove the turkey from the oven, give it one last basting, and let it rest for 15 to 20 minutes before carving.

MAPLE GLAZED CHICKEN WITH ROASTED COUNTRY VEGETABLES

MAKES: 4 servings   **COOK:** 1 hour 20 minutes

2   tablespoons honey mustard dressing

1   tablespoon spicy brown mustard

2   tablespoons canola oil

1   pound baby carrots

1   pound Brussels sprouts, halved

1   pound red baby potatoes, halved

1   (3½- to 4½-pound) chicken

1   tablespoon chicken seasoning—McCormick

Salt and pepper, to taste

FOR THE GLAZE:

¼   cup maple syrup

¼   cup orange juice

1   tablespoon spicy brown mustard

3   tablespoons butter

Salt and pepper, to taste

1. **Preheat oven to 375°F.**

2. In a small bowl, whisk together the dressing, mustard, oil, and salt and pepper to taste. Toss with vegetables and spread them on the bottom of a roasting pan.

3. Rinse chicken under cold water and pat dry with paper towels. Season chicken with the chicken seasoning. Place chicken on top of vegetables in roasting pan. Roast for 50 minutes to an hour until golden and a thermometer reads 150°F when inserted in the thickest part of the thigh.

4. While chicken is roasting, whisk together all ingredients for the glaze in a pot over medium-high heat. Bring to a simmer and cook until thickened slightly. Season with salt and pepper to taste.

5. When chicken is nearly cooked through, completely coat the outside with glaze using a pastry brush. Pour any remaining glaze over vegetables. Roast for an additional 15 to 20 minutes or until a thermometer reads 175°F when inserted in the thickest part of the thigh. Let rest for 10 minutes before serving.

MAYFLOWER CORNISH HENS WITH ROASTED POTATOES

MAKES: 4 servings   **COOK:** 1 hour

FOR THE POTATOES:

  Nonstick cooking spray

1 (30-ounce) bag frozen potato wedges—Ore-Ida®

2 tablespoons minced garlic

1 teaspoon salt

½ teaspoon coarse ground black pepper

FOR THE HENS:

4 whole Cornish game hens

2 teaspoons ground cumin seed

1 tablespoon dried oregano

3 tablespoons lemon pepper seasoning

½ cup scallions, cut in 1-inch pieces

2 whole lemons, halved

  Extra-virgin olive oil (for basting if necessary)

1. Preheat oven to 400°F. Spray a 9 × 13-inch baking pan with cooking spray and set aside.

2. For the potatoes, toss the frozen potatoes with garlic, salt, and pepper in the baking pan. Set aside to defrost slightly while assembling the hens.

3. For the hens, rinse the hens inside and out and pat dry with paper towels. Combine the cumin with the oregano and lemon pepper seasoning and rub 1 tablespoon of the mixture on each hen, including the cavity. Stuff each with ¼ of the scallions and plug with a lemon half. Do not truss the hens, or they will cook too slowly.

4. Place hens in 9 × 13-inch baking pan, legs pointing outward. Put pan in the oven and immediately turn heat down to 350°F. Bake for 45 minutes to 1 hour or until the internal temperature reads 180°F at the thigh.

5. After about 35 minutes, brush the hens with drippings that gather in the bottom of the pan. If the potatoes have absorbed all the liquid, brush hens with a bit of extra-virgin olive oil.

RED WINE HARVEST FILETS

MAKES: 4 servings **COOK:** 14 minutes

4 (8 ounces each) beef tenderloin steaks

1 (1.06-ounce) packet Zesty Herb Marinade—McCormick Grill Mates

1½ cups Merlot wine

1 tablespoon chopped fresh rosemary

Fresh rosemary sprigs, for garnish

1. Rinse steaks under cold water and pat dry with paper towels. In a large zip-top bag, combine all ingredients except rosemary sprigs. Squeeze out air and seal bag. Massage bag until well combined and marinade mix is dissolved. Marinate in refrigerator for a minimum of 1 hour, or for as long as overnight. Remove steaks from refrigerator 30 minutes before cooking.

2. Remove steaks from marinade and discard marinade. Preheat broiler. Place steaks on a foil-lined baking sheet or broiler pan. Broil 6 to 8 inches from heat source for 5 to 7 minutes per side for medium rare (135°F). Let steaks rest 5 minutes before serving.

ROASTED BEEF LOIN WITH POTATO AND CHIVE GRATIN

MAKES: 4 servings   **COOK:** 55 minutes

Nonstick cooking spray

2 pounds center-cut beef tenderloin

1 tablespoon garlic salt—Lawry's

2 teaspoons ground black pepper

1 tablespoon herbes de Provence—
McCormick

1 (24-ounce) container garlic mashed
potatoes—Country Crock

4 tablespoons butter

2 eggs

¼ cup sour cream

1 (8-ounce) container whipped chive cream
cheese—Philadelphia

4 teaspoons finely chopped chives, divided
use

1 teaspoon salt

¼ teaspoon pepper

½ cup seasoned dressing mix—
Mrs. Cubbison's, crushed
About 2 cups canola oil, for cooking

1. Preheat oven to 400°F. Spray a 1½-quart casserole dish with cooking spray and set aside.

2. Trim away any excess fat from beef, rinse under cold water, then pat dry with paper towels. Season with garlic salt, pepper, and herbes de Provence. Set aside.

3. Heat mashed potatoes and butter, covered, in microwave on 100 percent power for 2½ minutes. Remove, stir, and set aside. Beat eggs in a large bowl with electric mixer on low speed for 10 seconds. Add mashed potatoes and sour cream and beat until combined. Add cream cheese, 2 teaspoons chives, salt, and pepper. Beat until fluffy on medium speed, about 30 seconds. Scoop into prepared dish. Sprinkle crushed dressing mix over top. Set aside.

4. Heat ⅛ inch of oil in a heavy-bottomed or cast-iron skillet over high heat. When oil is very hot, add beef and brown for 2 to 4 minutes per side. Transfer to a roasting pan with a wire rack. Place roasting pan and casserole dish in oven and bake for 35 to 45 minutes or until internal temperature of roast reaches 135°F for medium rare.

5. Remove roast to a platter and tent with foil for 10 minutes before serving. Garnish gratin with fresh chives. Slice beef into 4 thick servings. Serve immediately with potato and chive gratin.

ROASTED CHICKEN WITH PORT AND FIGS

MAKES: 4 servings   **COOK:** 1 hour 15 minutes

1¾   cups ruby port

2   tablespoons honey

Nonstick cooking spray

1   (20-ounce) bag frozen roasted potatoes—Ore-Ida®

1   (16-ounce) bag frozen pearl onions

¾   cup chopped dried Mission figs

¾   cup pitted Kalamata olives, cut in half

¼   cup olive oil

1   (3-pound) chicken

1   teaspoon chicken seasoning

Salt and pepper, to taste

1. Preheat oven to 400°F.
2. In a small saucepan over medium-high heat, reduce the port by ½ or until syrupy, coating the back of a spoon. Remove from heat, stir in honey, and cool.
3. Spray a roasting pan with oil. Coat the potatoes with olive oil and place in the bottom of roasting pan. Top with onions and sprinkle figs and black olives over all.
4. Rinse chicken inside and out, pat dry with paper towels, and rub with salt and pepper. Place chicken on top of vegetables in roasting pan. Baste the bird with half the reduced port.
5. Reduce heat to 350°F and place chicken in the oven. After 30 minutes, baste chicken several more times or until the mixture is gone. If chicken begins to become too brown, cover loosely with foil. Roast for a total of 1 hour to 1 hour 15 minutes or until a thermometer registers 165°F when inserted in the breast.

ROASTED MEDITERRANEAN STYLE TURKEY

MAKES: 12 servings **COOK:** 3 hours

4   sprigs rosemary

2   large fennel bulbs

¾   cup butter, softened

1   (0.87-ounce) packet garlic, herb, and wine marinade mix—McCormick Grill Mates, divided use

1   tablespoon lemon juice

1   (12-pound) turkey, thawed if necessary

1   (8-ounce) bag baby carrots, divided use

6   stalks celery, divided use

1   (32-ounce) container less-sodium chicken broth

1   (14-ounce) bag frozen pearl onions

2   tablespoons extra-virgin olive oil

1. Preheat oven to 450°F. Place a roasting rack in a large roasting pan.

2. Strip rosemary leaves and finely chop enough for 2 teaspoons, then place in a small bowl. Remove fronds from fennel stems and finely chop enough for 2 tablespoons; add to bowl. Add butter, 2 teaspoons marinade mix, and lemon juice to the bowl. Blend with a fork until combined.

3. Rinse turkey inside and out with cold water and pat dry with paper towels. Use your fingers to loosen skin around the entire bird. Take half of the butter mixture and rub underneath the skin. Take the remaining butter mixture and rub over the outside. Use 2 teaspoons marinade mix and season inside of turkey. Place turkey breast-side up on roasting rack.

4. Chop fennel stems, ½ cup carrots, 1 celery stalk, and 2 sprigs rosemary into 1-inch pieces and stuff inside turkey cavity. Truss legs if desired. Place in oven and reduce temperature to 325°F. Roast for 1 hour and then baste with pan juices every 20 minutes. Add enough broth to pan for basting as needed. Roast turkey until the internal temperature of the thigh reaches 180°F and the juices run clear, about 3 hours total.

5. Chop remaining celery into 2-inch pieces and add to a large mixing bowl with onions and remaining carrots. Cut fennel bulbs into eighths through the root ends and add to bowl. Remove leaves from remaining rosemary sprig and finely chop. Toss vegetables with rosemary, olive oil, and remaining marinade mix to coat. After turkey has roasted for 2 hours, scatter vegetables around roasting pan. Stir vegetables every time turkey is basted.

6. Let turkey rest 10 minutes before carving. Meanwhile, strain and defat pan drippings. Serve hot with pan drippings and vegetables.

ROASTED RACK OF LAMB WITH MINT PESTO

MAKES: 4 servings **COOK:** 24 minutes

1 (2 ½ to 3-pound) frenched rack of lamb
Salt and pepper

FOR THE MINT PESTO:

1 bunch fresh mint, leaves only
2 tablespoons mint jelly
2 tablespoons chopped walnuts
1 tablespoon chopped garlic
1 tablespoon extra-virgin olive oil
1 tablespoon apple cider vinegar
¼ teaspoon red pepper flakes
Salt and pepper, to taste

1. Season the lamb all over with salt and pepper. Cover and let the meat come to room temperature, about 30 minutes.
2. Preheat oven to 350°F.
3. Heat a skillet over medium-high heat. Place the lamb, fat-side down, in skillet and cook until it is browned, about 2 minutes. Turn over and sear the other side for 2 minutes. Place the lamb, bone-side down, into a shallow roasting pan and roast until medium rare or until the internal temperature reaches 125 to 130°F, about 15 to 20 minutes. Remove lamb from oven, cover it with foil, and let it rest for about 10 minutes.
4. For the mint pesto, add the mint leaves, jelly, walnuts, garlic, oil, vinegar, and red pepper flakes to a bowl of a food processor. Process until almost smooth. Taste, and adjust the taste with salt and pepper.

ROASTED TURKEY WITH CITRUS BUTTER

MAKES: 8 servings **COOK:** 3 hours 30 minutes

1 (12- to 14-pound) turkey, thawed if frozen
1 lime
1 lemon
1 orange
1 stick (½ cup) butter, softened
1 pound leeks, green parts only
Salt and pepper, to taste

1. Preheat oven to 350°F. Let the turkey sit at room temperature, covered, for 30 minutes before preparing.
2. Zest and juice the lime, lemon, and orange. Reserve the juice and rinds. Mix the butter with the citrus zest and salt and pepper to taste. Rinse turkey under cold water and pat dry with paper towels. Rub the seasoned butter all over the turkey, inside and out, as well as under the skin. Put the citrus rinds and leeks into the cavity. Tie up the legs and put the turkey, breast-side up, on a rack in a roasting pan. Pour ½ cup water into the pan and roast, basting with pan juices every 15 to 20 minutes. Cook until the internal temperature is 165°F in the breast and 180°F in the thigh, about 15 to 20 minutes per pound.
3. Remove turkey from oven and let it rest for 15 to 20 minutes before carving. Pour off the juices, skim off the fat, and serve with the bird.

SMOKED TURKEY BREAST WITH CINNAMON APPLES

MAKES: 12 servings   **COOK:** 2 hours 15 minutes

FOR THE TURKEY:

- 1   whole (4- to 6-pound) turkey breast
- 1   stick (½ cup) butter, softened
- 1   tablespoon Montreal chicken seasoning—McCormick Grill Mates
- 1   (0.74-ounce) packet spiced apple cider mix—Alpine
- 2   teaspoons crushed garlic
- ¼   teaspoon liquid smoke, optional
      Salt and pepper, to taste

FOR THE APPLES:

- ⅓   cup brown sugar
- 1   teaspoon cinnamon
- ⅓   cup chopped pecans
- ⅓   cup golden raisins
- 3   tablespoons butter
- 6   Granny Smith apples, quartered and cored

1. Rinse turkey breast under cold water and pat dry with paper towels. Set aside. In a small bowl, blend together butter, chicken seasoning, cider mix, and garlic with a fork. Loosen skin of turkey breast around the neck end and work your hands under the skin, leaving the skin attached at the edges. Rub most of the butter under the skin and rub some over the skin, as well.

2. Preheat oven to 325°F. For a smoked flavor, add ¼ teaspoon liquid smoke to butter mixture. Place turkey in roasting pan and roast for 1½ to 2¼ hours or until internal temperature reaches 170°F.

3. In a small bowl, blend together sugar, cinnamon, pecans, raisins, and butter with a fork. Sprinkle over quartered apples and add to roasting pan during the last 30 minutes of roasting.

4. Transfer turkey to a platter and let rest for 10 minutes. Slice and serve hot with cinnamon apples.

THANKSGIVING LEFTOVER PIE

MAKES: 4 servings   **BAKE:** 35 minutes

Nonstick cooking spray

1½ cups diced roasted turkey

1 cup premade stuffing

1 (10-ounce) package frozen corn, thawed

½ cup low-sodium chicken broth

¾ cup turkey gravy

1 tablespoon chopped fresh parsley

2 cups store-bought mashed potatoes

1. Preheat oven to 350°F. Spray an 8 × 8-inch baking dish with nonstick cooking spray.

2. In a large bowl, fold together the turkey, stuffing, corn, broth, gravy, and parsley. Pour into prepared baking dish and smooth out the top. Cover with mashed potatoes, making sure to cover completely. Bake until the mixture is bubbling and the top is lightly browned, about 30 to 35 minutes. Let rest for 5 minutes before serving.

VEAL ROAST WITH WILD RICE AND PECAN STUFFING

MAKES: 8 servings   **COOK:** 2 hours 20 minutes

1   (4-pound) boneless veal loin

⅓   cup chopped fresh parsley

1   tablespoon chopped fresh rosemary leaves

1   tablespoon steak seasoning

2   (8.8-ounce) pouches precooked long grain and wild rice—Uncle Ben's Ready Rice

½   cup chopped pecans

1   teaspoon chopped garlic

2   cups white wine

2   sprigs rosemary

1. Rinse roast with cold water and pat dry with paper towels. Combine parsley, rosemary, and steak seasoning. Coat veal with herb mixture and set aside.

2. Heat both packages of rice in microwave for 2 minutes. Empty into a bowl and stir in pecans and garlic. Cut a wide slit into the side of the roast. When rice is cooled, stuff into the pocket made in the roast. Tie roast at 1-inch intervals with butcher's twine.

3. Set up grill for indirect cooking over medium heat (no heat source under meat). Pour wine into drip pan and add rosemary sprigs. Oil grate when ready to start cooking. Place roast over drip pan on hot, oiled grill. Add a handful of wood chips to each pile of coals or to smoke box. Cover and cook for 1½ to 2¼ hours or until internal temperature reaches 150° for medium. If using charcoal, add 10 briquettes and more wood chips to each pile of coals after one hour.

4. Remove from grill and tent with foil for 10 minutes before slicing. Slice and serve hot.

5. *Indoor*: Prepare roast with stuffing as directed. Preheat oven to 325°F. Place roast on a wire rack in a roasting pan (omit wine and garlic sprigs). Roast for 1½ to 2¼ hours or until internal temperature reaches 150 degrees for medium. Let stand 10 minutes and serve as directed.

MINI APPLE PIES

MAKES: 4 servings   **BAKE:** 20 minutes

4   whole wheat flour tortillas

1   (21-ounce) can apple pie filling

1   tablespoon milk

1   teaspoon sugar

1. Preheat oven to 350°F.

2. Warm the tortillas in a microwave to make them pliable. Divide the apple filling among the 4 tortillas. Fold in ends and roll up each tortilla like a burrito. Place on an ungreased baking sheet and make slashes to allow steam to vent. Brush tops with milk and sprinkle with sugar. Bake for 20 minutes or until lightly browned.

MINI FIG FINANCIERS

MAKES: 6 servings   **COOK:** 30 minutes

Nonstick cooking spray

1 stick (½ cup) butter

½ cup plus 2 tablespoons almonds

⅓ cup cake flour

1¼ cups powdered sugar, plus more for garnish

¾ cup liquid egg whites, room temperature

½ cup fig preserves

1. Preheat oven to 350°F. Spray 6-cup mini Bundt pans with cooking spray.

2. Melt butter in a medium saucepan over medium heat until a dark golden color, about 6 minutes, swirling pan occasionally. Remove and cool to room temperature, but still in liquid form.

3. Grind almonds in a food processor into coarse powder. Combine with cake flour and powdered sugar in a large bowl.

4. Pour egg whites into flour mixture and beat with an electric mixer on medium speed for 3 minutes. Scrape down sides of bowl and add fig preserves. Beat for 30 seconds on low speed. Scrape down sides of bowl and add cooled butter. Beat for 3 minutes more on medium speed.

5. Pour into prepared pans and bake for 20 to 24 minutes or until a tester comes out clean. Remove from oven and cool completely. Invert pan and place on serving plate. Dust with powdered sugar and serve immediately.

PUMPKIN MAPLE BREAD PUDDING

MAKES: 10 servings **BAKE:** 1 hour 10 minutes

Butter-flavored cooking spray
1 (16-ounce) loaf cinnamon-raisin swirl bread, cut into ½-inch cubes
½ cup chopped pecans
1¼ cups milk
½ cup cream
4 eggs
2 teaspoons pumpkin pie spice
½ cup maple syrup
1 (15-ounce) can solid packed pumpkin—Libby's
1 (4.5-ounce) jar brandied hard sauce—Crosse & Blackwell
1 teaspoon maple extract

1. Lightly spray a 3-quart casserole dish with butter-flavored cooking spray. Toss together cubed raisin bread and pecans in casserole dish. Set aside.
2. In a large bowl, whisk together remaining ingredients, except hard sauce and maple extract. Pour over bread cubes. Let soak for 1 hour in the refrigerator.
3. Preheat oven to 350°F.
4. Bake bread pudding in preheated oven for 1 hour to 1 hour 10 minutes or until knife inserted into center comes out clean.
5. Remove lid from hard sauce and place jar in a microwave-safe bowl. Fill bowl with water halfway up the side of the jar. Heat on high in microwave for 30 to 45 seconds. Pour into a bowl and stir in maple extract. Drizzle over bread pudding. Serve warm or at room temperature.

SPICED COFFEE MERINGUES

MAKES: 18 servings **BAKE:** 1 hour 5 minutes

1   tablespoon instant coffee crystals

4   large egg whites

⅛   teaspoon salt

¼   teaspoon cream of tartar

1   teaspoon ground cinnamon

½   cup packed brown sugar

½   cup sugar

½   teaspoon almond extract

½   cup slivered almonds, toasted

1. Preheat oven to 250°F. Line baking sheet with parchment paper and set aside.
2. Beat instant coffee, egg whites, salt, cream of tartar, and cinnamon in a medium bowl with an electric mixer until soft peaks form. Add both sugars and almond extract and beat until stiff (but not dry) peaks form. Fold in toasted slivered almonds.
3. Drop by heaping teaspoons 1½-inches apart onto prepared baking sheet. Bake in preheated oven for 30 to 35 minutes. Turn off heat and leave meringues in oven for an additional 30 minutes.
4. Remove parchment and meringues from the baking sheet and let cool completely on the counter. Peel cookies from parchment to serve.

PUMPKIN TIRAMISU

MAKES: 8 servings

1   (15-ounce) can pumpkin puree

1   (8-ounce) block cream cheese, softened

¾   cup packed brown sugar

1   tablespoon plus 1 teaspoon pumpkin pie spice, divided use

1½   cups heavy cream

¼   cup powdered sugar

1   teaspoon vanilla

1   cup orange spice tea, brewed with 1 tea bag and cooled

½   cup orange juice

3   tablespoons spiced rum

1   (7-ounce) package ladyfingers

½   cup chopped walnuts

1. In a mixing bowl, beat together pumpkin puree with cream cheese, brown sugar, and 1 tablespoon pumpkin pie spice.
2. In a separate bowl, beat heavy cream with powdered sugar and vanilla to medium peaks. Fold ¼ of the whipped cream into the pumpkin mixture.
3. To assemble, combine tea with juice and rum in a bowl. Dip ladyfingers in tea mixture and place in a single layer on the bottom of a 3-quart trifle bowl. Spread half of the pumpkin mixture in an even layer on top of the ladyfingers. Repeat with another layer of ladyfingers and remaining pumpkin mixture. Top with a layer of whipped cream, sprinkle with chopped walnuts, and dust with teaspoon of pumpkin pie spice. Cover with plastic and refrigerate for 3 hours before serving.

STRAWBERRIES 'N CREAM CAKE

MAKES: 24 servings **BAKE:** 35 minutes

Nonstick baking spray

2 (18.25-ounce) boxes vanilla cake mix

6 eggs

⅔ cup vegetable oil

2½ cups strawberry nectar

1 teaspoon strawberry extract

1¼ cups seedless strawberry preserves

3 (16-ounce) cans cream cheese frosting

2½ cups sliced fresh strawberries

3 cups mini vanilla meringue cookies

3 cups fresh strawberries

1. Preheat oven to 350°F. Lightly spray two 9-inch and two 6-inch round cake pans with baking spray.

2. For each cake mix, combine 1 cake mix, 3 eggs, ⅓ cup vegetable oil, 1¼ cups nectar, and 1 teaspoon strawberry extract in a large mixing bowl. Beat together on low speed for 30 seconds, scrape down sides of the bowl, then beat on medium speed for 2 minutes. Transfer to the 4 prepared pans so that the height of the batter is the same in each pan. Bake in preheated oven for 30 to 35 minutes or until a tester inserted in center of cakes comes away clean. The 6-inch cakes will finish about 5 minutes before the others. Cool in pan for 5 minutes before turning out onto a wire cooling rack to cool completely.

3. Level the cakes if they have crowned, and split each layer horizontally with a serrated knife. Stack the 9-inch cake layers, spreading about ¼ cup preserves, ½ cup frosting, and ½ cup sliced strawberries between the layers. Stack the 6-inch cake layers on a 6-inch cardboard cake round, repeating the filling between layers using about 2 tablespoons preserves, ¼ cup frosting, and ¼ cup sliced strawberries. Place the 6-inch cake centered on top of the larger cake. Frost the outside of the tiered cake.

4. Place meringue cookies in a plastic zip-top bag, and crush them with a rolling pin. Press the whole mini meringues or crushed meringue cookies in 8 evenly spaced "columns" up the sides of the cakes, around the base of the bottom layer, and a ½-inch border around the top of the cake. Decorate the center of the top cake and the top perimeter of the bottom cake.

SWEET POTATO BANANA CASSEROLE

MAKES: 6 servings **BAKE:** 30 minutes

Nonstick cooking spray

1 (24-ounce) bag Steam n' Mash Cut Sweet Potatoes—Ore-Ida®

1 cup mashed ripe bananas (about 3 medium)

1 (8-ounce) can crushed pineapple

1 egg, lightly beaten

¼ cup light coconut milk

¾ teaspoon Caribbean jerk seasoning—McCormick

¼ teaspoon ground allspice

½ teaspoon salt

1 cup miniature marshmallows

¾ cup sweetened coconut

1. Preheat oven to 350°F. Lightly spray a 1½-quart casserole dish with cooking spray.

2. Microwave sweet potatoes according to package directions. Add to a large bowl with bananas, pineapple, egg, coconut milk, seasoning, allspice, and salt. Beat with electric mixer until light and very fluffy. Turn into casserole dish. Top casserole with miniature marshmallows, then coconut.

3. Bake at 350°F for 30 minutes or until puffed and lightly browned.

DECEMBER

CHIVE BUTTER MASHED POTATOES

MAKES: 4 servings **COOK:** 12 minutes

- 1 (24-ounce) bag Steam 'n Mash potatoes—Ore-Ida®
- 6 tablespoons butter, softened, divided use
- ¾ cup heavy cream
- 2 sprigs thyme
- 2 tablespoons fresh chives
- 1 tablespoon prepared horseradish
   Salt and pepper, to taste

1. Microwave potatoes according to package directions.
2. In a small saucepan, heat 2 tablespoons butter with cream and thyme sprigs. Bring to a simmer, then remove from heat. Remove thyme sprigs and discard. Set aside.
3. In a small bowl, combine remaining butter and chives. Season with salt and pepper to taste. Mix until well incorporated.
4. Mash potatoes lightly with a potato masher. Add in cream mixture and horseradish, continuing to mash until desired consistency is reached. Do not overmix or potatoes will become gummy. Season with salt and pepper to taste. Transfer to a serving bowl and top with chive butter.

CHRISTMAS ENDIVE BITES

MAKES: 4 servings

- 2 endives
- 1 large green zebra or yellow tomato, chopped
- 1 cup grated mozzarella
- ¼ cup chopped fresh basil leaves
- ¼ cup balsamic vinaigrette salad dressing
   Kosher salt and freshly ground black pepper
- ¼ cup grated Parmesan

1. Separate the leaves of the endive and set aside the larger leaves.
2. In a bowl, gently mix together the tomatoes, mozzarella, basil, and dressing, and season with salt and pepper, to taste. Fill the leaves with the mixture and sprinkle with a little Parmesan. Arrange the bites on a serving platter and serve.

HAM AND CHEESE PINWHEELS

MAKES: 12 pinwheels **BAKE:** 25 minutes

3   tablespoons olive oil
1   tablespoon crushed garlic
2   teaspoons Italian seasoning
    Flour, for cutting board
1   (13.8-ounce) can refrigerated pizza
    crust dough
1½ cups shredded mozzarella cheese
⅓   pound sliced deli ham
1   large egg

1. Preheat oven to 375°F.
2. In a small bowl, whisk together the olive oil, garlic, and Italian seasoning.
3. Roll out the pizza dough onto a lightly floured cutting board. Brush the entire surface with the seasoned olive oil. Top with 1 cup of shredded cheese, an even layer of ham, then the remaining ½ cup of cheese.
4. Starting from the bottom edge, tightly roll up the dough to form a log. Using a sharp serrated knife, slice the roll in half, and then each half into 6 pieces. Place rolls on their side on a nonstick or lightly oiled baking sheet.
5. In a small bowl, whisk together the egg with 2 tablespoons water. Brush the tops and sides of rolls with egg wash. Bake until golden brown, about 20 to 25 minutes.

HOLIDAY DEVILED EGGS

MAKES: 12 pieces **COOK:** 15 Minutes

1   dozen eggs
¼   cup mayonnaise
1   tablespoon Dijon mustard
1   lemon, zested
2   teaspoons chopped jalapeños
1   teaspoon smoked paprika
2   tablespoons crumbled bacon, for garnish
2   tablespoons chopped fresh chives

1. Place eggs in a large pot and cover with cold water. Bring to a boil, turn off heat, cover, and let sit for 15 minutes. Drain water from pot and fill with cold water to cool eggs. Change water twice so eggs cool quickly.
2. Peel eggs and slice off the bottoms so that eggs will stand upright. Slice the top third off each (save tops). Carefully remove egg yolks with a small spoon and place in a medium bowl. Break up the yolks with a potato masher. Add all remaining ingredients except bacon and chives. Mix until well blended and smooth.
3. Transfer mixture to a resealable bag, cut off a corner of the bag, and pipe the filling into each egg. Sprinkle each with chopped chives and bacon bits. Place the tops back onto the eggs. Transfer to a platter and serve.

ITALIAN GREEN BEANS

MAKES: 4 servings   **COOK:** 8 minutes

1   (12-ounce) bag Steamfresh whole green beans—Birds Eye
2   tablespoons olive oil
¼   teaspoon crushed red pepper flakes
2   teaspoons Italian seasoning
2   teaspoons chopped garlic
     Salt and pepper, to taste

1. Cook green beans in microwave according to package directions.
2. Heat olive oil in a large skillet over medium heat. Add red pepper flakes, Italian seasoning, garlic, and a generous pinch of salt and pepper, and sauté for 2 minutes. Add green beans, toss to coat them in the oil, and sauté another 2 minutes. Serve hot.

PEPPERED GOAT CHEESE MASHED POTATOES

MAKES: 8 servings   **COOK:** 12 minutes

2   (24-ounce) bags Steam n' Mash potatoes—Ore-Ida®
2   cups light cream
½   stick (4 tablespoons) butter
6   sprigs fresh thyme
8   ounces peppered goat cheese, at room temperature
2   teaspoons salt
1   teaspoon pepper

1. Microwave Steam n' Mash potatoes according to package directions.
2. While the potatoes are cooking, warm the cream with the butter and thyme in a medium pot over medium heat. Don't let it boil.
3. Place the potatoes in a large pot and mash with a potato masher. Strain half the cream mixture into the warm potatoes and add the cheese in chunks. Mix together, adding more strained cream to get a creamy consistency. Keep covered and serve warm.
4. Bake for 30 to 35 minutes or until crust is golden and potatoes are cooked through. Allow to cool for 5 minutes before slicing.

ROASTED PARSNIP MEDLEY

MAKES: 8 servings   **COOK:** 40 minutes

1 large head cauliflower

2 pounds parsnips, peeled

2 pounds white potatoes

¼ cup plus 2 tablespoons olive oil

1 tablespoon lemon pepper seasoning

1. Preheat oven to 400°F.
2. Cut the large thick stems off the cauliflower. Break up into small florets. Slice the potatoes and parsnips in approximately 1-inch-thick pieces. Place all the vegetables into a large bowl and add oil and lemon pepper seasoning. Toss to coat, then transfer to 2 baking sheets. Roast for 35 to 40 minutes until lightly browned and tender. If the vegetables start to brown too quickly, loosely cover with foil. Transfer to a serving bowl and serve with pork crown roast.

ANCHO-RUBBED GAME HENS WITH PICKLED ONIONS

MAKES: 4 servings   **COOK:** 25 minutes

FOR THE PICKLED ONIONS:

- 1 large red onion, sliced
- 1 tablespoon diced jalapeños
- 1 clove garlic, smashed
- ½ cup lime juice
- ½ teaspoon salt

FOR THE HENS:

- 4 (1 to 1½-pound) game hens
- 2 tablespoons Montreal chicken seasoning— McCormick Grill Mates
- 1 tablespoon chili powder
- 1 teaspoon finely ground coffee
- 2 teaspoons salt
- 2 teaspoons brown sugar
- 1 tablespoon ancho chili powder

1. For pickled onions, place onion slices in a large bowl. Cover with boiling water, let stand for 1 minute, and drain. Add jalapeño, garlic, lime juice, and salt. Stir to combine. Transfer to a smaller container just large enough to hold onion mixture. Cover and refrigerate for at least 2 hours, stirring occasionally.

2. For the hens, remove the backbones with kitchen shears. Open up the hens and, from the inside, run a knife along each side of the breastbone. Run your finger along the breastbone, pull out, and remove. Cut off wing tips and excess skin. Rinse hens under cold water and pat dry with paper towels. Set aside.

3. In a bowl, combine remaining ingredients, and thoroughly pat spice mixture over all sides of each hen. Let cure 15 to 30 minutes.

4. Preheat broiler. Place hens on foil-lined baking sheet or broiler pan. Broil 6 to 8 inches from heat source for 10 to 12 minutes per side, or until no longer pink at the bone and the juices run clear (180°F at the thigh). Transfer hens to a platter and let rest for 5 minutes before serving. Serve hot with pickled onions.

CHICKEN POT PIES

MAKES: 4 servings   **COOK:** 1 hour 15 minutes

- 1 box pie crust mix
- 2 chicken breasts (about 1 lb. each)
- 5 cups water
- 1 tablespoon canola oil
- ½ medium onion, diced
- 3 stalks celery, diced
- 2 carrots, sliced
- ⅓ cup all-purpose flour
- ½ teaspoon poultry seasoning
- 1 teaspoon chopped fresh thyme
- 1 cup frozen peas
- 1 tablespoon milk
- Salt and pepper

1. Prepare pie crust according to package directions. Divide into 4 equal portions and refrigerate. Preheat oven to 350°F.

2. Put chicken breast in a medium pot, cover with water, bring to a boil, and add salt. Gently cook for 20 minutes or until chicken is completely cooked through. Skim any fat that rises to the surface. Remove chicken. Once cool enough to handle, remove meat and dice into ½-inch cubes. Reserve liquid the chicken was cooked in as stock.

3. In a medium pot, heat oil over medium heat. Add onion, celery, carrots, salt, and pepper and cook until onion is translucent, about 5 minutes. Add flour, poultry seasoning, and thyme, and cook for 2 minutes, stirring constantly. Add 4½ cups reserved stock and whisk to remove any lumps. Stir in chicken and peas. Bring to a boil and remove from heat. Divide among four 14-ounce ramekins. (Alternately, pot pie can be made in a single 9-inch pie pan.)

4. Roll out the 4 pieces of pie dough to ¼-inch-thick rounds. Brush edges of ramekins with milk. Place dough over top of each ramekin and press around edges to seal. Cut steam vents in the top of each, brush with milk, and place on a baking sheet. Bake for 40 to 45 minutes or until crust is golden brown and interior is bubbling.

CHICKEN CACCIATORE

MAKES: 3 servings   **COOK:** 35 minutes

¼   cup all-purpose flour

2   teaspoons Italian seasoning, divided use

2   chicken legs and 2 chicken thighs

¼   cup canola oil

1   cup sliced mushrooms

1   green bell pepper, diced

2   cups tomato soup

½   cup chicken broth

1   tablespoon chopped fresh parsley
    Salt and pepper, to taste

1. Rinse chicken under cold water and pat dry with paper towels. In a large bowl or zip-top bag, mix flour with salt, pepper, and Italian seasoning. Add chicken and toss to coat.

2. In a large high-sided skillet with a lid, heat oil over medium-high heat. Shake off excess flour from chicken and fry in oil until golden brown on all sides, about 5 minutes. Remove chicken and reserve.

3. To pan, add mushrooms and bell pepper and cook for 2 minutes until slightly softened. Add 1 teaspoon Italian seasoning, tomato soup, and chicken broth. Bring to a boil, reduce to a simmer, and return chicken to pan. Cover with lid and cook for about 20 to 25 minutes until chicken is completely cooked through. Remove lid and simmer for 5 minutes to reduce sauce slightly. Transfer the cacciatore to a serving platter, then sprinkle with parsley and serve.

CHICKEN NOODLE CASSEROLE

MAKES: 4 servings   **COOK:** 35 minutes

Nonstick cooking spray

4   tablespoons butter (2 tablespoons melted)

2   tablespoons all-purpose flour

1½   cups milk

1   (18.6-ounce) can Rich & Hearty Chicken Pot Pie Style soup—Progresso

½   cup bread crumbs

1   tablespoon chopped parsley

½   (16-ounce) package egg noodles, par-cooked and drained

¾   cup shredded mozzarella cheese
    Salt and pepper, to taste

1. Preheat oven to 350°F. Spray a casserole dish with cooking spray.

2. Melt 2 tablespoons of butter in a saucepan over medium heat. Whisk in flour and cook, stirring constantly, for 2 minutes, to cook out the raw flour taste. Add the milk while whisking, and continue until you have a smooth sauce. Stir in the soup and bring to a simmer.

3. In a small bowl, add the bread crumbs, the 2 tablespoons of melted butter, parsley, and salt and pepper to taste. Stir to combine and set aside.

4. In a large bowl, combine the mixture and the noodles. Stir in the cheese and pour it into the casserole dish.

5. Sprinkle the bread crumb mixture over the top of the casserole and bake until the top is golden brown, about 20 to 30 minutes.

CHRISTMAS DAY SANDWICH

MAKES: 4 sandwiches   **COOK:** 20 minutes

2   tablespoons canola oil, divided use

½   cup sliced onions

1   cup sliced potatoes

1   cup roughly chopped precooked pork roast

1   tablespoon spicy brown mustard

4   slices rye bread, toasted

½   cup shredded cheddar cheese

   Salt and pepper, to taste

1. Preheat broiler.

2. In a large nonstick skillet over medium heat, heat 2 tablespoons canola oil. Add onions and cook for 2 minutes until just becoming translucent. Add potatoes, season with salt and pepper, and cook for 10 minutes, until potatoes are cooked through and lightly browned. Stir in pork and cook 2 minutes to heat through.

3. Spread mustard on one side of each slice of bread and place on a sheet pan. Divide sautéed pork mixture among the slices of bread. Sprinkle 2 tablespoons of cheese over top of each and broil until cheese is melted and bubbling.

CRANBERRY GLAZED TURKEY

MAKES: 12 servings   **COOK:** 3 hours

1   (12-pound) turkey

1½ sticks (¾ cup) butter, softened

3   tablespoons fines herbes, divided use

1   tablespoon crushed garlic

2   tablespoons plus ½ cup orange marmalade, divided use

2   tablespoons dehydrated onion flakes—McCormick

2   tablespoons salt

1   tablespoon pepper

2   oranges, sliced

2   leeks, washed and sliced

1   tablespoon poultry seasoning

1   (32-ounce) container low-sodium chicken broth

½   cup orange juice

1   can jellied cranberry sauce

½   cup Cointreau

1. Preheat the oven to 450°F. Remove giblets and neck from turkey and rinse inside and out with cold water. Pat dry with paper towels; set aside.

2. In a small bowl, combine softened butter, 1 tablespoon fines herbes, crushed garlic, 2 tablespoons marmalade, and onion flakes. Use a fork to mix together until well combined.

3. In a small bowl combine poultry seasoning, 1 tablespoon fines herbes, and salt and pepper.

4. Use your hand to carefully loosen the skin around the entire bird. Work half of the butter mixture under the skin of the entire turkey. Rub the remaining butter on the outside of the skin and season with the poultry seasoning mixture inside and out. Stuff the inside of the turkey cavity with oranges and leeks. (Truss if desired.) Add any leftover oranges and leeks to a shallow roasting pan; pour in broth and set aside. Insert a pop-up thermometer at an angle about 3-inches down from the neck cavity and 2-inches from the breastbone, in the thickest part of the breast. Place turkey breast side up on a rack over the vegetables in the roasting pan. Place in oven and reduce temperature to 325°F.

5. Combine orange juice, remaining marmalade, jellied cranberries, and remaining fines herbes in a small saucepan and simmer until jelly melts. Continue simmering until mixture thickens, about 15 minutes; keep warm.

6. After the turkey has cooked for 2 hours, brush on the glaze mixture. When the thermometer pops up or until an instant-read thermometer inserted into the thigh registers 180°F, about 3 hours total.

7. Remove from oven and let turkey rest 15 minutes before carving.

GARLIC AND MUSTARD PORK ROAST

MAKES: 4 to 6 servings   **COOK:** 3 hours

- 1   tablespoon chopped garlic
- 1   teaspoon ground garlic
- 2   teaspoons finely chopped rosemary, plus 2 sprigs
- ¼   cup spicy brown mustard
- 1   tablespoon brown sugar
- 2   tablespoons canola oil
- 1   (5- to 6-pound) pork shoulder, deboned, rolled, and tied securely
  Salt and pepper, to taste

1. **Preheat oven to 325°F.**
2. In a medium bowl, whisk together garlic, rosemary, mustard, sugar, and canola oil. Place pork roast on a rack fitted in a roasting pan. Season pork well with salt and pepper. Using a brush or your hands, completely coat pork with mustard-and-garlic paste. Thread rosemary sprigs through center of roll on each end.
3. Roast until internal temperature reaches 145°F, 2½ to 3 hours. Remove from oven, cover loosely with foil, and allow to rest for 15 minutes before slicing. Serve with pan drippings poured over top.

HERB ROASTED HENS

MAKES: 4 servings   **COOK:** 55 minutes

- 4   Cornish game hens
- ½   cup red wine vinaigrette dressing
- 1   teaspoon chopped fresh thyme leaves, plus 4 sprigs
- 1   teaspoon chopped fresh parsley, plus 4 sprigs
- 1   teaspoon chopped fresh oregano, plus 4 sprigs
- 1   teaspoon chopped fresh rosemary, plus 4 sprigs
- 1   tablespoon grill seasoning
- 1   lemon, zested and cut into quarters
- 1   (16-ounce) bag baby carrots
- 1   (16-ounce) bag frozen pearl onions, thawed
- ½   pound red potatoes, cut into small chunks
  Salt and pepper

1. **Preheat oven to 375°F.** Line a baking sheet with foil and put a baking rack on top.
2. Rinse the body and cavity of hens under cold water and pat dry. Mix together the dressing, herbs, seasoning, and lemon zest. Reserve 2 tablespoons of herb-and-dressing mixture and rub the rest on hens, inside and out. Stuff each hen with a sprig of each herb and a piece of lemon.
3. In a large bowl, combine carrots, onions, and potatoes with the reserved dressing mixture and a pinch of salt and pepper. Toss to coat. Place the vegetables in a large roasting pan and place the hens on top of the rack. Roast for 50 to 55 minutes or until an instant-read thermometer reads 165°F when inserted in the thickest part of the thigh. Cover with foil and let rest for 5 minutes before serving.

NORTH STAR HAM

MAKES: 20 servings   **COOK:** 2 hours 30 minutes

1 (7-pound) ham, fully cooked

20 whole cloves—McCormick

1 (15-ounce) can dark sweet cherries—Oregon

1 habanero chili, stem and seeds removed

1 tablespoon minced ginger—Gourmet Garden

¼ cup dark brown sugar

1 tablespoon cornstarch

¼ cup ginger preserves—Robertson's®

1. Preheat oven to 325°F. Line a roasting pan with aluminum foil and set aside.
2. Cut the thick layer of fat and skin from ham and discard. Score the ham in a diamond pattern and insert whole cloves in center of diamonds. Place in roasting pan and roast in preheated oven for 1 hour.
3. Meanwhile, drain cherries and reserve juice. Finely chop the cherries, place in a medium bowl, and stir in chili and ginger. Combine sugar and cornstarch in a medium saucepan. Add enough water to cherry juice to equal 1 cup; slowly stir into sugar mixture. Bring to a boil over medium heat. Add cherry mixture and preserves and return to a boil. Reduce to a simmer, stirring frequently, for 10 minutes. Remove from heat.
4. After ham has cooked for 1 hour, baste with glaze and continue roasting. Baste ham every 15 minutes until the internal temperature reaches 130°–140°F, about another 1½ hours.
5. On a large platter, slice half of the ham, brush slices with any remaining glaze, and rest slices against the unsliced portion.

PORK CROWN ROAST WITH ROYAL GLAZE AND GRAVY

MAKES: 8 servings   **COOK:** 3 hours 30 minutes

1   (7- to 8-pound) pork crown roast

2   tablespoons grill seasoning

3½   cups chicken broth, divided use

⅓   cup apple butter

3   tablespoons spicy brown mustard

2   teaspoons peeled and chopped ginger

1   teaspoon chopped garlic

1   tablespoon Worcestershire sauce

¾   cup Canadian whisky

1   bunch fresh parsley, for garnish

1. Preheat oven to 325°F.

2. Sprinkle the grill seasoning over the pork, making sure it is thoroughly covered. Place the pork into a roasting pan, bone-ends up. Wrap the bone ends with aluminum foil to prevent them from browning too quickly. Pour 2 cups broth into the pan. Roast uncovered for 20 to 25 minutes per pound of meat, about 2½ to 3½ hours, until the internal temperature is 150°F. Make sure to baste with pan drippings every 20 minutes for the first 2 hours.

3. While roast is cooking, into a saucepan whisk together 1 cup of chicken broth, apple butter, mustard, ginger, garlic, Worcestershire sauce, and ¼ cup whisky and place over medium-low heat. Simmer for about 12 minutes until thick and reduced by one-third. Brush the glaze onto the pork every 15 minutes for the last hour of cooking.

4. Remove roast from oven, transfer to a serving platter, and let rest for 10 minutes before slicing.

5. Place the roasting pan over medium heat and deglaze with the remaining ½ cup of whisky and 1 cup of chicken broth, scraping up the browned bits with a flat-edged spoon. Add the remaining glaze, simmer, and reduce by half or until thickened. Pour into a gravy boat and serve with roast.

SHEPHERD'S BRISKET

MAKES: 8 servings **BAKE:** 4 hours 30 minutes

1 (2½- to 3-pound) beef brisket

1 (1.5-ounce) packet meat loaf seasoning mix—McCormick, divided use

2 cups frozen pearl onions

1 (16-ounce) bag baby carrots

1 (8-ounce) package baby bella mushrooms

1 cup dry red wine

1 (24-ounce) bag Steam n' Mash garlic seasoned potatoes—Ore-Ida®

1 teaspoon herbes de Provence—McCormick

1 cup sour cream

2 tablespoons butter

1 (12-ounce) jar beef gravy

1 (14.5-ounce) can petite diced tomatoes, drained

2 tablespoons finely chopped chives

1. Preheat oven to 325°F.

2. Rinse brisket under cold water, pat dry with paper towels, and place in a small roasting pan. Reserve 1 tablespoon meat loaf seasoning mix. Season both sides of brisket with seasoning. Add onions, carrots, and mushrooms to the pan. Pour red wine over brisket. Cover tightly with foil and bake in preheated oven for 3 to 4 hours or until fork-tender.

3. Remove roasting pan from oven and transfer the meat to a cutting board and the vegetables to a bowl. While brisket cools, microwave potatoes according to package directions. Empty potatoes into a medium bowl and mash. Stir in herbes de Provence, sour cream, butter, and remaining meat loaf seasoning. Set aside.

4. Increase oven temperature to 350°F. Shred or chop brisket and place in a large mixing bowl. Skim fat from pan juices, stir gravy into juices, and pour into bowl with meat. Add vegetables and tomatoes and stir to combine. Transfer back into baking dish. Spread potatoes over meat mixture and sprinkle with chives. Bake for 25 to 30 minutes or until bubbling.

SLOW COOKER BRISKET WITH BROWN GRAVY

MAKES: 6 servings   **COOK:** 6 hours

About 2 cups canola oil, for searing

1   (2 ½- to 3-pound) beef brisket

2   medium onions, chopped

2   stalks celery with leaves, chopped

1   bay leaf

1   bunch parsley, stems reserved and leaves
    chopped

2   cups red wine

1   (14.5-ounce) can beef broth

2   tablespoons tomato paste

1   packet brown gravy mix

2   large carrots, sliced

2   (8-ounce) packages mixed wild mushrooms

1   (1.3-ounce) packet pot roast seasoning—
    McCormick Slow Cooker

1   cup water

    Salt and pepper

1. Heat oil in a large skillet over medium-high heat. Season brisket on both sides with a generous pinch of salt and pepper. Sear for about 4 minutes per side.

2. To a slow cooker, add the onions, celery, bay leaf, and parsley stems. Place the seared brisket on top of the vegetables. In a large bowl, combine the wine and broth and whisk in tomato paste and pot roast seasoning. Pour over brisket and cook for 4 to 6 hours on low. Add the carrots and mushrooms and cook for another hour or until the carrots are tender.

3. Remove the meat, carrots, and mushrooms from the slow cooker and set aside. Strain the liquid into a medium pan over medium-high heat. Whisk together the gravy mix with 1 cup cold water. Turn the heat to medium and whisk in the gravy mix a bit at a time. Cook until thickened, about 2 minutes. To serve, slice the brisket and serve with carrots, mushrooms, and gravy. Garnish with reserved chopped parsley leaves and serve.

SLOW ROASTED CHRISTMAS HEN WITH DRESSING

MAKES: 6 servings **COOK:** 1 hour 45 minutes

1 (about 3-pound) whole chicken
1 tablespoon herb rub
¼ cup ruby port
¼ cup balsamic vinegar
¼ medium yellow onion, roughly chopped
¼ cup dried currants
½ cup dried cranberries
1 stick (½ cup) butter
1 (6-ounce) package seasoned dressing mix—Mrs. Cubbison's
¾ cup less-sodium chicken broth
2 inside ribs celery, including tops, minced
½ cup crumbled blue cheese

1. Preheat oven to 325°F.
2. Rinse chicken in cold water inside and out and pat dry on all sides with paper towels. Place in roasting pan and pat in roasting rub.
3. Place port, vinegar, onion, currants, cranberries, and butter in a blender or food processor fitted with the steel blade. Process until smooth, pulsing about 5 or 6 times, and pour into a small bowl.
4. Sprinkle the dressing mix with chicken broth and toss with celery and blue cheese. Stuff cavity and neck area of chicken with the dressing mixture. Pull the legs together, secure with kitchen twine, and secure the neck flap with sturdy toothpicks.
5. Baste the bird with one half of port mixture and place in oven.
6. While roasting, baste occasionally, first with the port mixture in the pan, then with the remainder of the mixture in the bowl, and then with pan juices. Roast about 1 hour 45 minutes or until the hen is mahogany in color and meat thermometer registers 180°F when inserted in the thigh. To serve, spoon stuffing onto each plate with sliced chicken or carved chicken pieces.

TURKEY BREAST WITH PEAR, PROSCIUTTO, AND PINE NUT STUFFING

MAKES: 8 servings   **COOK:** 1 hour 30 minutes

1   stick (½ cup) butter, softened

4   teaspoons chopped garlic, divided use

3   teaspoons poultry seasoning—The Spice Hunter, divided use

1   (5½- to 6-pound) whole turkey breast

1   (8 count) box frozen Garlic Texas Toast

1   tablespoon olive oil

1   (4 ounce) package prosciutto, chopped

¾   cup frozen seasoning blend—PictSweet

½   cup pine nuts

1   (8.25-ounce) can pear halves in light syrup—Del Monte, drained

½   cup vegetable broth Chopped fresh flat-leaf parsley, for garnish
    Salt and pepper, to taste

1. Preheat oven to 425°F. Spray a 2-quart casserole dish with cooking spray and set aside.

2. Rinse turkey under cold water and pat dry with paper towels. In a small bowl, combine butter, 2 teaspoons garlic, and 2 teaspoons poultry seasoning. Use a fork to mix together until well combined. Use your fingers to carefully loosen the skin around the entire breast. Work half of the butter mixture under the skin and rub the remaining butter on the outside of the turkey. Season with salt and pepper. Place in a shallow roasting pan and set aside.

3. Line a baking sheet with foil and arrange toast on top. Bake in preheated oven for 10 minutes. Remove and cool completely. Cut into 1-inch cubes and set aside.

4. Place turkey, uncovered, in the oven and immediately reduce temperature to 375°F. Roast for 1 to 1¼ hours or until a thermometer inserted into the thickest portion of the breast reaches 165°F. Remove turkey from oven and let rest 15 minutes before carving.

5. Heat oil in a medium skillet on medium-high heat. Sauté prosciutto until crispy. Remove prosciutto and drain on paper towels. Add seasoning blend, remaining garlic, and remaining poultry seasoning and sauté for 4 minutes. Transfer to a large bowl. Stir in pine nuts, pears, reserved pear juice, vegetable broth, prosciutto, and toast cubes until well combined. Transfer to prepared casserole dish. Cover with foil.

6. Starting 30 minutes before turkey is finished cooking, bake stuffing for 30 minutes. Remove foil and bake for another 15 minutes while turkey rests. Slice turkey and serve with any pan drippings and stuffing. Garnish with chopped parsley.

VEAL OSSO BUCCO WITH SPICY POLENTA

MAKES: 4 servings   **COOK:** 8 hours

2   tablespoons canola oil

1½ pounds veal stew meat (cut from the shoulder)

¼   cup all-purpose flour

1   (15-ounce) can chicken broth

1   medium onion, chopped

2   large carrots, sliced

3   stalks celery, chopped

1   tablespoon chopped garlic

4   sprigs thyme, plus more for garnish

1   teaspoon Italian seasoning

1   (14-ounce) can diced tomatoes

1   (8-ounce) package polenta

1   teaspoon red pepper flakes

¼   cup grated Parmesan cheese

2   tablespoons butter

    Salt and pepper, to taste

1. Put a large skillet over medium-high heat and add the oil. Season the veal with salt and pepper and dredge in flour, shaking off any excess. Cook until browned on all sides, about 8 minutes. Set aside. Pour ½ cup of the broth into the skillet and scrape up all the browned bits on the bottom. Put this liquid into a slow cooker.

2. Add half the vegetables to the slow cooker and nestle the meat on top. Add the thyme and seasoning and put the remaining vegetables over the meat. Pour in the rest of the broth plus 2 cups of water and the tomatoes. Cover, and turn the cooker on to low. Let cook for 6 to 8 hours.

3. About 30 minutes before you will be ready to eat, make the polenta according to package directions but adding red pepper flakes to the water before polenta. Once the polenta has thickened, remove from heat and stir in the cheese and butter. To serve, put a big spoonful of polenta onto a plate and top with some meat, vegetables, and sauce. Garnish with fresh thyme leaves.

JACK FROST CAKE

MAKES: 12 servings **BAKE:** 35 minutes

Nonstick cooking spray

1 (18.25-ounce) box spice cake mix—
Betty Crocker

1⅓ cups eggnog

½ cup vegetable oil

3 eggs

2 store-bought muffins

1 teaspoon cinnamon extract

2 (12-ounce) containers whipped white
frosting

FOR THE CANDY TO DECORATE
THE SNOWMAN:

1 (7.5-ounce) bag starlight mints

1 gumdrop

5 black jelly beans

1 foot Fruit by the Foot

1 marshmallow

1 pretzel rod

1. Preheat oven to 350°F. Spray two 8-inch round
cake pans with cooking spray and set aside.

2. In a large bowl, beat cake mix, eggnog, oil, and
eggs with an electric mixer on low speed for
30 seconds. Scrape down sides of bowl and
beat for 2 minutes on medium speed. Pour
batter into prepared pans.

3. Bake in preheated oven for 25 to 35 minutes or
until a tester comes out clean. Let cool in pans
for 5 minutes, then transfer to a wire cooling
rack to cool completely.

4. When cakes are completely cool, place rounds
side by side on a serving tray or large cutting
board. Place muffins side by side at one end of
a cake round for snowman's hat. Stir cinnamon
extract into frosting in a medium bowl until
well combined. Frost both cakes and muffins.

5. To decorate snowman, place rows of starlight
mints, starting at the top of cake and working
up to the two muffins, to look like a snowman's
hat. Decorate the cake to look like a face, using
2 black jelly beans for eyes, a gumdrop for a
nose, and 3 black jelly beans for a mouth.
Drape fruit strips across where the two cake
rounds meet, to make a scarf. Use
marshmallows for arms. Place a pretzel rod
with a marshmallow at one end for a broom to
rest between the marshmallow arms. Arrange
mints as buttons placed down the center of
the snowman's body.

MISTLETOE MERINGUES

MAKES: 34 meringues **BAKE:** 2 hours 30 minutes

6 egg whites

¼ teaspoon cream of tartar

1 cup superfine sugar

1 teaspoon mint extract

10 drops green food coloring

Green sparkling sugar

Green sprinkles

1. Preheat oven to 200°F. Line baking sheet(s) with parchment paper and set aside.

2. Beat egg whites and cream of tartar in a large bowl on medium speed with an electric mixer until mixture has doubled in volume. Beat on high speed and gradually add the sugar, mint extract, and green food coloring. Beat until shiny, stiff peaks form.

3. Spoon meringue into a disposable piping bag and snip a small end off the bag. Pipe onto prepared baking sheet(s), spaced 2 inches apart. Sprinkle with sparkling sugar and sprinkles.

4. Bake in preheated oven for 1½ hours. Turn off oven and leave meringues in oven for another hour. Remove and cool completely.

PEANUT BUTTER PIE

MAKES: 8 servings **COOK:** 5 minutes

1 (8-ounce) package cream cheese, softened

½ cup creamy peanut butter

1 cup powdered sugar

1 cup heavy cream

2 teaspoons vanilla extract

1 (9-inch) graham cracker crust

¼ cup salted peanuts, roughly chopped

½ cup chocolate chips

¼ cup milk

1. In a large bowl, beat together cream cheese with peanut butter and powdered sugar using an electric mixer on high speed. In a separate bowl, beat together heavy cream with vanilla until doubled in volume and soft peaks form.

2. Stir one-third of whipped cream into peanut butter mixture to lighten it. Fold peanut butter mixture into whipped cream until just combined.

3. Spread mixture into graham cracker crust and sprinkle with chopped peanuts. Melt chocolate chips with milk in microwave, stirring at 20-second intervals, until chocolate is melted and smooth. Drizzle chocolate over top of pie in a crisscross pattern. Place pie in freezer to set up, about 3 hours.

SWEET BISCUIT CENTERPIECE WREATH

MAKES: 1 wreath **BAKE:** 17 minutes

½ cup sugar

1 tablespoon pumpkin pie spice

2 teaspoons ground cinnamon

1 (16.3-ounce) can refrigerated biscuits

1 tablespoon water

1 egg

1 cup powdered sugar, sifted

¼ cup maple syrup

1. Preheat oven to 350°F.
2. On a piece of kitchen parchment, trace the bottom of the serving bowl that will be in the center of your biscuit wreath. Turn the parchment over and use to line a baking sheet. Set aside.
3. In a bowl, stir to combine sugar, pumpkin pie spice, and cinnamon. Set aside.
4. Open can of biscuits and separate into individual pieces. Sprinkle a smooth surface with some of the sugar mixture. One at a time, press each biscuit into the bowl of sugar mixture. Roll each biscuit on sugared surface to a 5-inch diameter. Using 2-inch and/or 3-inch leaf cookie-cutters, cut leaf shapes for your wreath. Reserve dough scraps. Reroll extra dough to cut out single leaf shapes or to make mini individual wreaths. Position leaves on baking sheet, overlapping around the circle drawn on parchment. Set aside.
5. Lightly beat egg with 1 tablespoon of water. Using a pastry brush, paint egg wash between the leaves where they overlap.
6. Bake in preheated oven for 14 to 17 minutes. Remove from oven and cool completely before lifting from baking sheet.
7. While wreath is baking, stir together sifted powdered sugar and maple syrup until smooth. Cover and set aside.
8. Once wreath has cooled, use a clean paint brush to apply glaze to leaves, painting every other leaf so that they are separated.

WHITE WINTER SLEIGH RIDE

MAKES: 36 servings **BAKE:** 55 minutes

Nonstick cooking spray

3 (18.25-ounce) boxes white cake mix, divided use

9 egg whites, divided use

1 cup vegetable oil, divided use

3¾ cups white cranberry juice, divided use

3 teaspoons vanilla extract, divided use

1 cup seedless raspberry jam

4 cans fluffy white frosting, divided use

FOR THE COOKIES:

1 (17.25-ounce) package sugar cookie mix

½ cup all-purpose flour

4 tablespoons butter, softened

¼ cup cream cheese, softened

1 egg

1 teaspoon lemon extract

Flour, for dusting board

FOR SANTA'S SLEIGH, REINDEER, AND RAMP:

1 (17.5-ounce) package gingerbread cookie mix

1 stick (½ cup) butter, softened

1 egg

1. Preheat oven to 350°F. Lightly spray the bottom of a 9 × 13-inch cake pan with baking spray.

2. For each 9 × 13-inch cake, combine 1 cake mix, 3 egg whites, ⅓ cup oil, 1¼ cups cranberry juice, and 1 teaspoon vanilla extract in a large mixing bowl. Beat together on medium speed for 2 minutes. Pour batter in prepared pan and bake in preheated oven for 27 to 32 minutes. Let cool.

3. For the cookies, preheat oven to 375°F. Line baking sheet(s) with parchment paper. Whisk together cookie mix and flour in a large mixing bowl. Stir in butter, cream cheese, egg, and lemon extract with a wooden spoon until a soft dough forms. Split dough in half and shape each half into a disk. Roll out on a lightly floured surface to ¼-inch thickness. Cut out snowmen shapes with a cookie cutter and place on baking sheet. Chill cutout cookies in refrigerator for 15 minutes before baking. Bake in preheated oven for 9 to 11 minutes or until edges are just golden. Let cool. Repeat with remaining dough. Decorate cooled cookies with one can of frosting plus red and black decorating icing.

4. For Santa's sleigh, reindeer, and ramp, line a baking sheet with kitchen parchment. Prepare dough with gingerbread cookie mix, butter, and egg according to package directions. Roll out dough on a lightly floured surface and cut out 2 sleigh shapes for the outsides of the sleigh , plus three 2 × 3-inch rectangles. Place sleigh shapes on baking sheet, reversing one. Cut out 3 to 5 reindeer. For the ramp, cut out 2 triangles 3 inches high and 6 inches along the base, and two rectangles, one 4 × 3 inches and one 4 × 8 inches. Bake at 375°F for 10 to 12 minutes or until golden at the edges. Cool on pan. Decorate sleighs and reindeer. Use the 2-inch-wide rectangles and decorating icing to assemble sleigh and the 4-inch pieces for the ramp; use a serrated knife to trim cookie pieces.

5. To decorate, stack the 3 cakes using half of the jam and half of one can of frosting between layers, then frost the entire cake. Place the assembled ramp on top of cake and frost. Sprinkle ramp and top of cake with white sanding sugar. Use frosting to stand up reindeer and then place sleigh.

CHEERFUL CHERRIES JUBILEE

MAKES: 1 cocktail

Bing cherry, for garnish
¼ ounce cherry brandy
3½ ounces extra dry champagne

1. In a chilled champagne flute, add cherry and cherry brandy. Slowly top off with champagne.

HOLIDAY PUNCH BOWL

MAKES: 8 drinks

6 cups frozen strawberries
2 cups lemonade
1 cup lemon drop mixer
2 cups cream soda

1. In a punch bowl filled with ice, stir together frozen strawberries, lemonade, and lemon drop mixer. Pour in cream soda and serve immediately.

MERRY PEAR COCKTAIL

MAKES: 2 cocktails

- 3 ounces Peach Bellini mix—Stirrings
- 1 ounce pear brandy
- 6 ½ ounces extra dry champagne

1. Stir together Bellini mix and pear brandy in a chilled glass. Divide into 2 rocks glasses filled with crushed ice. Top with chilled champagne.

SPICED APPLE COCKTAIL

MAKES: 4 servings

- 1 cup apple cider
- 1 cup cranberry juice
- 2 cups ginger ale
   Orange slices, for garnish
- 6 ounces spiced rum, optional

1. Stir together all ingredients in a large pitcher. Pour over ice-filled glasses and garnish each with a slice of orange. Pour 1 ½ ounces rum in each drink if desired.

Index